OCS Study
MMS 2005-033

ANALYSIS OF COVARIANCE OF
FALL MIGRATIONS OF BOWHEAD WHALES IN RELATION TO
HUMAN ACTIVITIES AND ENVIRONMENTAL FACTORS,
ALASKAN BEAUFORT SEA: PHASE I, 1996–1998

by

environmental research associates

and

Western EcoSystems Technology Inc.

for

 U.S. Department of the Interior
Minerals Management Service
Alaska Outer Continental Shelf Region

MMS Contract 1435-01-02-CT-85133

LGL Report TA2799-3

March 2007

This Phase I study was completed in March 2004. The report prepared then was updated in early 2007 to take account of MMS comments on the initial report. However, this revised 2007 report does not cite or discuss most of the related publications and reports released after March 2004.

Suggested Format for Citations:

Manly, B.F.J., V.D. Moulton, R.E. Elliott, G.W. Miller and W.J. Richardson. 2007. Analysis of covariance of fall migrations of bowhead whales in relation to human activities and environmental factors, Alaskan Beaufort Sea: Phase I, 1996–1998. OCS Study 2005-033; LGL Rep. TA2799-3. Rep. from LGL Ltd., King City, Ont., and WEST Inc., Cheyenne, WY, for U.S. Minerals Manage. Serv., Anchorage, AK. 128 p.

ANALYSIS OF COVARIANCE OF
FALL MIGRATIONS OF BOWHEAD WHALES IN RELATION TO
HUMAN ACTIVITIES AND ENVIRONMENTAL FACTORS,
ALASKAN BEAUFORT SEA: PHASE I, 1996–1998

by

Bryan F.J. Manly [c], **Valerie D. Moulton** [b], **Robert E. Elliott** [a],
Gary W. Miller [a,d], and **W. John Richardson** [a,e]

[a] **LGL Ltd., environmental research associates**
22 Fisher St., POB 280, King City, Ont. L7B 1A6
(905) 833-1244; wjr@lgl.com

[b] **LGL Ltd., environmental research associates**
388 Kenmount Rd., POB 13248, Stn A, St. John's, Nfld. A1B 4A5
(709) 754-1922; vmoulton@lgl.com

and

[c] **Western EcoSystems Technology Inc.**
2003 Central Ave., Cheyenne, WY 82001
(307) 634-1756; bmanly@west-inc.com

LGL Report TA2799-3

March 2007

This study was funded by the U.S. Department of the Interior, Minerals Management Service (MMS), Alaska Outer Continental Shelf Region, Anchorage, Alaska, under Contract Number 1435-01-02-CT-85133, as part of the MMS Alaska Environmental Studies Program.

The opinions, findings, conclusions, or recommendations expressed in this report are those of the authors and do not necessarily reflect the views of the U.S. Department of the Interior, nor does mention of trade names or commercial products constitute endorsement or recommendation for use by the Federal Government.

_____

[d] Deceased.
[e] Author to whom correspondence should be sent.

ii

TABLE OF CONTENTS

EXECUTIVE SUMMARY

This study develops an approach for exploratory analysis to investigate whether and how the distribution of bowhead whales (*Balaena mysticetus*) in the Alaskan Beaufort Sea during autumn is affected by human activities, while simultaneously investigating and allowing for the influences of natural environmental factors on bowhead distribution and sightability. This study is based on analysis of aerial survey, industrial activity, and environmental data from the 1996, 1997 and 1998 autumn migration seasons. It was designed as Phase I of a study initiated by the Minerals Management Service (MMS). Phase II, if it proceeds, would expand and apply the approach to incorporate data from additional years, and to address additional questions and hypotheses about influences of natural and anthropogenic factors. The results from Phase I concerning potential effects of various variables should be considered preliminary, given the exploratory nature of the analysis, the limited number of years considered, and the fact that the statistical models were not fully optimized given the preliminary nature of the work.

Prior to the start of the present project, numerous objectives and hypotheses were formulated as part of a Feasibility Study. These objectives and hypotheses concerned the influences of seismic surveys, offshore drilling, ice breaking, shallow-hazards surveys, and subsistence whaling, plus the combined influences of some of these activities, on bowhead distribution. Objectives were also formulated concerning the influences of natural factors like ice cover, distance from shore, bottom slope, water depth, longitude, date, and year on bowhead distribution and numbers. Also included were various objectives and hypotheses concerning the influences of sightability factors like sea state, visibility, survey altitude, aircraft type, and survey type on the numbers of bowhead whales expected to be seen during aerial surveys.

This Phase I study attempted to address 7 of the 17 Objectives/Hypotheses outlined in the Feasibility Study. Most of those not included were deferred because the anthropogenic activities involved in those particular objectives (offshore drilling, icebreaking, etc.) did not occur during the three years considered in the Phase I work.

The decision to base Phase I on the 1996-98 data was a key decision made early in Phase I. Aerial survey data were available from numerous sources covering a wide range of years (1979-1998), during which a variety of types of industry activity occurred. For Phase I, we selected data from 1996-98 based on criteria discussed in a Study Plan that was refined in consultation with MMS. The offshore activities in 1996-98 were mainly limited to marine seismic operations. Aerial survey data for Phase I were available from three sources: from MMS's annual aerial surveys of the Alaskan Beaufort Sea, and from industry- and MMS-sponsored projects conducted by LGL. • The MMS surveys covered a broad geographic area each year. • The LGL surveys for BP Exploration (Alaska) Inc. and Western Geophysical Inc. in 1996-98 provided intensive survey coverage over a relatively small geographic area focused on areas with seismic surveys. • LGL's aerial surveys during the MMS-sponsored bowhead feeding study occurred in the eastern portion of the Alaskan Beaufort Sea. In addition to aerial survey data, other types of data used in the study included bathymetry, seismic shotpoint, and whaling information. Data from these various sources were standardized, validated, and compiled into one final data set. These data were organized to provide bowhead sighting, human activity, and environmental data for many sample units, each of which nominally consisted of a segment of aerial survey transect 5 km long. We considered bowhead sightings within a cross-track distance of 5 km (2.5 km on each side of the aircraft), for a total of 25 km^2 per sampling unit

A Poisson regression analysis was proposed and applied to quantify effects of human activities (primarily seismic surveys) on the number of bowhead groups sighted in a sample unit while simultaneously allowing for and quantifying the influences of other potentially relevant variables. A Poisson regression can theoretically show whether and how the number of bowhead whales seen at a given location changes as a result of industrial, environmental, and sightability factors, and also "occurrence of whaling". During the development of the analysis approach, several complications arose associated with the large number of covariates, quantifying the variable amount of seismic activity, deriving an appropriate heterogeneity factor, dealing with potential serial correlation, and deciding whether to assume a maximum range of influence of seismic sources. Much of the work in Phase I was directed toward finding solutions for some of these complications.

"Objective 1" of the study was to quantify the numbers of bowhead sightings relative to distance and direction (E, W, N, S) from a seismic source, the amount of exposure to sound pulses, and time since exposure. In practice, airgun activity was quantified for the periods 0-1, 1-2, 2-3, 3-6, 6-12, and 12-24 h prior to the aerial survey. "Objective 3" was to assess whether the seismic effect, if any, is reduced or absent if there is a barrier island or shallow water between the airguns and the survey area. Ultimately, two Poisson regression models were chosen to describe the data after dealing with various complications mentioned above. These models assumed that seismic effects might extend as far as 70 km in each direction from a seismic source. The models included quadratic terms for seismic effects, scaled using the seismic activity levels. One of the models included the covariates for the 0-1 hour seismic effect, i.e., considering seismic activity that had occurred in the hour leading up to the aerial survey. The other included covariates representing seismic activity 12-24 hours prior to the survey. Maps showing the distribution of the expected number of bowhead sightings were generated based on the estimated coefficients of the regression models. These maps were useful in helping to "visualize" the results of the analyses and to validate them against what is already known about the pattern of bowhead whale migration across the Alaskan Beaufort Sea.

In addition to the Poisson regression analysis, a circular randomization test was developed to test for differences in the headings of traveling bowhead whales during periods with vs. without seismic activity ("Objective 2"). It was of interest to assess the extent to which the headings of bowheads at various distances and directions from the seismic vessel are deflected from the typical WNW migration direction when airguns were operating.

The preliminary Poisson models suggest that, of the **natural covariates,** only distance from shore and water depth were significantly (at the 5 % level) related to the number of bowhead sightings during at least one of the three years considered. After allowance for other variables, there were no statistically significant relationships between bowhead occurrence and any of the following: percent ice cover, bottom slope, date within season, and year. More bowheads appeared to be sighted in intermediate water depths, and in some years sightings occurred at intermediate distances from shore as compared with close to and far from shore. These preliminary results are consistent with what one would expect, given the known tendency for the bowhead migration corridor to be concentrated over the middle and outer continental shelf, at least in years with low to moderate ice cover. The inclusion of more years of data in analyses similar to those done during this study, and the refinement of certain covariates (i.e., bottom slope), would be helpful in refining the understanding of relationships between natural covariates considered in Phase I and the expected number of bowhead sightings.

The preliminary Poisson models suggest that, of the **sightability covariates,** only survey type (MMS vs. LGL) was significantly (at the 5 % level) related to the number of bowhead sightings. After allowance for other variables (see below), there were no statistically significant relationships between bowhead occurrence and any of the following: sea state, visibility, survey altitude, and aircraft type. However, the relationship to visibility was positive and very close to significant at the 5 % criterion. With larger sample size (after inclusion of additional years), additional relationships would likely become evident.

With regard to *Objective 1*, **seismic surveys** within the general area tended to reduce the number of bowhead whale groups that were sighted per sample unit. The reduction is statistically significant in the present preliminary statistical models. However, further investigation of the goodness-of-fit of the models, and associated model refinements, are required before specific conclusions can be drawn about the spatial scale, directional properties, and magnitude of seismic effects. While the results of analyses to date indicate that nearby seismic activity results in a reduction in bowhead numbers, probably both along the north-south axis and the east-west axis, the spatial extent of the effect cannot be determined with confidence from the preliminary models.

With regard to *Objective 3*, the analysis did not show any appreciable improvement in the predictions of sighting probability when **minimum water depth** between the seismic vessel and observation area was taken into account. This was somewhat surprising, given earlier indications that the closest sightings of migrating bowheads to operating seismic vessels tended to occur in circumstances with shallow water (or gravel bars) between the vessel and the whales. The lack of clear evidence (from the preliminary Poisson regression models) for such an effect may be a result of low sample size in the most critical conditions. Alternatively, it may mean that the "minimum water depth" measure that we used was not a very good measure of the sound attenuating effect.

With regard to *Objective 2*, overall, there was some evidence that the **headings** of traveling bowhead whales were significantly different during periods with vs. without seismic activity. However, the evidence was not very convincing within any one specific distance and direction category relative to the seismic vessel. Consideration of data from additional years would provide larger sample sizes.

Overall, the results of Phase I are encouraging and we recommend that Phase II of this study proceed. Several recommendations for Phase II, particularly pertaining to data structure and the Poisson regression approach, are provided in the Discussion section of this report.

INTRODUCTION

This report describes the results of Phase I (of potentially two Phases) of a study initiated by the Minerals Management Service (MMS) for the purposes of assessing the effects of industry and natural factors on the distribution of bowhead whales (*Balaena mysticetus*) in the Alaskan Beaufort Sea during late summer and early autumn. This preliminary and exploratory study suggests an analysis approach for investigating whether and how the distribution of bowhead whales in the Alaskan Beaufort Sea during their autumn migration has been affected by human activities, while simultaneously allowing for the influences of natural environmental factors on bowhead distribution and sightability.

Background

Hydrocarbon exploration and development activities have been conducted in the Alaskan Beaufort Sea for over 25 years. These activities have included shallow-hazard surveys, seismic exploration, construction of artificial islands and causeways, drilling for exploration and production, construction of underwater pipelines, vessel traffic, aircraft traffic, and numerous other associated activities. Much concern has been expressed about the possible effects of this offshore industrial activity on the Bering-Chukchi-Beaufort stock of bowhead whales. This population is currently listed as Endangered under the U.S. Endangered Species Act, and is classified as a strategic stock by the U.S. National Marine Fisheries Service (Angliss et al. 2001). In addition there is a subsistence hunt by Alaskan aboriginals during the spring and autumn migration of the bowhead whale. Along the Alaskan Beaufort Sea coast, subsistence hunts occur at Barrow during spring, and at Kaktovik, Cross Island, and Barrow during autumn.

Annual studies of the timing and routes of autumn bowhead migration through the Alaskan Beaufort Sea have been funded since 1979 by the MMS or, in early years, the Bureau of Land Management (e.g., Ljungblad et al. 1988; Treacy 2002b). These studies, based on broad-scale aerial surveys, were conducted in part to monitor the effects of offshore industrial activities on bowhead whale distribution and behavior. MMS also funded multi-year studies of bowhead feeding ecology in the eastern Alaskan Beaufort Sea, and those studies involved aerial surveys for bowheads in that portion of the Alaskan Beaufort Sea. In addition to the MMS studies, there have been numerous site-specific industry-funded studies of the effects of industrial activities (e.g., geophysical exploration or offshore drilling) on bowhead whale distribution and behavior during autumn migration. Most of these studies have included intensive site-specific aerial surveys in parts of the Alaskan Beaufort Sea (e.g., LGL and Greeneridge 1987; Hall et al. 1994; Miller et al. 1999).

MMS recently funded the compilation of a Human Activities Database (HAD) (Wainwright 2002). The general objective of that study was to compile a readily-accessible and quantitative HAD for the Alaskan Beaufort Sea for the years 1979 through 1998. One component of that project was an examination of the feasibility of using the HAD and existing aerial survey data to analyze bowhead whale distribution during the fall migration vs. human activities and "natural" factors (Richardson et al. 2001—see Appendix A of this report). This Feasibility Study concluded that adequate information was available for a meaningful analysis of some questions of interest, and recommended that MMS proceed with the then-planned "analysis of covariance" of bowhead distribution relative to industrial and environmental factors.

The present study uses some of the data available in the HAD, along with a 3-year sample of the MMS and industry-funded aerial survey results, to develop and test an approach for examining the relationships between the distribution of sightings of bowhead whales during their autumn migration across the Alaskan Beaufort Sea and, on the other hand, human activities and environmental factors. Analysis of available data to address specific hypotheses about influences of industry and environmental factors on bowhead distribution may reduce the need for (and help focus) additional field studies. This Phase I study analyses a subset (1996-98) of the years (1979-1998) included in the HAD. Phase II, if it proceeds, is expected to include a larger subset of the years covered by the HAD.

Approach

This study builds upon the HAD and the objectives outlined in the Feasibility Study (Appendix A). The study was designed to occur in two phases. The primary purpose of Phase I was to provide useful guidance as to the best analysis approaches, and a basis for judging the likelihood that a follow-up multi-year analysis (in Phase II) would be successful in characterizing relationships of whale distribution to a number of natural and anthropogenic factors. The original intention for Phase I was to consider the effects of multiple types of industrial activity on bowhead whale distribution during a single year. A primary purpose would have been to develop the structure of a multivariate model that could later be expanded to include data from additional years. However, after careful consideration in consultation with MMS, it was decided to use data from three years (1996-98) during Phase I. During those years, the most prevalent offshore industrial activity was marine seismic surveys (see Methods for further detail about data selection).

A Poisson regression model was proposed and used to quantify, in a preliminary way, effects of human activities (primarily seismic surveys) on the number of bowhead groups sighted. A Poisson regression analysis can theoretically show whether and how the number of bowhead whales seen at a given location changes as a result of industrial, environmental, and sightability factors, and also "occurrence of whaling". Industrial factors considered in Phase I include seismic surveys at various times up to 24 hours before the whales were observed. Both North-South and East-West components of location relative to the industrial activity were considered. Assuming that an effect on the number of bowhead sightings will occur close to the activity while it is active and for some time thereafter, this approach should make it possible to determine how far away, in space and time, the effect extends. More specifically, the approach is designed

- to determine the 'no effect' distance in all directions away from each type of activity, and a 'no effect' time after activities cease; and
- within that distance and time, to characterize the strength of effect as a function of distance and direction from each type of activity.

It is recognized, however, that to fully address these questions, additional years' data and further refinement of the model-selection procedures would be necessary beyond what was possible in Phase I.

The approach also included provision to quantify the effects of various environmental and sightability variables on the likelihood of finding whales at a given location. This study differs from previous statistical approaches used to examine bowhead densities relative to industry (e.g., Davies 1997; Miller et al. 1999; Schick and Urban 2000) in that it simultaneously accounts for environmental and sightability effects on the probability of sighting whales at a given location. Also, unlike most previous analyses (Miller et al. 1999 was an exception), the present analysis uses both (a) MMS aerial survey data from the Alaskan Beaufort Sea as a whole and (b) site-specific aerial survey data acquired during projects funded by industry — specifically BP Exploration (Alaska) Inc. in 1996-97 and Western Geophysical Inc. in 1998 — and by MMS.

This report also documents how aerial survey data were standardized, structured, validated, and stored. The Objectives and Hypotheses of the study are presented in the next section. In the Discussion, we make recommendations as to whether and under what circumstances Phase II should proceed.

Objectives/Hypotheses

The objectives of this study relate specifically to bowhead whales in the Alaskan Beaufort Sea during late summer and autumn. The influences of human-activity and natural factors in other areas and seasons, when bowheads are often engaged in different activities, may differ. There is increasing evidence that responsiveness of bowheads (as for other cetaceans) can vary depending on the activity of the animals. Much is already known about the influences of some natural, sightability, and industry factors on the likelihood of seeing bowhead whales at specific locations. We know that these factors all do influence the distribution of bowhead whales (or bowhead sightings). Therefore, it can be argued that it is not meaningful to formulate questions about these influences as conventional "null vs. alternate" hypotheses. In many cases, previous studies have already convincingly rejected the null hypothesis. In these cases, the primary reason for conducting additional analyses is to better quantify the magnitude, geographic extent, and duration of effects that are already known to exist, taking account of more data than in past studies, and allowing for the influences of confounding factors to a greater extent than in the past. In these cases, rather than list a null vs. alternate hypothesis, we now state the objectives of the analysis, which are generally (a) to better quantify the known effects, and (b) to take those effects into account when attempting to test for and/or quantify the effects of other factors. For other factors whose influence (if any) on the probability of sighting bowhead whales is uncertain, the objectives are stated in the terms of a "null vs. alternate hypothesis" formulation. A nominal 5% level of significance is used for tests, although we also regard the P-value as a general measure of the strength of the evidence against the null hypothesis.

The Objectives/Hypotheses were originally presented in the Feasibility Study (Richardson et al. 2001), modified slightly in the Study Plan (LGL Ltd. 2003), and modified once again here to reflect a change in statistical analysis approach (Poisson vs. logistic regression). However, to facilitate cross-referencing, the numbering sequence adheres to that presented in the Feasibility Study. Objectives/Hypotheses are organized into three main groups; those that address (1) natural environmental, (2) sightability, and (3) human activity influences on the likelihood of sighting a bowhead whale. They are listed in this order because, conceptually, the intent is to assess the influence of human activities after allowing for the influences of natural environmental and sightability variables. Some objectives/hypotheses outlined in the Study Plan could not be addressed in Phase I given the limited scope of this Phase; these are listed in Appendix B. During Phase I, we attempted to address in part or full 7 of the 17 Objectives/Hypotheses outlined in the Study Plan, based on data from 1996-98. These Objectives/Hypotheses are described below.

Natural Factors

Many natural factors are known or expected to influence the distribution of migrating bowheads, or the probability of detecting them, or both. Previous studies have not attempted to take simultaneous account of the wide variety of factors (natural and industrial) suspected to influence sighting rates of bowhead whales during aerial surveys. Also, most previous analyses of natural factors affecting sighting rates have been based on the MMS area-wide surveys and have not used the results of industry-funded site-specific surveys. Objectives 13, 15, and 16 address the potential influences of natural factors like ice cover, distance from shore, water depth, longitude, date, and year on the expected number of bowhead sightings. The factor 'year' was not included in the Study Plan for Phase I as the original intent was to analyze data from one year only. However, with the decision to use data from three years in Phase I, "year" became a relevant factor. Also, Objective 13 has been further modified to subdivide it into two components, one dealing with natural factors and the other with sightability factors.

<u>Objective 13 (Natural Factors)</u>

> To quantify the number of bowhead sightings expected to be observed relative to percent ice cover, distance from shore, bottom slope, water depth, longitude, date within season, and year.

<u>Objective 15</u>

> To quantify the relationship between the preferred distance from shore (or preferred water depth) and date within season, and the effect of this interaction on the number of bowhead sightings expected to be observed.

<u>Objective 16</u>

> H_a: Peak number of bowhead sightings expected to be observed occurs progressively later in the season with increasing longitude.

> H_o: Peak number of bowhead sightings expected to be observed does not occur progressively later in the season with increasing longitude.

Sightability Factors

During an aerial survey, environmental conditions like sea state, visibility, and ice cover are known to affect an observer's ability to detect bowheads. The effects of these factors on bowhead sighting probability (specifically, the fall-off in detectability with increasing lateral distance) have been investigated as part of the MMS-funded bowhead feeding study (see Thomas et al. 2002). The feeding study also investigated the influence of aircraft type and survey altitude on lateral distances of the bowheads sighted. Aircraft type, survey altitude, and survey type (MMS vs. LGL) are all covariates considered in Phase I of this study. The factor 'survey type' was not included in the Study Plan. As previously mentioned, Objective 13 as originally formulated dealt with both natural factors affecting bowhead distribution and sightability factors affecting probability of detecting bowheads that are present. Objective 13 has been revised to distinguish these two types of factors.

<u>Objective 13 (Sightability Factors)</u>

> To quantify the number of bowhead sightings expected to be observed relative to sea state, visibility, survey altitude, aircraft type, and survey type.

Human Activities

For Phase I, only objectives concerning influences of marine seismic surveys and subsistence whaling on bowhead density are considered. Objectives concerning influences of drilling, icebreaking, and shallow-hazards surveys, and the combined influences of some of these (and seismic) activities, could be addressed in Phase II incorporating data from other years with more variable industry activities. (Those other types of activities were absent or infrequent in 1996-98, the years considered in Phase I.) Effects of "regular" boat traffic could not be addressed because available data on boat movements were incomplete. If reactions of bowheads to other vessels could have been considered, this presumably would have accounted for some of the residual variability and would have improved the ability to characterize the influences of seismic surveys and other factors. However, given the known large scale responses of migrating bowheads to seismic surveys (Miller et al. 1999) as compared with their responses to other vessels (Richardson et al. 1985, 1995), it was assumed that seismic effects could be modeled even without consideration of other boat traffic.

Objectives concerning potential disturbance effects from human activities are worded in terms of distance from the source of disturbance. They could, in theory, be reworded in terms of received sound levels. However, as discussed in the Feasibility Study (Appendix A) and in Marko (2001), many of the necessary geoacoustic data are not available at the present time. Also, there is merit in expressing the results in terms of easy-to-visualize distances rather than sound levels.

Seismic.—The potential effects of seismic survey activities were considered in terms of time and space. For example, it is hypothesized that the effects of a seismic survey within the hour preceding the aerial survey of a given location on the probability of observing a whale there depend on how far north and east (or south and west) of that location the seismic survey is located. Similarly, the effects of seismic surveys occurring at other times in the past will depend on these distances, though probably not in the same specific way. The analysis approach accounted for the multiple 'questions' posed in Objective 1 (below). We also consider whether presence of "acoustic barriers" (i.e., barrier island or shallow water) between a seismic source and a survey location influences the probability of sighting a bowhead there.

Objective 1

Quantify the number of bowhead sightings expected to be observed relative to distance and direction (E, W, N, S) from a seismic source, amount of exposure to sound pulses, and time since exposure. More specifically, we assess the change in the number of bowhead sightings expected to be observed

- with distance inshore and offshore of the seismic vessel at times when the airguns are operating;
- with distance east and west of the seismic vessel at times when the airguns are operating; and
- with the passage of time since the termination of seismic surveys.

Objective 2

H_a: The distribution of headings for "traveling" bowheads is deflected from the typical WNW migratory direction at distances up to w km east of the seismic vessel at times when the airguns are operating. [Bowheads recorded as being engaged in activities other than "traveling" should not be considered when addressing this hypothesis about traveling bowheads.]

H_0: The distribution of headings for "traveling" bowheads is not deflected from the typical WNW migratory direction east of the seismic vessel at times when the airguns are operating.

Objective 3

H_a: Operating airguns have reduced or no effect on the number of bowhead sightings expected to be observed if there is a barrier island or shallow water between the airguns and the whale sighting. [This hypothesis has not been tested formally in previous studies, but there is evidence that it is true – see Miller et al. (1999).]

H_0: Operating airguns have the *same effect* on the number of bowhead sightings expected to be observed if there is a barrier island or shallow water between the airguns and the whales.

Subsistence Hunting.—Only very limited data were available on specific locations and timing of whaling activities in 1996-98. However, we have structured the preliminary statistical model to include an "approximate" measure of whaling activity that addresses Objective 17. If a similar analysis is done for future years when more specific information about whaling may be available, the possible effects of nearby whaling on the probability of sighting bowheads could be tested more effectively.

Objective 17

H_a: The number of bowhead sightings expected to be observed tends to be reduced within whale hunting regions during the date range when hunting occurred within the region and year in question.

H_o: The number of bowhead sightings expected to be observed does not tend to be reduced within whale hunting regions during the date range when hunting occurred within the region and year in question.

METHODS

Selection of Data for Phase I

Numerous criteria were evaluated to determine which year(s) of data to analyze in Phase I. The Study Plan (LGL Ltd. 2003) discusses these criteria and provides details of the selection process. The following text summarizes the selection process.

It was originally planned that Phase I would involve the analysis of a single year of data collected during the 1979-1998 period, and we initially sought to identify the most suitable year for consideration in Phase I:

- An "Index of Completeness and Adequacy of Information in the Human Activities Database" (see Table 1 in LGL Ltd. 2003) was generated. Information documenting the industrial activities was most complete and reliable for the years from 1990 to 1998.

- It was originally intended that, during Phase I, we would initiate studying the combined effects of multiple types of industrial activity on bowhead whale distribution. It was thought that developing an approach to investigate the influences of more than one type of industry activity on bowhead distribution would be useful in preparing for Phase II even though a single year of data probably would not, in itself, allow for a meaningful analysis. Rather, it would provide a basis for judging the likelihood that a follow-up multi-year analysis would be successful in characterizing relationships of whale distribution to a number of natural and anthropogenic factors.

- Within the 1990-98 period, the industrial activities considered most likely to have a major influence on bowhead whale distribution were seismic exploration and offshore drilling, particularly drilling from drillships. Only the years 1991 and 1993 had both seismic surveys and offshore drilling from drillships.

- Drillship operations typically require support from icebreakers. Because icebreaker operations could potentially influence bowhead distribution (Richardson et al. 1995a,b) and are not well documented in the HAD, the minimal data on icebreaker activity was considered an important limitation in the dataset, especially for 1991. The 1993 season had very light ice conditions and icebreaking services were not required during the autumn bowhead migration whereas drilling activities in 1991 did require icebreaking support. Therefore, for 1993 the absence of detailed information about icebreaking operations should not confound conclusions about the effects of either seismic surveys or drilling operations.

- In addition to considerable drillship and seismic activity, 1993 also included substantial aerial survey coverage by both MMS and COPAC, with numerous bowhead whale sightings (Hall et al. 1994; Treacy 1994). For example, MMS recorded 235 sightings of 353 bowheads according to the original dataset developed by Treacy (1994). Unfortunately, a serious limitation of 1993 as a "test" year is that the COPAC data we obtained were lacking the visibility and sea state data that were recorded during those aerial surveys. We attempted to obtain a more complete version of the COPAC dataset. However, those efforts were unsuccessful, and we concluded that, in the absence of the detailed COPAC data, it would be better to select another year (or years) for the Phase I study.

As an alternative, data from 1998 or combined years 1996-98 were considered suitable for Phase I. The offshore human activities during these years were mainly limited to marine seismic operations, in contrast to the more variable activities in 1993. However, the use of combined years 1996-98 would have the advantage of giving us the opportunity to work with multi-year data in Phase I, which would be helpful in preparation for possible multi-year analyses in Phase II. The combined 1996-98 data would also include a greater diversity of ice conditions than present in 1998 (which was an especially light ice year). We had already worked extensively with the 1996-98 data on behalf of industry (Miller et al. 1999). Those data would, therefore, require less preparation than would have been required to organize the 1993 data, thereby making it practical to work with 3 years rather than the planned 1 year during Phase I. We decided (with MMS concurrence) to base the Phase I analyses on data from combined years 1996-98.

Aerial Surveys

During the autumns of 1996-98, aerial surveys for bowhead whales (and other marine mammals) were conducted in the Alaskan Beaufort Sea by MMS, by LGL on behalf of industry (BP and Western Geophysical), and by LGL for a MMS-funded bowhead feeding study (only in 1998). The combined data obtained during these surveys are used in this study. Details about aerial survey procedures by MMS (reports by Treacy) and LGL (reports by Miller et al. and Thomas et al.) can be found in the following reports:

1996: Treacy (1997), Miller et al. (1997)

1997: Treacy (1998), Miller et al. (1998)

1998: Treacy (2000), Miller et al. (1999), Thomas et al. (1999).

Summary of MMS Survey Procedures

Similar procedures were used by MMS during each year of surveys (1996-98) and survey effort details are summarized in Table 1. MMS bowhead surveys have been conducted in the fall of each year since 1979 and encompass a large area extending between 140°W and 157°W longitude, and from the nearshore zone north to 72°N latitude. The MMS annual survey program is based on a design of randomly located transects (see p. 5-6 *in* Treacy 1997 for a description) within 12 established geographic blocks (see Figure 1 *in* Treacy 1997) spanning the Alaskan Beaufort Sea. The randomly-selected transects were oriented approximately north–south, with one transect per 1/2° of longitude (i.e., averaging about 19 km apart). The selection of survey blocks to be flown on a given day was non-random, based on factors like weather and survey coverage attained during recent days. Any one survey block was typically sampled on about one day per week. Transects flown in 1996-98 are shown in Figure 1.

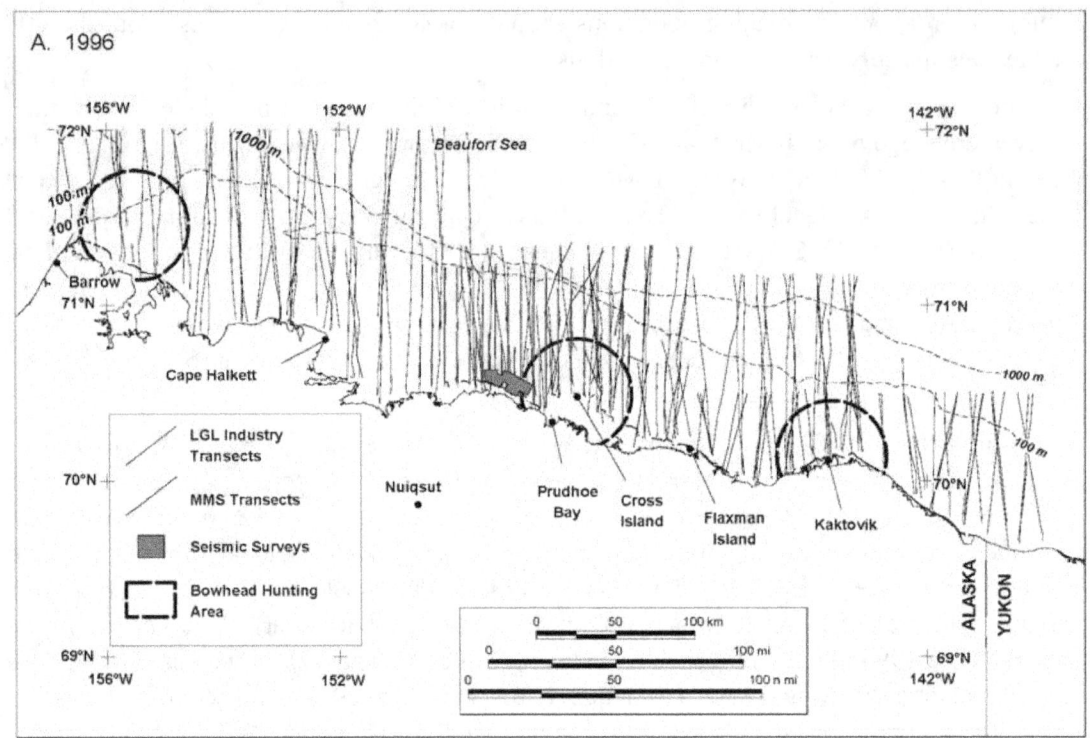

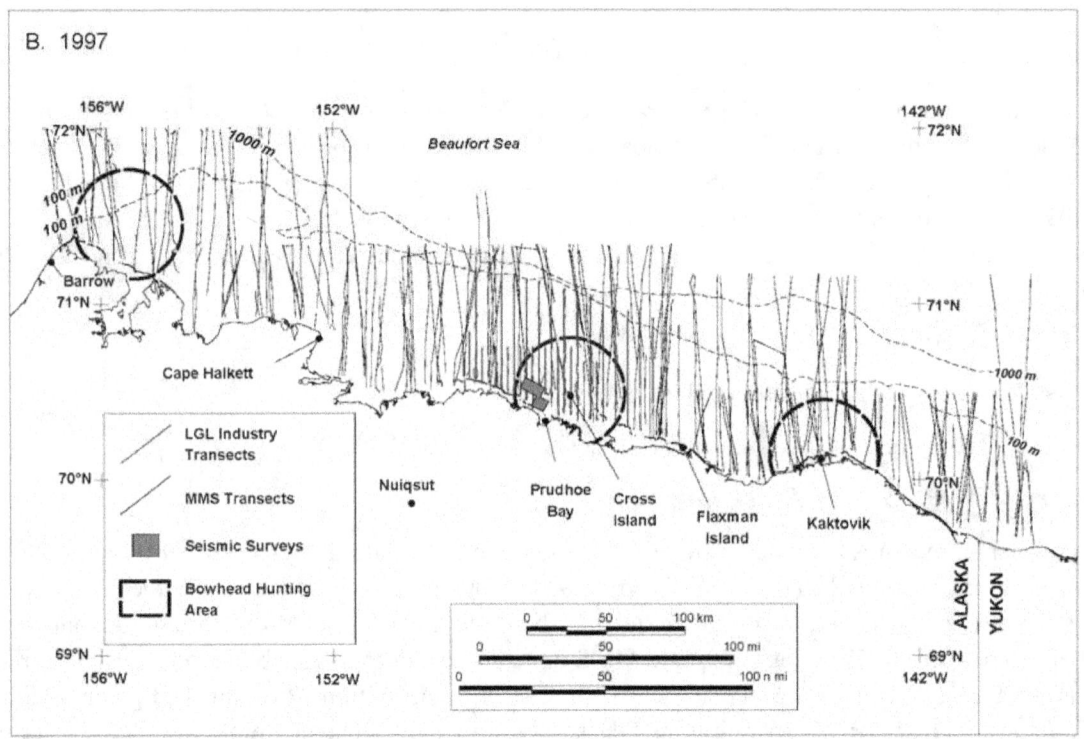

FIGURE 1. Locations of MMS, industry/LGL, and feeding study/LGL (only in 1998) aerial survey transects, seismic areas (gray shading), and approximate whaling areas in **(A)** 1996, **(B)** 1997, and **(C)** 1998.

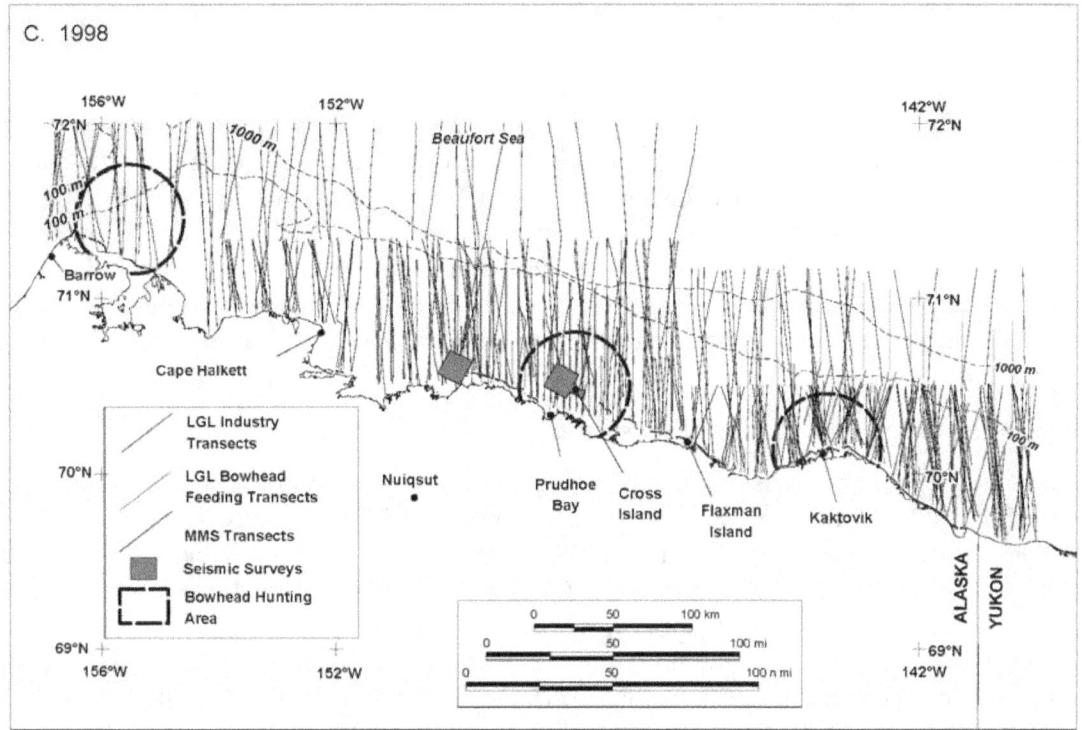

FIGURE 1. Concluded.

TABLE 1. Summary of dates flown and survey effort during MMS and LGL aerial surveys for bowhead whales in the Alaskan Beaufort Sea, fall 1996-98.

	Year		
	1996	**1997**	**1998**
MMS Surveys			
Dates Flown	1 Sep - 9 Oct	31 Aug - 19 Oct	31 Aug - 27 Oct
Linear Distance (km) [a]	13,056	13,604	21,302
Industry LGL Surveys			
Dates Flown	1-21 Sep	1-28 Sep	1 Sep - 15 Oct
Linear Distance (km) [b]	10,225	15,506	39,134
MMS LGL Feeding Study Survey			
Dates Flown			11-24 Sep
Linear Distance (km) [b]			3,187

[a] Only includes random-transect effort.
[b] Includes on-transect survey effort; does not exclude effort during periods of poor sightability.

In 1996-98, MMS surveys were conducted from a de Havilland Twin Otter Series 300 aircraft equipped with bubble windows. Surveys were conducted at a preferred altitude of 1500 ft (457 m) ASL (ranged from 1000 to 1500 ft) and a ground speed of 120 knots (222 km/h). Port observers included a primary observer at a bubble window, the pilot, and an occasional secondary observer-visitor, stationed aft at a flat window. Starboard observers included a data recorder-observer, a team leader, and a co-pilot. The team leader and co-pilot alternated between sitting at an aft bubble window and the copilot's seat. Observers recorded data on marine mammal sightings, environmental conditions (e.g., weather, sea state, ice cover), and start and end points of transects. Environmental conditions were recorded at turning points, when changes in environmental conditions were observed, and otherwise within 10-min intervals. Data were logged with a custom-written data-logging program that interfaced with an FMS 5000 GPS (Model GPS-505).

Summary of Industry/LGL Survey Procedures

Similar procedures were used by LGL during each year of surveys and survey effort details are summarized in Table 1. In 1996-98, surveys were conducted from a Twin Commander 680FL (twin engine high-wing aircraft) equipped with bubble windows. Surveys were conducted at a preferred altitude of 1000 ft (305 m) ASL (ranged from 900 to 1500 ft) and a ground speed of 120 knots (222 km/h). Two primary observers looked for bowhead whales; one occupied the front right (co-pilot's) seat and the other was on the left side of the aircraft, immediately behind the pilot. A third observer, who also operated a computerized data logger (GeoLink software interfaced with Trimble GPS), was positioned behind the co-pilot's seat. This third observer surveyed when not occupied with other duties. All observers sat at bubble windows. The two primary observers recorded environmental conditions every two minutes and all observers recorded details about whale sightings (number, species, activity, heading, swim speed, sighting cue, inclinometer angle, sighting cue, ice conditions, size/age/sex class, and altitude).

The industry-funded aerial surveys occurred in a much smaller geographic area than MMS surveys but provided more intensive survey coverage near marine seismic operations. A standard survey route was flown daily (weather permitting) that was "centered" on the location of seismic activity at that time. In 1996 and 1997, aerial surveys extended from ~30 km west of the western edge of the area where seismic work was underway east to ~50 km east of the eastern edge of that area. In 1998, aerial surveys extended from ~50 km west of the western edge to ~50 km east of the eastern edge of that area. During all three seasons, the surveys extended from the barrier islands north to 65-85 km offshore.

Within this study area, two series of systematic north-south transects were flown each day. The "extensive" grid nominally consisted of 12 transect lines in 1996-97 and 16 transect lines in 1998, all spaced 8 km apart. A smaller "intensive" grid over and near the area of seismic operations nominally consisted of 4 shorter transects spaced 8 km apart and midway between the nearby lines of the extensive grid. The survey grids for 1996-98 are included in Figure 1.

Summary of LGL/MMS 1998 Feeding Study Survey Procedures

Systematic aerial surveys were conducted during September of 1998 (and 1999-2000) as part of a study to assess the importance of the eastern Alaskan Beaufort Sea for feeding by bowhead whales. Those data are included in the Poisson regression analysis. The survey methods used in 1998 were very similar to those used in the LGL-industry surveys described above. The same type of aircraft was used and the survey procedures were similar, although the nominal survey speed was 200 km/h, rather than 222 km/h. The study area extended from 145°W east to the U.S./Canada border (as defined by the U.S.), which extends approximately NNE from the shoreline at 141°W. Standard transects were flown in two strata, the continental shelf stratum (from shore to the 200 m depth contour), and the continental slope stratum (depths 200-2000 m). Transect start positions were randomized and were oriented roughly perpendicular to the depth contours. There were 17 transects in the continental shelf stratum (totaling 1117 km), and 10 continental slope transects (totaling 516 km). During the 11-24 September 1998 study period, systematic surveys of the continental shelf stratum were flown three times (third survey only partially completed) on 11-14, 17, and 23-24 September. The continental slope stratum was surveyed once on 12 September. The survey transects are shown in Figure 1C.

Human Activities Summary

Seismic Surveys

Ocean Bottom Cable (OBC) seismic surveys were conducted in the nearshore waters of the central Alaskan Beaufort Sea during the open-water seasons of 1996-98. Although seismic programs began each year in late July, the time period of relevance to this study is September and October when seismic operations coincided with aerial surveys for bowhead whales. Seismic programs for 1996-98 are described in detail in Richardson (ed., 1997, 1998, 1999). In all three years, marine mammal observers (MMOs) were aboard the seismic vessel and were on watch at all times (day and night) with seismic surveys. Ramp-ups (soft starts) were used whenever airgun operations began, and the airguns were shut down when marine mammals were sighted within designated safety radii. Almost all shut downs in the 3 years were for seals near the seismic vessels; bowhead whales were very rarely sighted by vessel-based MMOs.

In 1996, seismic surveys occurred from 24 July through 19 September. The airgun array consisted of eleven 120 in^3 Bolt airguns totaling 1320 in^3 and primarily operated from the tug *Point Barrow*. Overall, a total of about 2946 km (355 h) of production seismic was shot. Of this, 1135 km (126 h) was shot during the period (September) when aerial surveys occurred. Surveys were conducted at various locations in and near the Northstar area northwest of Prudhoe Bay. These survey areas included waters from Prudhoe Bay West Dock out to about 45 km northwest of West Dock, and from the barrier islands out to as much as 13 km offshore of the barrier islands (see Fig. 1A). Water depths within the survey area ranged from 3 to 17 m.

In 1997, seismic surveys occurred from 26 July through 25 September. The airgun array consisted (at most times) of six Bolt airguns totaling 720 in^3 and primarily operated from the tug *Sag River*. The airgun array was operated for a total of 314.3 h in 1997. Surveys were conducted at various locations from the Northstar area (northwest of Prudhoe Bay) east to the Challenge Island – Flaxman Island area (see Fig. 1B). Water depths within the survey area ranged from 0 to 18 m. During September, the airgun array was operated for 93.6 h. From 1 to 20 September, operations were northwest of Prudhoe Bay in the West Dock and Northstar areas, west of Cross Island. From 21 to 25 September, operations were east of Prudhoe Bay.

In 1998, seismic surveys occurred from 24 July through 11 October. Two different airgun arrays were used alternately. These consisted of 16 sleeve-type airguns of various individual volumes totaling 1500 in^3 (towed by the primary source vessel *Arctic Star*) or eight sleeve-type airguns of equal volume totaling 560 in^3 (towed by the *Saber Tooth*, which operated in shallow waters). Overall, a total of about 4560 km of production seismic was shot. Seismic work was conducted at various locations in the central Alaskan Beaufort Sea from Flaxman Island west to the Spy Island area (near Oliktok Point; see Fig. 1C). Water depths within the survey area ranged from 2 to 24 m. During September and October, the airgun arrays were operated for 337.4 h. From 1 to 23 September, operations were northwest of Prudhoe Bay in the Jones Island area, ~ 65 km west of Cross Island. After 23 September seismic data were acquired near Cross Island.

Subsistence Hunting

Autumn subsistence hunts for bowhead whales in the Beaufort Sea occur near the communities of Kaktovik and Barrow. In addition the residents of Nuiqsut hunt bowheads near Cross Island, offshore of Prudhoe Bay. The typical hunting areas at each of these locations were mapped (see Fig. 1), based on historical harvest location data, information provided by the North Slope Borough (Craig George, Department of Wildlife Management, pers. comm.), and Galginaitis and Koski (2002). The actual or approximate hunting period for each community was determined for each year (1996-98), based on a variety of types of information, including field notes and personal observations (GWM), harvest dates, information provided by Tom Cook (Consultant to BP Exploration Alaska Inc. during 1996), and Galginaitis and Koski (2002). For the Kaktovik and Cross Island hunts, the actual start and end dates for the typically brief hunting periods were usually known. For Barrow, where the harvest in autumn is typically larger and the hunt is more prolonged, we used the date of the first and last whale harvest in each autumn season as the start and end dates, respectively, of the subsistence hunt.

Compilation of Data

Several types of data were used to derive the final database of 1996-98 survey effort, bowhead sightings, and covariates for use in the regression analysis. Data were acquired from marine mammal aerial surveys, bathymetric databases, and seismic shotpoint files from BP and Western Geophysical (now WesternGeco). Information concerning times and locations of subsistence whaling activity and a 'standardized' Beaufort Sea shoreline were also acquired and incorporated into the final regression analysis database.

Aerial Survey

For the period considered in Phase I (1996-98), the aerial survey data were derived from three sources: • the MMS BWASP database, which covers a broad geographic area; • industry-funded surveys that provide intensive survey coverage of relatively small areas varying from year to year; and • the MMS-funded bowhead feeding study conducted by LGL in the fall of 1998, which covered an area east of the area with industrial activity. (Details concerning aerial survey procedures are provided in the subsection "Aerial Surveys".)

MMS BWASP Dataset.—LGL Ltd. had worked extensively with a portion of the BWASP/NOSC data, those from areas east of ~150°W longitude (Harrison Bay), for other projects (e.g., LGL and Greene-ridge 1996; Miller et al. 1999, 2002). For this project, we acquired a complete version of the BWASP/NOSC database for 1979 to 2000, covering the entire geographic range of MMS surveys, via the National Oceanographic Data Center.

Site-Specific Industry-Sponsored Datasets.—The industry-funded (BP and Western Geophysical) survey data collected by LGL during the 1996-98 seismic programs were available in a useable digital format. For each of those three years, there were agreements for two-way sharing of aerial survey data collected by MMS and for industry. The MMS data had already been made available by MMS for use in industry-sponsored analyses (e.g., Miller et al. 1999). This analysis and report represents the first use of the industry-sponsored data in an MMS project.

1998 Feeding Study Dataset.—LGL Ltd., on behalf of MMS, conducted aerial surveys during the fall of 1998 in the eastern Alaskan Beaufort Sea as part of a bowhead whale feeding study (Miller et al. 2002). As a result, we had the data in a useable digital format.

Seismic Shotpoint Data

LGL had previously worked with seismic shotpoint databases that were collected by seismic contractors on behalf of BP in 1996 and 1997 and by Western Geophysical in 1998 (see subsection Seismic Surveys). Shotpoint data consisted of date, time, latitude, and longitude for only those shotpoints when the airgun array was firing at or above 'specification' levels. In 1997 and 1998, two vessels were used to acquire seismic data; a primary source vessel which operated the airgun array for the majority of operations and a secondary source vessel that acquired relatively less data. The primary and secondary source vessels did not operate simultaneously in any survey year. Typically, during the 1996-98 seismic programs, airguns were fired at 20 sec intervals. These shotpoint files had been used by LGL in previous analyses of ship-based and aerial survey data collected as part of marine mammal monitoring programs. Raw shotpoint datasets had also been included in the HAD, with industry permission. However, the version of the shotpoint files included in the HAD did not contain interpolated values for unrecorded shots fired during "ramp ups", certain line changes, and lines that had to re-shot. The versions of the shotpoint files used for the analyses described in LGL's reports for BP and Western Geophysical were considered more complete because they contained interpolated shotpoint locations for times when actual shotpoints were not specifically documented. Therefore, the latter shotpoint files (rather than those in the HAD) were used in deriving the measures of seismic activity used in this study.

Bathymetry Data

Bathymetry data for the study area were acquired from two sources: the National Ocean Survey Bathymetry database and the International Bathymetric Chart of the Arctic Ocean database. As part of other studies LGL had conducted concerning the Alaskan Beaufort Sea, we had constructed a grid-based bathymetry dataset at a resolution of 200 m x 200 m, including both water depth and bottom slope estimates for each grid cell. This dataset was derived from precise nearshore bathymetry values derived from the National Ocean Survey Bathymetry database for areas <20 km (approximately) from shore, and the more general offshore International Bathymetric Chart of the Arctic Ocean database. The two bathymetry databases were merged and water depth values were interpolated to provide grid cell coverage for the entire study area.

Subsistence Whaling Data

As discussed previously, information on the approximate locations and dates of subsistence whaling activity in 1996-98 were acquired from several sources. Traditional whale hunting areas in the Beaufort Sea were constructed from historical whale kill locations at each of three main hunting areas, Kaktovik, Cross Island, and Barrow and were combined with the time periods when the hunting seasons occurred (Table 2). These data were later incorporated into the regression analysis database.

Metadata

Details about the aerial survey, seismic shotpoint, bathymetry, and whaling data used in Phase I are fully documented. To do this, we retrieved documentation concerning the original coding scheme and survey methods used in each project, especially the methods used to record environmental conditions. Information obtained from this process formed part of the metadata included with the datasets used during Phase I. The metadata also include all variable names and a description of the codes used.

TABLE 2. Summary of dates used for 1996-98 whaling seasons at Kaktovik, Cross Island and Barrow.

Location	Year	First Day of Whaling Season	Last Day of Whaling Season	First Harvest Date	Last Harvest Date	Source of Information (First Day; Last Day)
Kaktovik						
	1996	07-Sep	17-Sep	12-Sep	12-Sep	Notes from Tom Cook; Notes from Tom Cook
	1997	03-Sep	27-Sep	03-Sep	27-Sep	Galginaitis and Koski 2002; Field notes (GWM)
	1998	04-Sep	15-Sep	04-Sep	14-Sep	Galginaitis and Koski 2002; Field notes (GWM)
Cross Island						
	1996	7 Sept.	17-Sep	12-Sep	15-Sep	Notes from Tom Cook; Notes from Tom Cook
	1997	02-Sep	22-Sep	05-Sep	20-Sep	Assumed that whaling started the day after Labor Day; Field Notes (GWM)
	1998	08-Sep	18-Sep	12-Sep	17-Sep	Assumed that whaling started the day after Labor Day; Field Notes (GWM)
Barrow						
	1996	10-Sep	26-Sep	10-Sep	26-Sep	First Harvest Date; Last Harvest Date
	1997	11-Sep	21-Oct	11-Sep	21-Oct	First Harvest Date; Last Harvest Date
	1998	19-Sep	07-Oct	19-Sep	07-Oct	First Harvest Date; Last Harvest Date

Standardization of Data

The aerial survey datasets were examined carefully, along with their accompanying documentation, before data manipulation began. Data were validated through several procedures that are described in Appendix C. Variables that were coded differently in the different aerial survey datasets were harmonized to a common coding scheme. The variables that were re-coded are described below.

Recoding of Variables

The MMS and LGL aerial surveyors coded several environmental variables somewhat differently. Variables that needed standardization included visibility, altitude, ice cover, and distance from shoreline.

Visibility was re-coded to account for differences between subjective sightability ratings and visibility codes included in the LGL aerial survey data as compared with the visibility values recorded in the MMS data (see Table 3). In the MMS dataset, visibility estimates were recorded mainly when changes in environmental conditions were observed. During LGL surveys, visibility estimates (in km) were recorded by observers at the start and end of each transect, but in addition a sightability rating was provided for each 2-min time interval along each transect. These sightability codes were converted to visibility estimates in km. For the purposes of the regression analysis database, a new "Visibility" variable was created that had values ranging from 0 to 4 that incorporated both the LGL and MMS aerial survey data (Table 3).

'Survey altitude', as recorded in the LGL and MMS datasets, was standardized to have all values expressed in meters (vs. feet) above sea level.

Ice cover during most aerial surveys was coded as a percentage ranging from 0 to 100%. During 1996 industry-funded surveys, ice cover was recorded using an unequal interval scale (Table 4). These data were re-coded to percent ice cover by taking the midpoint of the interval as the percent ice cover.

Database Structure

The Feasibility Study (see Appendix A) concluded that logistic regression would be the analysis of choice for the "Analysis of Covariance". It was initially thought that logistic regression would be most

TABLE 3. Summary of visibility coding scheme used in the regression analysis database and the corresponding codes in the LGL and MMS aerial survey databases.

New 'Visibility' Coding Scheme for Regression Analysis Database	LGL Sightability Code	MMS Visibility Code
0 (<1 km)	Impossible	0 (0 km); 1 (<1 km)
1 (1-2 km)	Seriously impaired	2 (1-2 km)
2 (2-3 km)	Moderately impaired	3 (2-3 km)
3 (3-5 km)	Good	4 (3-5 km)
4 (>5 km)	Excellent	5 (6-10 km); 6 (>10 km)

TABLE 4. Summary of the ice cover coding scheme used in the 1996 LGL industry-funded aerial surveys and the corresponding ice cover values used in the regression analysis database.

'Ice Cover' Values (%) for Regression Analysis Database	LGL Ice Cover for 1996	
	Code	Value Range (%)
0.5	0	0 - 0.9
2.5	1	1-5
15.5	2	6-25
38.0	3	26-50
63.0	4	51 - 75
83.0	5	76 - 90
95.0	6	91 - 99
100.0	7	100

suitable because, when aerial surveys are subdivided into sampling units sufficiently small to provide adequate spatial resolution, bowhead whales are detected in only a small minority of the sampling units. Also, when whales are detected, most sightings consist of individuals or small groups. Standard logistic regression approaches are appropriate for "presence–absence" data of this type. Initially, we tried creating sampling units 1 km in length but found the number of records produced to be prohibitively large and difficult to process with desktop computers. As such, we explored the effect of increasing the sample unit size to segments 5 km in length. Although this did not produce many transect segments with multiple bowhead whale sightings, a few sample units included up to 5 individual sightings. Consequently, the analysis approach was changed from logistic to Poisson regression, in which the dependent variable is the number of whale sightings in a sampling unit. Poisson regression is appropriate for a situation such as this, where the number of sightings per unit is sometimes more than 1, but always small.

As with the logistic regression approach, the use of Poisson regression requires that the aerial survey coverage be divided into sample units and that the predictor variables ("covariates") be defined and coded in a standard way across all aerial surveys considered in the analysis. The following section discusses the types of databases generated from the various aerial survey, bathymetry, and shotpoint files.

It also discusses how sample units, predictor variables, and the dependent variable were defined and coded.

Regression Analysis and Sightings Databases

The Poisson regression analysis was based on one final and overall database referred to as the "regression analysis" database. As noted in the Study Plan (LGL Ltd. 2003), the format of this database was kept simple, basically a flat ASCII file with each record (row of data) representing a sample unit that was nominally 5 km of survey transect. In this file, one column contained the number of bowhead sightings in that segment of transect, and the remaining columns contained predictor variables (covariates) that would potentially be used in the regression procedure. In addition, five bowhead sightings databases were generated: one for each of the three annual industry-funded surveys, one for the combined 1996-98 MMS surveys, and one for the 1998 LGL Bowhead Feeding Study survey. Each of these sighting databases had an index number at the beginning of each record to reference (match) the sighting with a particular sample unit in the "regression analysis" database. Only sightings that were considered on-transect were extracted to the final regression analysis database.

Sample Units

Not all of the bowheads that are present along aerial survey tracklines are seen during aerial surveys. Bowheads may be missed by observers because of obstruction by parts of the aircraft structure, poor sighting conditions, limitations of observers in seeing and recognizing animals, and because they are below the surface and invisible for a significant amount of time (Thomas et al. 2002).

One factor that affects the probability of sighting a bowhead at the surface is the distance of that bowhead from the survey trackline. This factor has a bearing on the selection of the size of the sample unit. We selected a sample unit that extends laterally to 2.5 km from the survey trackline (on each side). Thomas et al. (2002) found that on average, 5% of bowhead sightings were sighted beyond 2 km from the trackline. An area extending slightly more than 2 km laterally would include most of the whale sightings.

As noted, the standard length of a sample unit (along the trackline) was 5 km. This limited the spatial resolution of the analysis to ~5 km. That is reasonable in an analysis concentrating on the effects of seismic surveys on bowheads. Previous univariate analyses of the same 1996-98 data have showed that most migrating bowheads avoided the area within 20 km of the operating seismic vessel (Miller et al. 1999; Richardson et al. 1999). Thus, a 5 km spatial resolution should be sufficient for this analysis. If there were specific interest in smaller-scale effects, which could be the case in Phase II, then it might be desirable to work with smaller transect segments, e.g., 1 km × 1 km, despite the practical difficulties in dealing with the larger dataset (see above).

The environmental and sighting data required for use in the Poisson regression model were derived from the aerial survey databases maintained by MMS and LGL. A Visual Basic (version 4) program was developed that processed the raw datasets (three different formats) with the associated files of GPS location data (if applicable). The result was an intermediate database that contained summaries of environmental variables and bowhead whale sightings within 5-km segments of survey transects. A series of 5-km segments began at the start of a transect line and progressed until the end of the transect line. The last segment of transect was usually substantially less than 5 km in length. (In the Poisson regression analyses, these shorter-than-normal segments were handled by introducing an offset into the models—see 'Assessing Model Fit' later.)

The Visual Basic program loaded the details of each survey transect into an array along with details about bowhead sightings. Sightings detected at lateral distances greater than 2.5 km from the survey trackline were excluded. Also, for LGL surveys, only the sightings recorded by the primary observers on the left and right sides of the aircraft were included. For MMS surveys, we included all sightings because it was not clear at the time of this study which sightings were recorded by primary vs. other observers. Initially, the program summarized environmental variables (visibility, ice cover, sea state) and numbers of individuals and groups of bowheads on each side of the aircraft separately. For analysis in the Poisson regression model, visibility, percent ice cover and sea state were averaged for the left and right observers, and the numbers of bowhead individuals and groups seen by the left and right observers were summed. Data from the two sides of the plane were combined to reduce the sample size and concerns about spatial correlation. Because data from the left and right sides of the survey plane were pooled, each sample unit nominally consisted of an area of 5 km length × 5 km width (2.5 + 2.5 km) = 25 km². In most cases, the segment at the end of a transect was smaller.

Extracting Spatial Covariates

Each record (sample unit) in the database included water depth and bottom slope values. Using MapInfo (a GIS), a geographic lookup was performed for bathymetry and slope values for every sample unit within the dataset. Water depth and slope values were estimated for the center of the sample unit. In addition, the minimum distance between the standardized shoreline and the center of each sample unit was calculated (via a macro in MapInfo). An additional variable was added to indicate whether the sampling unit overlapped temporally and geographically with whaling activity during the year in question.

Generating Seismic Terms

To address Objective 1, which involved assessing the change in bowhead numbers relative to distance and direction (E, W, N, S) from a seismic source, amount of exposure to airgun pulses, and time since exposure, a series of terms characterizing exposure to seismic surveys were generated. As suggested in the Study Plan, we considered the amount and location(s) of seismic activity during the time periods 0-1, 1-2, 2-3, 3-6, 6-12, and 12-24 hours before the aerial survey of the sample unit in question. For each sample unit, a Visual Basic program was used to search through the databases of primary and secondary seismic shotpoints (shotpoints acquired from primary and secondary seismic source vessels— see subsection Seismic Shotpoint Data) to identify those shots that occurred within each of the above time intervals before the sample unit was surveyed. For each sample unit, we kept separate tallies for each time interval (and separately for the primary and secondary seismic sources) of the

- number of shots,
- number of shotpoints with poor position estimates (positions that were interpolated and suggested the occurrence of a shot outside a known area of seismic survey activity),
- east offset (m) from the longitude of the sample unit to the average shot location for a particular time interval (west offsets negative),
- north offset (m) from the latitude of the sample unit to the average shot location for a particular time interval (south offsets negative),
- actual distance (m) from the center of the sample unit to the average shot location for a particular time interval,

- azimuth from the center of the sample unit to the average shot location for a particular time interval, and

- seismic activity level based on the assumption that a standard seismic survey included 1 shot every 20 seconds, i.e., 180 shots per hour if the seismic survey was continuous. To derive a measure of the seismic activity level, the actual number of shots in the time period was divided by the number expected if the rate were 180 /hr. For example, if a seismic source operated at 200 shots per hour, then the seismic activity value was $\theta = 200/180 = 1.11$. If shooting occurred at 200 shots per hour for half of the "3-6 hr before survey" period (i.e., for 1.5 h), then the corresponding activity level would be $(200 \times 1.5) / (180 \times 3) = 0.56$.

If only shots with poor position estimates were found in a time interval, the record was not used in regression analyses that tested for seismic effects.

It was necessary to combine data from primary and secondary seismic sources in order to assess the additive effects of two seismic sources that both operated (albeit not simultaneously) within a given time period. A new variable was generated for each time interval, which represented the combined activity of both primary and secondary seismic sources; θ values for primary and secondary sources were summed. Similarly, east and north offset variables were combined for primary and secondary sources for each time interval. This was accomplished by summing east and north offset values for the primary and secondary seismic source offsets. Note that combining east and north offset values (and corresponding θ values) for two seismic sources in an exponential function (i.e., Poisson regression) effectively reduces the combined offset values relative to either of the individual source offset values.

The seismic terms described above are perhaps better explained with the use of theoretical regression equations. Seismic effects were modeled by including terms of the form $b_0I + b_1E + b_2N + b_3EN + b_4E^2 + b_5N^2$ in the Poisson regression model. Here $I = 1$ if a seismic effect is present, and is otherwise 0. E is the (signed) distance east from the source, and N is the (signed) distance north from the source. Distances west and south would be negative. For a sample unit without a seismic effect, E and N (like I) are 0. Higher order terms (X^3 etc.) were sometimes included to assess potential cubic relationships. If a source only operates for a fraction θ of the time interval being considered, then I, E, N, EN, E^2 and N^2 would be reduced to θI, θE, θN, θEN, θE^2 and θN^2, to give a fraction θ of the full effect. If two seismic sources (primary and secondary) are both occurring in the same time interval, then initially their effects will be assumed to be additive. Using the subscripts 1 and 2 to denote the two sources, operating for fractions θ_1 and θ_2 of the hour, then the additive effects would be represented by $b_0I(\theta_1 + \theta_2) + b_1(\theta_1E_1 + \theta_2E_2) + b_2(\theta_1N_1 + \theta_2N_2) + b_3(\theta_1E_1N_1 + \theta_2E_2N_2) + b_4(\theta_1E_1^2 + \theta_2E_2^2) + b_5(\theta_1N_1^2 + \theta_2N_2^2)$. Here the sample unit is at position (E_1,N_1) relative to the first source and position (E_2,N_2) relative to the second source.

Another consideration in generating the seismic terms was determining the minimum water depth between the sample unit and the seismic source. Minimum water depth values were derived for each sample unit if seismic activity had occurred during a given time interval. Based on this measure, we attempted to investigate whether barrier islands and/or shallow water areas ("acoustic barriers") reduced the effects of seismic surveys on bowhead distribution. For this preliminary analysis, we assumed that if the minimum water depth was

- less than 2 m, then the potential for a seismic effect was negligible,
- more than 20 m, then there was no reduction in seismic effects, and
- d, where 2 m $< d <$ 20 m, then the seismic activity value θ was multiplied by $(d - 2)/18$.

This then gives a linear scaling effect between 0 with minimum depth ≤2 m and 1 with minimum depth ≥20 m. Minimum water depth scaling was applied as an additional scaling after the θ scaling (for seismic activity), as described above.

Dependent Variable

The dependent variable for the Poisson regression is the number of bowhead sightings per sample unit (nominally a 25 km^2 area defined above). Either a single bowhead or a group of bowheads was counted as one sighting.

Predictor Variables

The names of the predictor variables used in the analysis are listed below. Predictor variables have been categorized into three groups: (1) natural, (2) sightability, and (3) human activity variables. If any of the predictor variables were missing for a transect segment then that transect segment was not used for fitting any of the Poisson model runs. All variables in the Poisson regression except survey year, visibility, aircraft type, survey type, and whaling activity were considered continuous. Quadratic terms were included for the continuous predictor variables water depth, distance from the shore, longitude, bottom slope, and date to investigate possible non-linear trends. Cubic terms were considered for some seismic variables.

(1) Natural Variables

Ice Cover (%)	Ice data, on a percentage basis, were standardized for all surveys and coded as integers ranging from 0 to 100 %. Linear and quadratic terms were included.
Distance to Shore (km)	This covariate was calculated based on the distance in km from the 'standardized' shoreline to the center of the sample unit. Linear and quadratic terms were included.
Water depth (m)	This covariate was calculated as the water depth at the center of the sample unit. Linear and quadratic terms were included.
Date	The day number with 30 August = –1 (earliest date), 1 Sep = 1, …, 26 Oct = 56 (latest date). Linear and quadratic terms were included.
Year	This covariate was coded as 1996 = 1, 1997 = 2, and 1998 = 3.
Longitude	This variable was coded in degrees, with minutes and seconds of longitude converted to decimal degrees. For each sample unit, longitude was taken at the center of a sample unit. For the regression analysis longitude was standardized based on a reference value of 150°.
Bottom Slope (Degrees)	The slope of the ocean bottom was calculated as an absolute value derived at the center of the sample unit. It was calculated as the number of degrees from a horizontal plane. (MapInfo estimated the maximum slope angle across the four corners of each 200 x 200 m bathymetry grid cell.)

(2) Sightability Variables

Sea State	Sea state conditions were recorded as Beaufort wind force and coded as integers ranging from 0 to 9.

Visibility	Visibility conditions were standardized for all surveys and coded as values ranging from 0 to 4. The codes 0-4 represent <1, 1-2, 2-3, 3-5, and >5 km, respectively.
Aircraft Type	This is a factor with one level for each aircraft type. For LGL surveys the Twin Commander 680FL was coded as 1 and for MMS surveys the DHC Twin Otter was coded as 2.
Altitude (m)	Aircraft altitude was coded in meters for all survey data.
Survey Type	This is a factor with one level for each survey type. LGL surveys were coded as 1 and MMS surveys were coded as 2. This variable essentially duplicated the "Aircraft Type" variable given the consistent use of two specific aircraft types by LGL and MMS during the years in question.

(3) Human Activity Variables

Seismic Survey Activities	The potential effects of seismic survey activities were considered in terms of time and space. For example, it is hypothesized that the effects of seismic surveys occurring within the last hour on the expected number of whale groups in a sample unit depend on how far north and east (or south and west) of the unit the activity is located. Similarly, the effects of seismic surveys occurring at other times (e.g., 1-2 h, 2-3 h, etc.) in the past will depend on these distances, although not necessarily in the same manner. We distinguished and considered the possible effects of seismic surveys that occurred in the time intervals 0-1, 1-2, 2-3, 3-6, 6-12 and 12-24 hours before the observation time. We also considered the influences of minimum water depth between a seismic source and sample unit. See subsection "Generation of Seismic Terms" (above) for more detail.
Within Whaling Season and Area	Survey effort in each 5-km bin was coded as to whether (1) or not (0) it was within an autumn bowhead hunting range during the hunting season associated with that range in that year. The hunting areas near Kaktovik, Cross Island, and Barrow were considered.

Analyses

Data Excluded

Only on-transect survey effort and sightings data were considered in the analysis. MMS effort and sightings collected during "Search" and "Connect" flight segments were excluded. All sightings (MMS and LGL surveys) >2.5 km from the survey trackline were excluded. For LGL (industry and bowhead feeding) aerial surveys, only bowhead sightings by primary observers were used in analyses. For MMS aerial surveys, sightings by all observers were used, as described previously. If any of the predictor variables were missing for a transect segment then that transect segment was not used for fitting any of the Poisson model runs. This resulted in the exclusion of ~7 % of the transect segments (1696 of 24,393 segments) from analyses.

Data were not excluded based on Beaufort sea state or visibility conditions. However, surveys were not usually flown in wind force conditions >5 for LGL surveys and >4 for MMS surveys. Also, covariates were included to account for the expected reductions in sightability with high wind force and low visibility.

Descriptive Statistics

The means and standard deviations, and minimum and maximum values, were calculated for each predictor variable based on the data included in the Poisson regression analysis. The number of bowhead sightings on-transect during periods with and without seismic activity was also calculated. All descriptive statistics were determined for each year (1996-98) separately and overall.

Poisson Regression

Poisson regression is also known as log-linear modeling. It is a standard approach for the analysis of count data, and is analogous to the multiple regression approach commonly applied to continuous data. With multiple regression, the model assumed is

$$Y = ß_0 + ß_1X_1 + ß_2X_2 + ... + ß_pX_p + \epsilon,$$

where Y is a dependent variable, the Xs are covariates (explanatory variables), and the error ϵ is assumed to be normally distributed with mean zero and a constant variance. This means that Y itself is assumed to be normally distributed with an expected value (mean) of

$$E(Y) = ß_0 + ß_1X_1 + ß_2X_2 + ... + ß_pX_p.$$

A Poisson regression is similar, but the dependent variable Y is a count that is assumed to have an expected value given by the equation

$$E(Y) = \exp(ß_0 + ß_1X_1 + ß_2X_2 + ... + ß_pX_p).$$

Here the X variables are still thought of as accounting for variation in Y. However, it is assumed that Y has a Poisson distribution instead of a normal distribution. An important assumption for both the standard multiple regression model and the Poisson regression model is that the errors in observations, Y - E(Y), are independently distributed for all of the observations.

There are two reasons for using a Poisson regression model with count data in preference to the standard multiple regression model. First, the use of the exponential function ensures that negative expected counts cannot occur. Second, the discrete Poisson distribution is more appropriate than the continuous normal distribution for count data. The theory and applications of this model are described in considerable detail by McCullagh and Nelder (1989) and Cameron and Trivedi (1998).

The expected value of Y for a Poisson regression model can be written in the alternative form

$$E(Y) = \exp(ß_0) \cdot \exp(ß_1X_1) \cdot \exp(ß_2X_2) \cdot ...\exp(ß_pX_p).$$

This emphasizes that the effects of the covariates are assumed to operate multiplicatively rather than additively. That is to say, there is a basic frequency $\exp(ß_0)$, which is modified by being multiplied by the factors $\exp(ß_1X_1)$, $\exp(ß_2X_2)$, ... $\exp(ß_pX_p)$ to account for the effects of the variables X_1, X_2, ..., X_p, respectively.

Fitting a log-linear model is usually done by maximum likelihood. This involves finding the values of the ß parameters so as to maximize the probability of obtaining the observed data. This is more complicated than fitting a multiple regression equation, and usually requires iterative calculations. Computer programs for these calculations often allow the observed counts to depend on both quantitative variables and factors, and interactions between these. For example, the coefficient of the covariate X_1

might be assumed to vary with the year that the data are collected when the data are collected over a number of years.

Assessing Model Fit

In assessing a log-linear model for a set of data, there are four aspects of the fit that can be considered:

(a) The goodness of fit of the model can be measured by one or both of the log-likelihood statistic

$$X_L^2 = 2 \Sigma \, O_i \, \log_e(O_i \, / \, E_i),$$

and the Pearson chi-squared statistic

$$X_P^2 = \Sigma \, (O_i - E_i)^2 \, / \, E_i.$$

Here O_i represents an observed count, E_i represents an expected count, and the summation is over all of the counts in the data. The degrees of freedom (df) associated with these statistics are $n - p - 1$, where n is the total number of data records (sample units in this study) and p is the number of covariates in the model. If one of these statistics is significantly large in comparison with tables of percentage points of the chi-squared distribution, then there is evidence that the model being considered does not fit the data. The statistic X_L^2 is commonly referred to as the deviance for a model.

(b) The residuals $O_i - E_i$ can be studied to see whether there are some observed frequencies that are fitted particularly poorly by the model. Since the standard deviation of O_i is approximately $\sqrt{E_i}$, the ith standardized residual can be defined to be

$$R_i = (O_i - E_i)/\sqrt{E_i}.$$

Then one simple way to detect a poor fit is to isolate the residuals that are more than two standard deviations from zero, i.e., cases where $|R_i| \geq 2$. These residuals are significantly large at approximately the 5% level.

(c) The most important regression variables can be determined by comparing the estimated ß values with their standard errors. Any estimate that is more than two standard errors from zero, which is shown by

$$|(\text{Estimate})/(\text{Standard Error})| > 2,$$

is significantly different from zero at approximately the 5% level.

(d) The improvement in the fit that is obtained by adding one or more extra covariates into the model can be assessed by considering the reduction in the deviance that is obtained by adding the extra variables. The significance of this reduction can be determined by comparing it with the percentage points of the chi-squared distribution using as df the number of extra X variables involved. A significantly large reduction indicates that the extra X variables make a useful contribution to the model. This method of assessing the value of X variables is sometimes called the analysis of deviance.

It is common to find that even the model with all possible covariates included does not fit the data well. This may just reflect the fact that few models are perfect, so that a significant lack of fit can be expected with most large data sets. However, an alternative explanation is that the observed frequencies do not follow a Poisson distribution. If the latter explanation is correct then the variance of an observed count may exceed its expected value, so that there is extraneous variance present.

One reason for extraneous variance is that the observations may not really be independent, which is a basic assumption of the Poisson regression model. Extraneous variance can occur because there is a tendency for larger-than-expected counts to occur with observations taken at about the same time. The effect of this is to raise the variance of each of the data counts above what is expected for a sample of independent observations.

One way of taking into account extraneous variance involves assuming that the variances of all the data counts are multiplied by the same heterogeneity factor, H, which can be estimated by either

$$\hat{H}_L = X_L{}^2 / (n - p - 1),$$

based on the deviance, or

$$\hat{H}_P = X_P{}^2 / (n - p - 1),$$

based on the Pearson chi-squared statistic. In either case the calculation should be made for a model that is believed to be reasonable, except that it may contain one or more covariates that do not in fact influence the counts.

The variances of the estimated coefficients of the X variables in the model are adjusted for extraneous variance by multiplying all of them by $\hat{H}_L$ or $\hat{H}_P$. McCullagh and Nelder (1989) suggest that $\hat{H}_P$ is probably best for this purpose. In addition, the analysis of deviance described in (d) above is modified. Instead of comparing the reduction in deviance due to adding m covariates with the chi-squared distribution with m df, this reduction is divided by $\hat{H}_L$ and assessed for significance in comparison with the F-distribution with m and n - p - 1 df.

Occasions do arise where there is a reason to believe that expected counts will be proportional to some known constants in the absence of any effects of the predictor variables used in a Poisson regression model. This can be allowed for using what is called an offset. For example, with the bowhead whale data considered in this report, the sample unit was in most cases a 5 km segment of a transect. However, for most transects, there was a segment of less than 5 km length at the end of the transect. A reasonable assumption is that the number of groups of whales expected to be seen in a transect length of D < 5 km will be proportional to D/5. Hence if the expected number of whale groups for a stretch of length 5 km is

$$E(Y) = \exp(\beta_0 + \beta_1 X_1 + \beta_2 X_2 + ... + \beta_p X_p),$$

then for the stretch of length D this will become

$$E(Y) = (D/5)\exp(\beta_0 + \beta_1 X_1 + \beta_2 X_2 + ... + \beta_p X_p),$$

or

$$E(Y) = \exp\{\log_e(D/5) + \beta_0 + \beta_1 X_1 + \beta_2 X_2 + ... + \beta_p X_p\}.$$

The offset is then $\log_e(D/5)$, which is a reasonable allowance for the shorter-than-usual transect length. Many computer programs for Poisson regression allow an offset variable, in this case containing the values of $\log_e(D/5)$, to be defined and used in the analysis.

The methods used in Poisson regression are reliable when most of the expected counts are not very small for the data set being analyzed. The precise conditions for the methods to be reliable are not clearly defined. However, for the bowhead whale data, most of the expected counts are very small indeed, and almost all of the observations (5-km segments) contain no whale sightings. It is therefore clear that with these data the standard methods may not be reliable, particularly in terms of the standard errors of parameter estimates and tests of significance. This problem can be overcome by the use of simulation, bootstrap, and randomization methods, depending upon the circumstances (Manly 1997). For example, to estimate a heterogeneity factor many sets of data can be generated based on a fitted model but with the data following Poisson distributions. An estimate of the heterogeneity factor is then provided by the observed deviance for the fitted model divided by the mean deviance for the simulated sets of data. Alternatively, the Pearson chi-squared statistic for the observed data could be divided by the mean value of this statistic from the simulated sets of data. See also the stratified bootstrap resampling analysis proposed by Manly and Chotkowski (2006) for count data with many zeros.

Correlation

There is potential that serial correlation (i.e., the tendency for spatially and/or temporally adjacent sampling units to have positively correlated numbers of sightings) in the Poisson regression model may affect the estimated coefficients and their standard errors. Although we did not account for correlation in the model, we did investigate the potential influences of serially correlated errors by simulating data from a relatively simple Poisson model (see Appendix D). Based on this analysis, it seemed that serially correlated errors should have minimal effect on estimated standard errors except when correlations are very strong.

Maps of Model Results

A series of maps were produced based on the fitted Poisson regression models. The maps allow us to visualize the results of the analyses based on the "actual" geographic setting where data were collected (Alaskan Beaufort Sea). Coefficients estimated by the Poisson regression models plus some selected predictor variable values were used to produce maps showing the number of whale groups expected to be seen in each sample unit under the specified conditions. The following predictor variables that were included in the final models and that were spatial in nature were considered in this process:

- water depth
- distance from shore
- longitude
- offset east (or west) from seismic
- offset north (or south) from seismic.

The non-spatial predictor variables that were "held constant" were chosen to represent average to good aerial survey conditions:

- "visibility" excellent (4),
- "Beaufort sea state" low to moderate (3),
- "ice cover" 0 %,
- "date" (held constant for a given map), and
- "survey type" was MMS surveys (2).

The spatial and non-spatial variables were processed by the regression equation for each 5 km x 5 km grid location within the Alaskan Beaufort Sea study area producing an estimate of whale groups expected to be seen at that location. The estimates were restricted to areas with distance from shore values > 0 km and < 185 km and areas with water depth < 2700 m; this essentially defines the MMS survey area and includes all of the industry/LGL survey areas.

Maps were chosen to highlight the capability of the Poisson model to demonstrate three things: (1) the nearshore migration corridor of bowhead whales, (2) the effects of seismic sources on the expected number of bowhead sightings, and (3) the temporal progression of the fall bowhead whale migration from east to west. A series of eight maps was produced for each year (1996-98), for a total of 24 maps. For each year, the fall progression of bowhead whale migration was shown on four maps representing four dates: 1 September, 15 September, 1 October, and 15 October. To demonstrate seismic effects, a seismic source was assumed to be located near Prudhoe Bay and, for each year, the estimated number of bowhead sightings was mapped separately for seismic time intervals 0-1 h and 12-24 h.

Circular (Randomization) Test for Whale Headings

Given the circular distribution of bowhead whale headings, with the dependent variable being the direction in degrees, Objective 2 cannot be tested with the Poisson regression approach discussed earlier. Instead a randomization test (Manly 1997) was designed to see whether there is a significant difference between the mean angle of movement (heading) for bowhead whales (sightings) recorded during periods with and without seismic activity. In this analysis, "no-seismic" and "seismic" periods are defined as in Miller et al. (1999). No-seismic periods include periods with no airgun operations at the time, or within the previous 3.5 h. Seismic periods include times 5 min after airgun operations started to 5 min after airgun operations ended. Only whales whose activity was recorded as "traveling" were included in the analysis. Any bowhead sightings made by MMS > 3 days after the end of seismic activity in 1996-98 were excluded from analyses. A special purpose FORTRAN program "DISTRND" was written to carry out this test.

The bowhead sightings were divided into six categories based on their distance from a seismic source. The distance categories used were as follows: (1) $\geq$60 km east of the source, (2) 30 km to less than 60 km east, (3) east of the source by <30 km, (4) 0 to 30 km west of the source, (5) >30 km and up to 60 km west, and (6) >60 km west. The "axis" used to differentiate bowhead sightings east vs. west of the seismic source, extended ESE-WNW from the (nominal) most recent shotpoint. The program DISTRND was designed to allow up to 20 distance categories, but six categories were considered a reasonable balance between having a large number of categories and keeping the number of observations in each category large.

With circular data, the standard way to calculate the mean of n angular observations involves first calculating

$$X = \sum \cos(a_i) / n$$

and

$$Y = \sum \sin(a_i) / n,$$

where a_i is the ith angle and the summation is over the n observations. Then the mean angle is

$$\bar{a} = \tan^{-1}(Y/X),$$

i.e., the mean angle is the one for which the tangent is Y/X (Batschelet 1981). It is necessary to calculate the mean angle in this way in order to take into account the fact that a heading of 0° and a heading of 360° are in fact exactly the same.

The randomization test involves comparing the mean bowhead headings with and without seismic activity for each of the six distance categories. For each, the difference between the mean heading angle with seismic activity and the mean heading angle without seismic activity is calculated. This gives six test statistics. In addition, the sum of the absolute differences for the six categories is calculated to give a seventh statistic that measures the overall seismic versus non-seismic difference. The randomization test compares these seven observed statistics with the distributions of the same statistics that are obtained by randomly reallocating the labels "seismic activity" and "no seismic activity" to the whales within the distance groups, keeping the numbers of whales with and without seismic activity constant within the groups. The randomization distributions are determined by generating a large number of sets of data with randomized labels.

The idea behind this test is that the significance level of the test statistics for the individual distance categories will indicate which distance ranges, if any, show seismic effects. The significance level for the overall test statistic will also indicate whether, for all the distance classes taken together, there is a difference between whale headings with and without seismic activity.

RESULTS

Exploratory Analyses

Natural and sightability conditions were in most cases similar in each survey year (Table 5). However, much more ice was present in 1996 (47.8 % average cover) than in 1997 and 1998, when there was little to no ice cover over most of the survey area. Also, on average, sea state conditions were calmer in 1996 than in 1997-98, presumably at least in part because of the dampening effect of ice on sea state.

Overall, 704 sightings of bowheads were included in the Poisson regression analysis. Of these sightings, 57, 298, and 349 were in 1996, 1997 and 1998, respectively. Of the ~22,000 sampling units in the analysis over the three years, bowheads were sighted within 440 sampling units. In those sampling units, the number of bowhead sightings per sampling unit ranged from 1 to 5.

Poisson Regression

The Approach

The fitting of a Poisson regression model was a multi-stage process, because of complications associated with the large number of covariates (particularly those for seismic effects), deciding how to allow for the activity level of a seismic source, and deciding whether to constrain the range of influence of seismic sources (i.e., to fix a maximum distance from the seismic source, beyond which the seismic effects are made to be zero).

Calculations were mainly carried out using the GenStat statistical package (NAG 2003). Initially, this program failed to identify all of the parameters correctly for some models. For this reason, three other statistical packages were also tried for the calculations. SAS (2003) completely failed to produce estimates, as did Matlab (2003). When S-Plus (MathSoft 2000) was used it did produce estimates for all the models considered, and the estimates were the same as for GenStat when GenStat identified the parameters correctly. It was then realized that S-Plus was always fitting models starting with no prior estimates of the coefficients. In contrast, GenStat was starting with the estimated coefficients from earlier models with some covariates included, and from there was deriving estimates for a revised model with additional covariates. When GenStat was forced to estimate in the same way as S-Plus, it also was always able to estimate all of the parameters correctly, and the results agreed with those for S-Plus. These computational difficulties were not anticipated. They illustrate that the analysis of a large data set (~22,000 cases and up to 89 covariates) using Poisson regression cannot even be attempted with some standard statistical software.

TABLE 5. Summary of predictor variables used in the Poisson regression analysis. Each 5-km segment of aerial survey transect contributed one observation to the dataset summarized here.

	Distance fr. Shore (km)	Water Depth (m)	Bottom Slope (degrees)	Ice Cover (%)	Date within Season [a]	Sea State [b]	Visibility Scale [c]	Altitude (m)
1996								
Mean	42.5	205	0.6	48	16.3	1.9	2.7	340
SD	28.69	500.4	1.42	36.7	9.24	1.55	1.11	76.6
Min	0.0	0.3	0.0	0.0	1	0	0	30.5
Max	152.1	3317.2	19.1	100.0	38	7	4	609.9
1997								
Mean	38.0	134	0.4	2	20.3	3.1	2.3	339
SD	26.24	365.3	1.18	13.1	12.07	1.80	1.29	83.0
Min	0.0	0.3	0.0	0.0	0	0	0	121.9
Max	157.9	2733.2	12.6	99.0	48	9	4	1097.3
1998								
Mean	38.3	149	0.4	1	21.6	3.3	2.5	343
SD	27.55	458.3	0.98	5.8	12.77	1.20	1.03	79.3
Min	0.0	0.3	0.0	0.0	-1	0	0	121.6
Max	184.3	3545.7	14.8	95.0	56	7	4	825.1

[a] This variable coded as Aug 30 = -1, Aug 31 = 0, Sep 1 = 1, Sep 2 = 2,....Oct 26 = 56.

[b] Sea state is Beaufort Wind Force scale.

[c] Visibility coded as 0 = < 1 km, 1 = 1-2 km, 2 = 2-3 km, 3 = 3-5 km, 4 = > 5 km.

A heterogeneity factor was estimated based on the Pearson chi-squared statistic. It was thought likely that extraneous variance, above that expected from the simple Poisson regression model, would be present, and that this method for estimating the heterogeneity factor should be more reliable than estimation based on the deviance function. Indeed, heterogeneity factors estimated using the deviance function are much less than one. As it is hard to believe that the variance of whale group counts is less than expected from the Poisson distribution, these estimates seem quite unrealistic. Using Pearson chi-squared statistics, the estimated heterogeneity factor varied depending on the assumptions made at different stages in the analysis, but always exceeded one. For the final models considered, the estimated heterogeneity values were quite large (~6). However, the very high proportion of zero values in the data means that heterogeneity factors estimated using Pearson chi-squared statistics may also have questionable properties. This is the first of several aspects of the data analysis described here that are in need of further consideration in the future. The stratified bootstrap resampling method of Manly and Chowkowski (2006) is worth examining in this respect.

Having found how to obtain reliable estimates, and after correcting a number of errors that were found in the data, various modifications to the Poisson regression model were tried, as follows:

(a) Initially, the potential range of influence of seismic activity was unbounded. As this produced apparently unrealistic estimates of seismic effects at great distances that were believed to be due to the chance clustering of whale groups, the assumed maximum distance for seismic effects was reduced to 100 km, 75 km, and finally to 70 km. There is a subjective element in the decision to restrict the range of influence like this, but it does appear to produce patterns that are reasonable. This is an element of the data analysis that should be revisited in the future.

(b) Because of the high correlations between the seismic covariates for different time periods, we considered pooling the first three intervals of 0-1 hours, 1-2 hours, and 2-3 hours into a single interval of 0-3 hours. This gave a worse model fit than the interval 0-1 hours alone, and was therefore not considered further. The idea of only using one of the six intervals was also considered. The argument in this case was that separate use of all six intervals resulted in an excessive number of covariates. This was especially so given that, because of correlation among the covariates for different intervals, each of the intervals represented all of the other intervals to some extent. When only one interval was considered in a given model, it was found that the best fit to the data was obtained using the covariates for the 12-24 hour interval, with the second best fit being based on the covariates for the 0-1 hour interval. At this point, it was decided to refine the model further using both the 0-1 hour and 12-24 hour seismic coefficients, but with any fitted model only containing the covariates for one of these periods. This approach should be revisited in future analyses.

(c) Initially, the activity level of a seismic source was scaled so that it was at the standard level if there was an average of one shot every 20 seconds, and therefore 180 shots per hour, over the full interval length. This level of seismic activity received a scale value of 1.0. If the average number of shots per hour differed from 180, then the seismic effect was multiplied by the number of shots per hour divided by 180. For example, if a seismic source operated at 200 shots per hour, then the assumed effect was the standard effect multiplied by $\theta = 200/180$. This scaling was achieved by multiplying the values for all the covariates that characterized seismic effects by θ.

As an alternative to this scaling, seismic effects were left unscaled if θ exceeded 0.1, or otherwise the seismic effects were set to zero. This alternative treatment of activity levels produced a slightly worse fit with both the 0-1 hour and 12-24 hour seismic effects. It was therefore decided to retain the original method of allowing for seismic activity levels. Nevertheless, future analyses should revisit the question of how best to take into account varying activity levels.

(d) The effect of using a scaling based on the minimum water depth between an observed stretch of transect and a seismic source was also investigated as an additional scaling applied after the θ scaling described in (c) above. This was done as described in the Methods, and resulted in a linear scaling effect between 0 at ≤ 2 m and 1 at ≥ 20 m. As this minimum depth scaling failed to improve the fit of the model using either the 0-1 hour seismic interval or the 12-24 hour seismic interval, its use was discontinued. This is another area that could be revisited in future analyses, possibly trying a range of limits as alternatives to the 2 m and 20 m ones used here for the linear scaling effect. Also, something other than a linear effect over the specified range of minimum depths may be appropriate.

(e) A check was made to see whether cubic functions of the seismic effect gave a significant improvement in fit over quadratic functions. This involves adding the four covariate terms E^2N, EN^2, E^3 and N^3 to the terms E, N, EN, E^2 and N^2 that are already in the quadratic model to describe the effect of a source with the standard level of activity with an easterly distance of E and a northerly distance of N from the source. Scaling by the activity level θ also applied to these four new covariates. The extra cubic function covariates gave no significant improvement in fit at the 5% level for either the 0-1 or 12-24 hour seismic effects. It was therefore concluded that the quadratic functions are adequate to describe the data, and cubic covariates are unnecessary. In any future analysis, it may be desirable to consider alternatives to the quadratic formulation.

(f) The effect of a hunting covariate was considered, where this was 1 if the sampling unit was within a hunting area on a date when hunting may have been taking place, or was otherwise 0. The estimated coefficients for this covariate were always positive, indicating a possible positive association between this variable and the presence of whale groups. However, the apparent effect was never significant at the 5% level. This variable was therefore not included in the final models chosen to describe the data. This decision should be reconsidered if more specific information about the timing and locations of hunting becomes available, e.g., if the analysis is redone at some future time for years when hunting activity is more specifically documented.

(g) No systematic attempt was made to see which, if any, of the covariates describing the distribution of whale groups in the absence of seismic activity could be removed from the model. It was, however, quite clear that considering the altitude of the survey aircraft did not significantly improve the fit of the equation. This covariate was therefore not included in the final models chosen to describe the data. In addition, some of the values for the bottom slope covariate were questionable given the limitations of the available bathymetric data. When all of the bottom slope covariates were removed from models the change in fit was not significant at the 5% level. Consequently, this covariate was also omitted from the final models chosen to describe the data. In future analyses, it may be appropriate to recompute the bottom slope over a spatial scale other than the 200 x 200 m used here, and then reconsider whether bottom slope is a useful predictor of bowhead sightings.

The outcome, after dealing with the considerations described by (a) to (g), was that two models were finally chosen to describe the data. These models assumed that seismic effects might extend as far as 70 km in each direction. They included quadratic terms for seismic effects, scaled using the activity levels θ, with the hunting, altitude, and bottom slope covariates omitted. One of the models included the covariates for the 0-1 hour seismic effect and the other included the covariates for the 12-24 hour seismic effects.

As discussed elsewhere in this report, the resulting preliminary models are of value primarily in indicating how such an analysis can be approached. Some of the specific results concerning relationships of whale sightings to natural and human-activity variables are likely meaningful. However, some other results probably are confounded by various data and model limitations, and it is not always clear which results are confounded in these ways. Inclusion of data from additional years, combined with further refinements of the modeling, would help resolve uncertainties and refine model predictions.

Natural and Sightability Covariates

The estimated parameters for the models are provided in Table 6 (0-1 h seismic effect) and Table 7 (12-24 h seismic effect). Considering the results for both models, it should be noted that most of the coefficients of the natural and sightability covariates are not significant at the 5% level. This suggests that the models could be simplified by removing some non-significant covariates. Natural and sightability covariates should be investigated further in the future, taking into account the fact that the apparent statistical significance of individual covariates depends very much on the presence or absence of other intercorrelated covariates in the model, and on the estimated heterogeneity factor. As noted above, the reliability with which the heterogeneity factor is estimated also needs further investigation. Nonetheless, the models provide indications concerning which natural and sightability covariates influenced the expected number of bowhead sightings in the 5-km sample units. Model results, organized by Objective number, are presented below.

TABLE 6. Estimates of Poisson regression coefficients for the model with 0-1 h seismic effects. P-values < 0.05 marked with * and boldface parameter name.

Parameter[a]	Estimate	Standard Error	t-statistic[b]	P-value
Constant	-2.510400	1.740070	-1.44	0.149
SurTp 2	0.762025	0.281118	2.71	0.007 *
Year 2	-0.307998	1.791380	-0.17	0.863
Year 3	-1.019860	1.761680	-0.58	0.563
DShr1.Year 1	-0.035925	0.092264	-0.39	0.697
DShr1.Year 2	0.096411	0.050710	1.90	0.057
DShr1.Year 3	0.035156	0.035124	1.00	0.317
DShr2.Year 1	-0.002716	0.001910	-1.42	0.155
DShr2.Year 2	-0.003162	0.000993	-3.19	0.001 *
DShr2.Year 3	-0.001126	0.000521	-2.16	0.031 *
Long1.Year 1	-0.260830	0.321399	-0.81	0.417
Long1.Year 2	0.113791	0.176704	0.64	0.520
Long1.Year 3	0.014876	0.101504	0.15	0.883
Long2.Year 1	-0.015655	0.027957	-0.56	0.576
Long2.Year 2	0.005244	0.012273	0.43	0.669
Long2.Year 3	0.000922	0.008718	0.11	0.916
DSLg.Year 1	0.002628	0.010276	0.26	0.798
DSLg.Year 2	-0.011674	0.005204	-2.24	0.025 *
DSLg.Year 3	0.000232	0.002410	0.10	0.923
WDth1.Year 1	0.013333	0.037803	0.35	0.724
WDth1.Year 2	-0.034864	0.016837	-2.07	0.038 *
WDth1.Year 3	-0.002911	0.005493	-0.53	0.596
WDth2.Year 1	-0.000061	0.000140	-0.44	0.663
WDth2.Year 2	0.000016	0.000024	0.67	0.505
WDth2.Year 3	0.000002	0.000002	1.00	0.319
IC1.Year 1	0.049947	0.055492	0.90	0.368
IC1.Year 2	-0.168738	0.257112	-0.66	0.512
IC1.Year 3	0.726140	1.063960	0.68	0.495
IC2.Year 1	-0.000468	0.000516	-0.91	0.364
IC2.Year 2	0.001619	0.002619	0.62	0.537
IC2.Year 3	-0.090466	0.173267	-0.52	0.602
DWS1.Year 1	-0.136077	0.214491	-0.63	0.526
DWS1.Year 2	0.018454	0.060028	0.31	0.759
DWS1.Year 3	0.027749	0.052482	0.53	0.597
DWS2.Year 1	-0.006967	0.007803	-0.89	0.372
DWS2.Year 2	-0.001177	0.001323	-0.89	0.374
DWS2.Year 3	-0.000841	0.000983	-0.86	0.392
DWLg.Year 1	0.004390	0.022251	0.20	0.844
DWLg.Year 2	-0.004032	0.005991	-0.67	0.501
DWLg.Year 3	-0.003000	0.003080	-0.97	0.330
DWDS.Year 1	0.010260	0.005889	1.74	0.081
DWDS.Year 2	0.001252	0.001498	0.84	0.403
DWDS.Year 3	0.000159	0.000791	0.20	0.841
SeaSt1	-0.320863	0.264711	-1.21	0.225
SeaSt2	0.019881	0.040254	0.49	0.621
Vis1	0.750959	0.408591	1.84	0.066

TABLE 6. Continued.

Parameter[a]	Estimate	Standard Error	t-statistic[b]	P-value
Vis2	-0.132814	0.085293	-1.56	0.119
B01	-1.979920	0.824200	-2.40	0.016 *
E1	0.041653	0.025435	1.64	0.101
N1	0.106996	0.061510	1.74	0.082
EN1	-0.001433	0.000921	-1.56	0.120
EE1	-0.000116	0.000307	-0.38	0.706
NN1	-0.001239	0.001159	-1.07	0.285

[a] Abbreviations for the covariates are as follows: **SurTp2** = Survey Type 2, an effect for an MMS survey instead of an LGL survey; **Year**i = Year i, an effect for the year i, with i = 1, 2 or 3; **DShr**i = (Distance to Shore)^i, where i = 1 or 2; **Long**i = (Longitude)^i, where i = 1 or 2; **DSLg** = (Distance to Shore)*(Longitude); **WDth**i = (Water Depth)^i, where i = 1 or 2; **IC**i = (Ice Cover)^i, where i = 1 or 2; **DWS**i = (Day Within the Season)^i, where i = 1 or 2; **DWLg** = (Day Within the Season)*(Longitude); **DWDS** = (Day Within the Season)*(Distance to Shore); **SeaSt**i = (Sea State)^i, where i = 1 or 2; **Vis**i = (Visibility)^i, for i = 1 or 2; **B01** is the constant term for the period 1 (0-1 hour) seismic effect, and **E1**, **N1**, **EN1**, **EE1** and **NN1** represent the linear product and squared terms E, N, EN, E^2, and N^2 for the seismic effect in the same interval. The longitude variable used was from a base reference to 150°W for the regression analysis.

[b] The t-statistics are the estimates divided by the standard errors. P-values are probabilities that t-statistics would be as far from zero as estimated by the model if the true value of the coefficient is zero. Because of the large number of residual degrees of freedom, these probabilities are calculated using the normal distribution.

Natural Covariates

Based on the Poisson regression models, the natural covariates that were significant (at least in one survey year) at the 5 % level included distance from shore, the interaction of distance from shore and longitude, and water depth.

Objective 13: Influence of Specific Natural Factors.—Objective 13 was to quantify the probability of observing bowheads relative to percent ice cover, distance from shore, bottom slope, water depth, longitude, date within season, and year (along with some other covariates described later under "Sightability"). The models suggest that, after allowance for the effects of other covariates, distance from shore and water depth were significantly ($P \leq 0.05$) related to the expected number of bowhead sightings in particular 5-km sample units during at least one of the three years considered. In contrast, there were no obvious relationships between bowhead occurrence and any of the following: percent ice cover, bottom slope, date within season, and year. It should be noted that, for each covariate summarized below, the results are based on the overall multivariate models, and represent apparent effects after allowance for all other variables. The simple bivariate relationship between any given variable and bowhead occurrence is not necessarily the same as the relationship after allowance for other factors.

- Percent *ice cover* was not significantly related to the expected number of bowhead sightings in any survey year. There was 'moderate' ice cover in 1996 (classified by MMS as a "light ice year") and almost no ice cover in 1997 and 1998 (Table 5). The inclusion of more years of data in the analyses may refine the relationship between ice cover and expected number of bowhead sightings.

- It appears that the covariate ***distance from shore*** (quadratic terms) was significantly related to the expected number of bowhead sightings in at least one survey year (1997) and perhaps in 1998 as well. The models suggest that more sightings are expected at some intermediate distance from shore as compared with close to and far from shore.

TABLE 7. Estimates of Poisson regression coefficients for the model with 12-24 h seismic effects. P-values < 0.05 marked with * and boldface parameter name.

Parameter [a]	Estimate	Standard Error	t-statistic [b]	P-value	
Constant	-2.274140	1.742960	-1.30	0.192	
SurTp 2	0.633823	0.285303	2.22	0.026	*
Year 2	-0.424501	1.785170	-0.24	0.812	
Year 3	-0.575392	1.760710	-0.33	0.744	
DShr1.Year 1	-0.041585	0.092538	-0.45	0.653	
DShr1.Year 2	0.095655	0.050741	1.89	0.059	
DShr1.Year 3	0.020871	0.035630	0.59	0.558	
DShr2.Year 1	-0.002772	0.001935	-1.43	0.152	
DShr2.Year 2	-0.003121	0.000990	-3.15	0.002	*
DShr2.Year 3	-0.000988	0.000525	-1.88	0.060	
Long1.Year 1	-0.214521	0.321134	-0.67	0.504	
Long1.Year 2	0.108006	0.177878	0.61	0.544	
Long1.Year 3	-0.011148	0.096716	-0.12	0.908	
Long2.Year 1	-0.019323	0.027953	-0.69	0.489	
Long2.Year 2	0.006407	0.012306	0.52	0.603	
Long2.Year 3	-0.001645	0.008757	-0.19	0.851	
DSLg.Year 1	0.002507	0.010417	0.24	0.810	
DSLg.Year 2	-0.011667	0.005187	-2.25	0.024	*
DSLg.Year 3	0.000696	0.002404	0.29	0.772	
WDth1.Year 1	0.009186	0.036678	0.25	0.802	
WDth1.Year 2	-0.036141	0.017118	-2.11	0.035	*
WDth1.Year 3	-0.003553	0.005670	-0.63	0.531	
WDth2.Year 1	-0.000045	0.000131	-0.35	0.730	
WDth2.Year 2	0.000016	0.000021	0.77	0.442	
WDth2.Year 3	0.000002	0.000002	1.05	0.294	
IC1.Year 1	0.036653	0.056611	0.65	0.517	
IC1.Year 2	-0.170215	0.257461	-0.66	0.509	
IC1.Year 3	0.709008	0.998320	0.71	0.478	
IC2.Year 1	-0.000394	0.000522	-0.76	0.450	
IC2.Year 2	0.001632	0.002622	0.62	0.534	
IC2.Year 3	-0.078083	0.156661	-0.50	0.618	
DWS1.Year 1	-0.084858	0.225493	-0.38	0.707	
DWS1.Year 2	0.015707	0.059234	0.27	0.791	
DWS1.Year 3	0.008994	0.051364	0.18	0.861	
DWS2.Year 1	-0.008203	0.008056	-1.02	0.309	
DWS2.Year 2	-0.001142	0.001325	-0.86	0.389	
DWS2.Year 3	-0.000625	0.000958	-0.65	0.514	
DWLg.Year 1	0.002997	0.022807	0.13	0.895	
DWLg.Year 2	-0.003964	0.006054	-0.65	0.513	
DWLg.Year 3	-0.002690	0.003045	-0.88	0.377	
DWDS.Year 1	0.010674	0.005969	1.79	0.074	
DWDS.Year 2	0.001267	0.001510	0.84	0.401	
DWDS.Year 3	0.000350	0.000787	0.44	0.656	
SeaSt1	-0.357062	0.267062	-1.34	0.181	
SeaSt2	0.023285	0.040898	0.57	0.569	
Vis1	0.788518	0.411917	1.91	0.056	

TABLE 7. Continued.

Parameter [a]	Estimate	Standard Error	t-statistic [b]	P-value
Vis2	-0.135382	0.085833	-1.58	0.115
B06	-3.803980	1.235630	-3.08	0.002 *
E6	0.083394	0.036965	2.26	0.024 *
N6	0.202932	0.088693	2.29	0.022 *
EN6	-0.002422	0.001228	-1.97	0.049 *
EE6	-0.000345	0.000391	-0.88	0.377
NN6	-0.002604	0.001631	-1.60	0.110

[a] Abbreviations are as for Table 6, except that the seismic variables B06, E6, N6, EN6, EE6 and NN6 are for seismic surveys during the period 12-24 hours before the aerial survey

[b] See footnote b in Table 6.

- *Bottom slope* was not significantly related to the expected number of bowhead sightings and this covariate was excluded from the final models. It is recommended (see Discussion) that the method for deriving bottom slope values should be revisited in future analyses.

- The models suggest that *water depth*, at least in 1997, was negatively related to the expected number of bowhead sightings. Fewer bowhead sightings were expected in deep than in shallow waters, other factors being equal.

- *Date within season* was not significantly (at the 5 % level) related to the expected number of bowhead sightings in any survey year.

- The factor *year* was also not significantly related to the expected number of sightings. This suggests that, after accounting for other covariates, there was no overall difference in expected bowhead numbers from year to year. This result, along with the lack of significance for date within season, should be treated cautiously given the limited number of survey years included in the analyses.

- Although the covariate *longitude* by itself (linear and quadratic terms) was not significantly related to the expected number of bowhead sightings in any particular survey year, its interaction with distance from shore was significant, at least in 1997. The negative coefficient (Tables 6 and 7) for this interaction suggests that more bowhead sightings would be expected close to shore in the western portion of the study area.

Objective 15: Distance from Shore vs. Date.—This objective concerned whether there was variation, over the duration of the migration season, in the typical distances offshore. The models suggest that the expected number of bowhead sightings in 1996-98 was not significantly (at the 5 % level) related to the interaction between distance from shore and date within season. However, in 1996, the interaction term approached statistical significance (Tables 6, 7). Once again, the analysis of more years of data would likely refine this relationship, as would the inclusion of data from a broader range of dates. (For 1996-98, there were almost no data from August.)

Objective 16: Longitude vs. Date.—This objective concerned whether the peak probability of observing bowheads occurs progressively later in the season with increasing longitude. The models suggest that the interaction between date within season and longitude was not significantly (at the 5 % level) related to the expected number of bowhead sightings in 1996-98. Based on the results of the preliminary models in this study, we would accept the null hypothesis that peak number of bowhead sightings does not occur progressively later in the season with increasing longitude. However, these results should be treated with caution given the preliminary nature of the models, the limited number of years considered, and the lack of early-mid August data. The distribution patterns shown in Figure 2 are suggestive of the westward seasonal progression that is known to exist.

Sightability Covariates

Objective 13 was to quantify the probability of observing bowheads relative to sea state, visibility, survey altitude, and aircraft type / survey type (MMS Twin Otter vs. LGL Twin Commander), as well as other "natural" factors described above. Based on the Poisson regression models, the only sightability covariate that was significant at the 5 % level (after allowance for other variables) was survey type, although the association with visibility was close to significant at the 5 % level.

- The models suggest that neither ***sea state*** nor ***visibility*** was significantly related (at the 5 % level) to the expected number of bowhead sightings. However, there was a nearly-significant positive relationship between visibility and bowhead sightings ($P = 0.066$ and $P = 0.056$, depending on interval since seismic). Also, the "association" between sea state and bowhead sightings was negative, as expected, though not very strong. The low degree of association between these two variables and bowhead sightings was unexpected, especially considering that the data analyzed in the Poisson regression models included sightability conditions that ranged from very poor (i.e., high sea states and low visibility) to good and excellent.

- ***Survey altitude*** was not significantly related to the expected number of bowhead sightings; this covariate was dropped from the final models as it clearly did not improve model fit.

- The covariates ***aircraft type*** and ***survey type*** are essentially the same variables given the consistent use of two different aircraft types by LGL and MMS during 1996-98. "Aircraft type" was not included in the final models but "survey type" was significantly related to the expected number of bowhead sightings in a sample unit. The models suggested that there tended to be significantly more bowhead sightings per sample unit during MMS than LGL surveys.

Sample Model Predictions

Figure 2 demonstrates the ability of the model to represent the nearshore migration corridor of bowhead whales and the temporal progression of the fall 1998 bowhead whale migration from east to west. (Similar maps for 1996 and 1997 are found in Appendix E.) Figure 2 shows the expected number of sightings per 5-km sampling unit at four times during the 1998 fall season, assuming no seismic activity, no ice, Beaufort state 3, and excellent visibility. Based on the Poisson regression model, early in the 1998 fall migration period (1 Sep; Fig. 2A), expected bowhead sightings are distributed evenly from the U.S./Canada border to Barrow in relatively low numbers close to the coast. As the season progresses (15 Sep and 1 Oct), expected numbers of bowhead sightings increase in the west and decrease in the east (Fig. 2B, C). Late in the migration season (15 Oct), very few sightings are expected east of Prudhoe Bay; more sightings are expected to occur near Barrow than farther east, but even near Barrow the expected number of sightings is reduced as compared with earlier in the autumn (Fig. 2D).

Human Activities

The Poisson regression models, although preliminary in nature, demonstrate an approach useful for this type of analysis, and indicate how (and if) seismic and whaling activity influenced the expected number of bowhead sightings in a sample unit. As previously mentioned, interpretations of the results should take into account the fact that the apparent significance of individual covariates depends very much on the estimated heterogeneity factor. The reliability with which this factor is estimated needs further investigation.

Seismic Surveys

The Poisson regression analyses suggest that seismic activity affected the number of bowhead sightings expected in a sample unit. We considered seismic activity during time periods 0-1, 1-2, 2-3, 3-6, 6-12, and 12-24 hours before the aerial survey of the transect segment in question, and also during the combined "0-3 h before" period. The best model fits occurred when we considered the seismic activity 0-1 h and 12-24 h before aerial surveys. As such, two final Poisson models were used, those including the seismic terms for the '0-1 h' and '12-24' seismic effects.

These models, in part, address Objective 1 concerning seismic effects on bowhead distribution, and Objective 3 concerning the possible mitigation of seismic effects by intervening shallow water ("acoustic barrier"). For both models, it was found that inclusion of a scaling factor for an "acoustic barrier" (shallow water) between the seismic vessel and the sample unit did not improve model fit. Therefore, the acoustic barrier factor was excluded from the final models. We recommend revisiting the approach to generating and including this acoustic barrier measure in potential future models, and cannot confidently reject or accept the null hypothesis presented in Objective 3.

0-1 h Seismic Effect.—Considering the amount of seismic activity 0-1 hour before aerial surveys, the only seismic term that was significant was B01 ($P = 0.016$; Table 6). That term is essentially an indicator whether seismic occurred or not, and does not account for distance from the seismic source(s). Although the other five seismic terms were not significant at the 5 % level, these terms still contributed to the overall fit of the model.

Figure 3 shows an example of the predicted effects of seismic activity occurring 0-1 hour before the aerial survey (in 1998) on the expected number of bowhead sightings. (Similar maps for 1996 and 1997 are found in Appendix E.) In Figure 3B, the seismic source was assumed to be operating near Prudhoe Bay for the complete one-hour period on 15 Sep. Relative to an otherwise comparable period when no airguns were operating (Fig. 3A), the expected numbers of bowhead sightings are reduced near the seismic source. There are also two areas where the expected numbers of sightings are increased; these areas are northwest and northeast of the seismic source (Fig. 3B vs. 3A).

12-24 h Seismic Effect.—Considering the amount of seismic activity 12-24 h before aerial surveys, the estimates for four of the six seismic coefficients are significant at the 5 % level, with the squared terms being non-significant (Table 7).

Figure 4 shows an example of the predicted effects of seismic activity that had occurred 12-24 h before the aerial survey (in 1998) on the expected number of bowhead sightings. (Similar maps for 1996 and 1997 are found in Appendix E.) In Figure 4B, the seismic source was assumed to be operating near Prudhoe Bay for the complete period 12-24 hours before the survey on 15 Sep. Relative to an otherwise comparable period when no airguns were operating (Fig. 4A), the expected numbers of bowhead sightings are reduced near the seismic source (Fig. 4B).

Subsistence Hunting

The Poisson regression analyses indicated that subsistence hunting, as "quantified" here, did not significantly influence the number of bowhead sightings. The hunting variable was not included in the final models as it did not significantly improve model fit. It is noteworthy that the estimated coefficients for this covariate were always positive, indicating a possible positive association between hunting and the

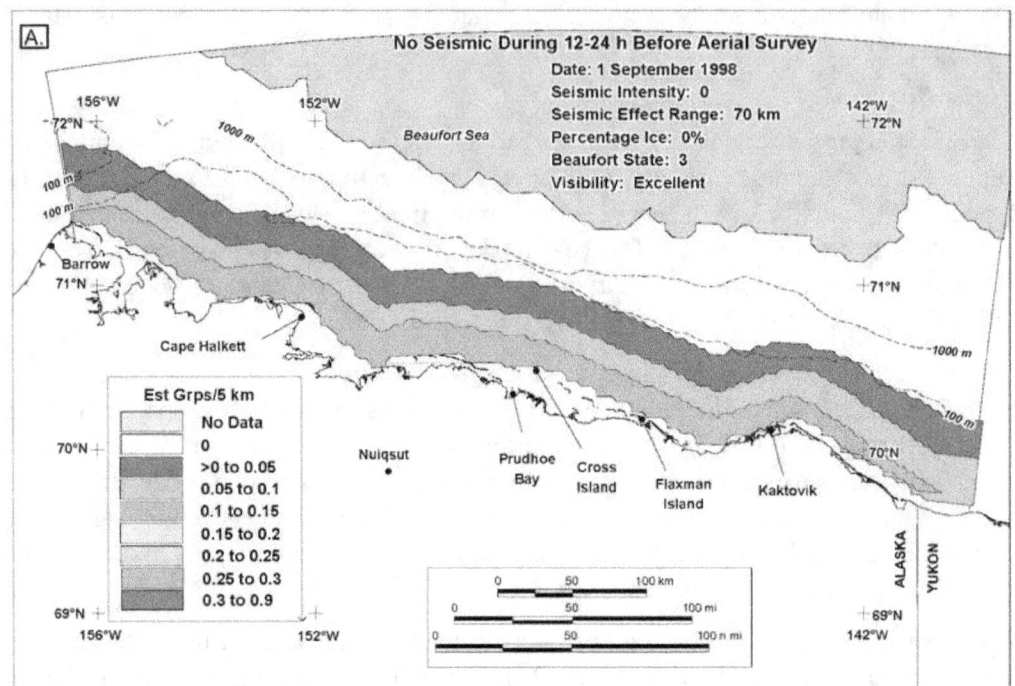

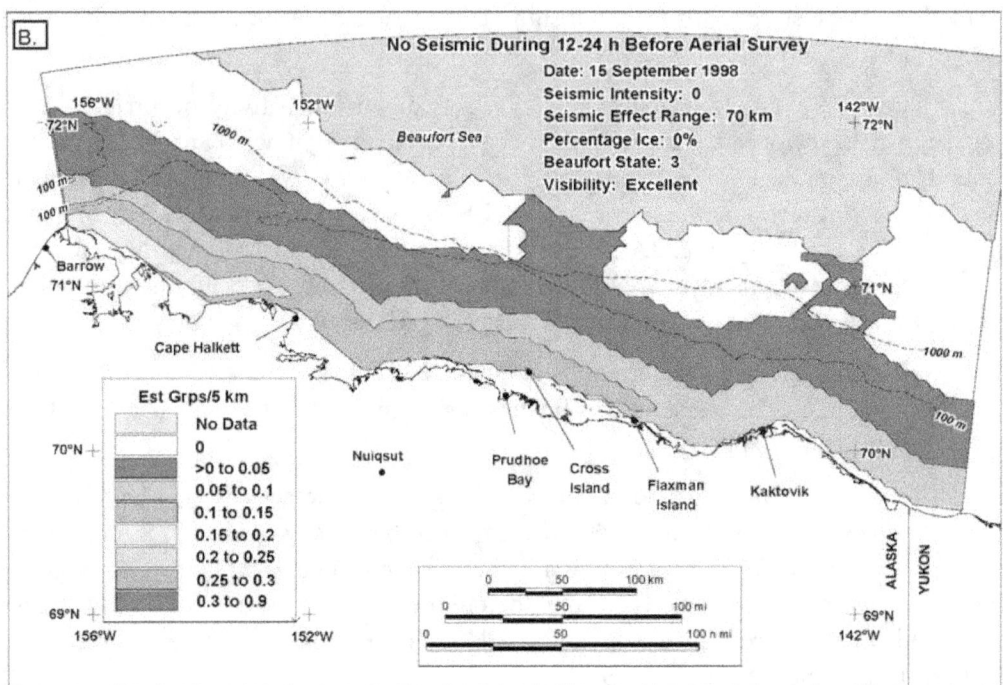

FIGURE 2. Distribution of expected number of bowhead whale sightings (per 5 km transect segment) on **(A)** 1 Sep, **(B)** 15 Sep, **(C)** 1 Oct, and **(D)** 15 Oct 1998. Expected numbers of sightings are based on the estimated coefficients of the Poisson regression model (12-24 h 'version', but assuming no seismic activity), and the additional assumptions that there was no ice, Beaufort state was 3, and visibility was excellent.

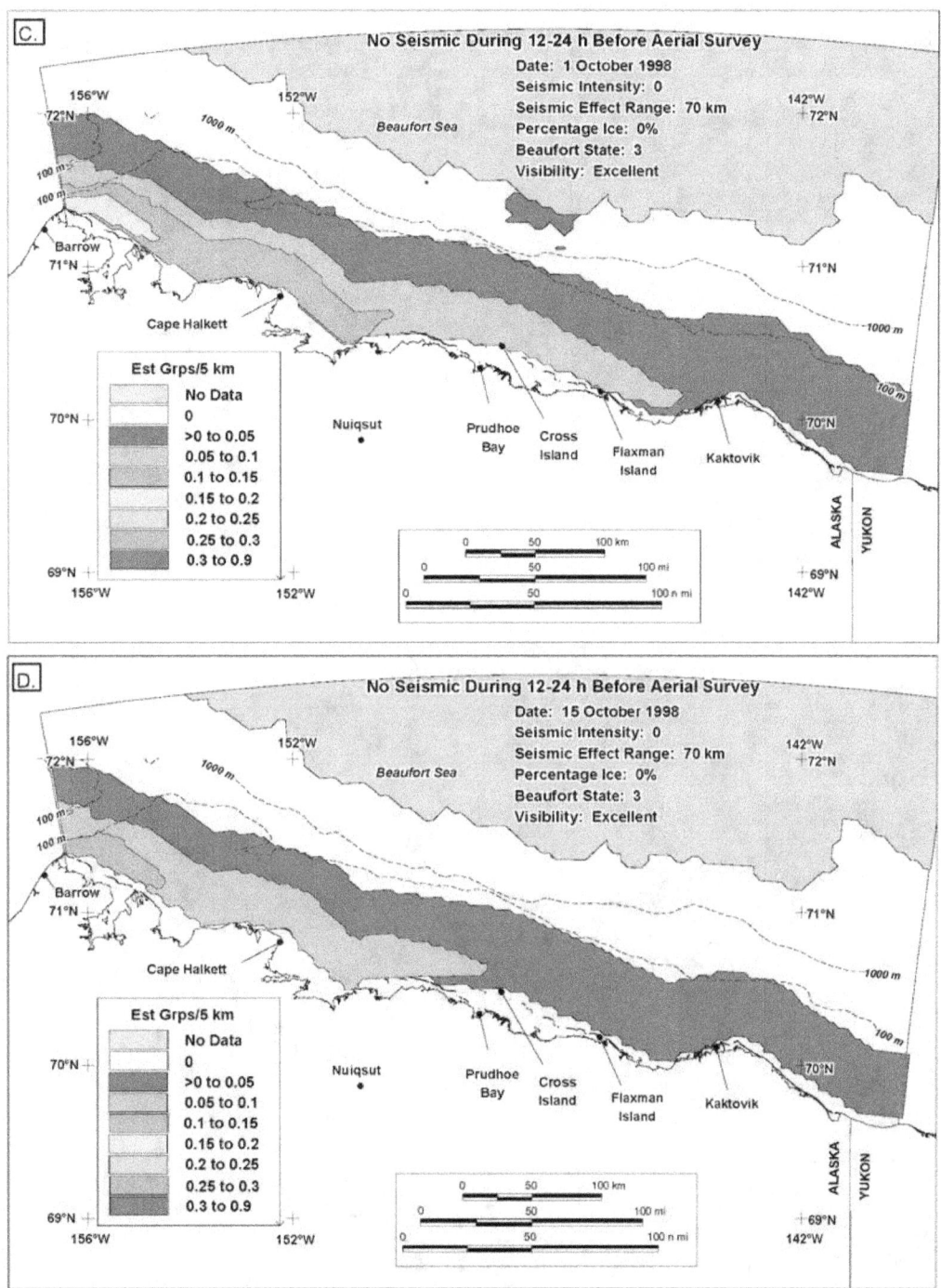

FIGURE 2. Concluded.

presence of whale groups. However, this effect was never significant at the 5 % level. A positive effect, if real, might be indicative of a tendency for hunting to occur in areas and at dates when bowhead abundance tends to be high, which is not surprising.

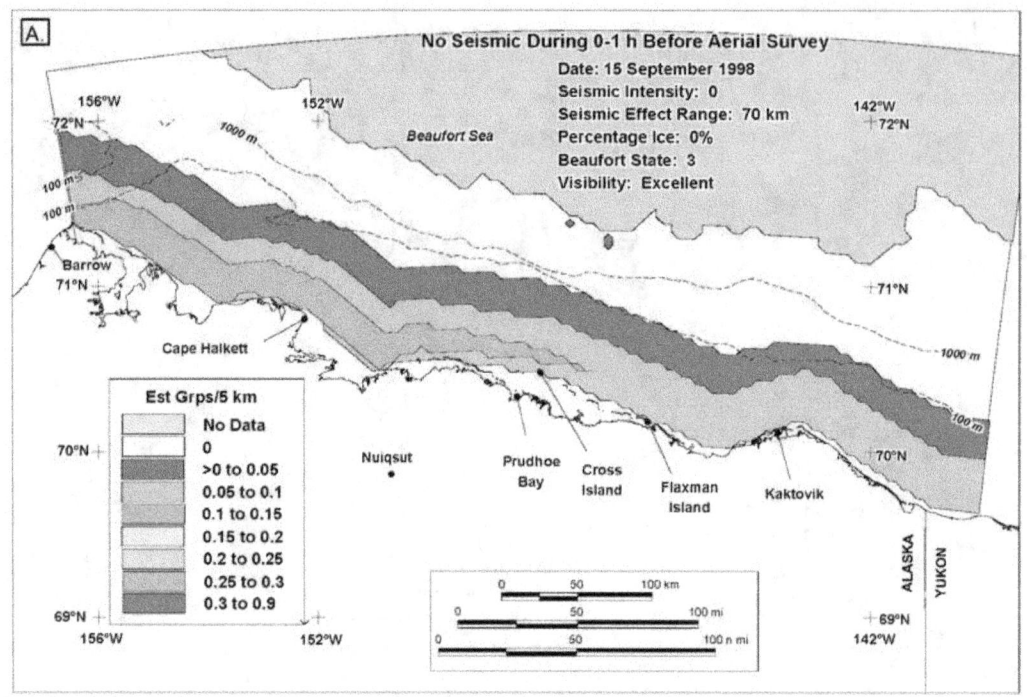

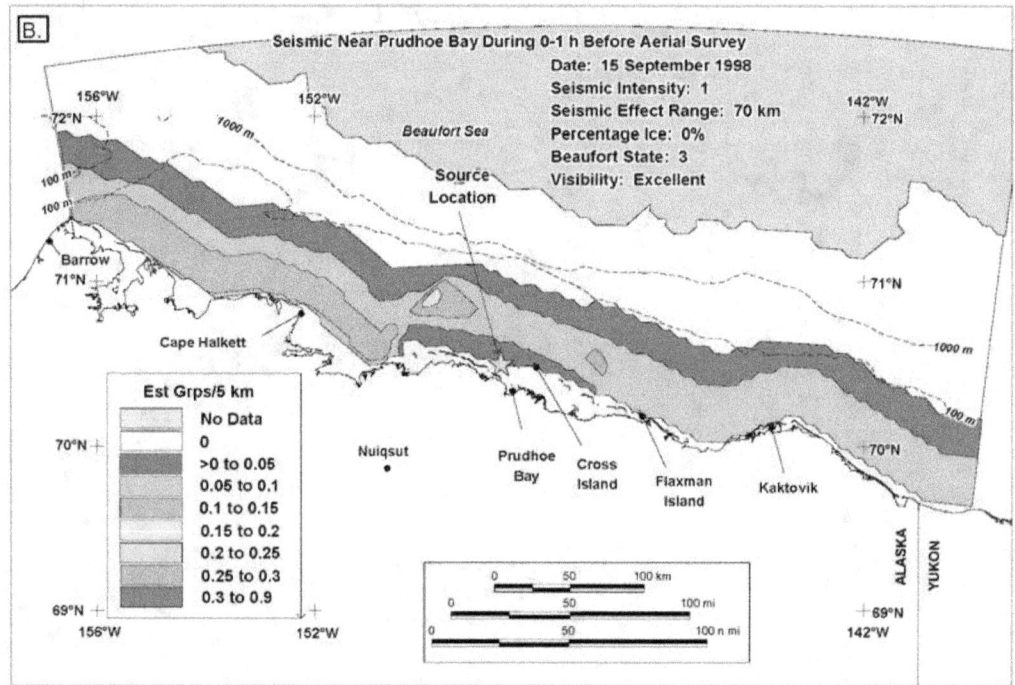

FIGURE 3. Distribution of expected number of bowhead whale sightings (per 5 km transect segment) in 1998 when **(A)** no seismic activity occurred during the hour before aerial surveys and when **(B)** a seismic source near Prudhoe Bay was active for the full hour before aerial surveys. Expected numbers of sightings are based on the estimated coefficients of the Poisson regression model (0-1 h 'version') and the assumptions that the date was 15 Sep 1998, there was no ice, Beaufort state was 3, and visibility was excellent.

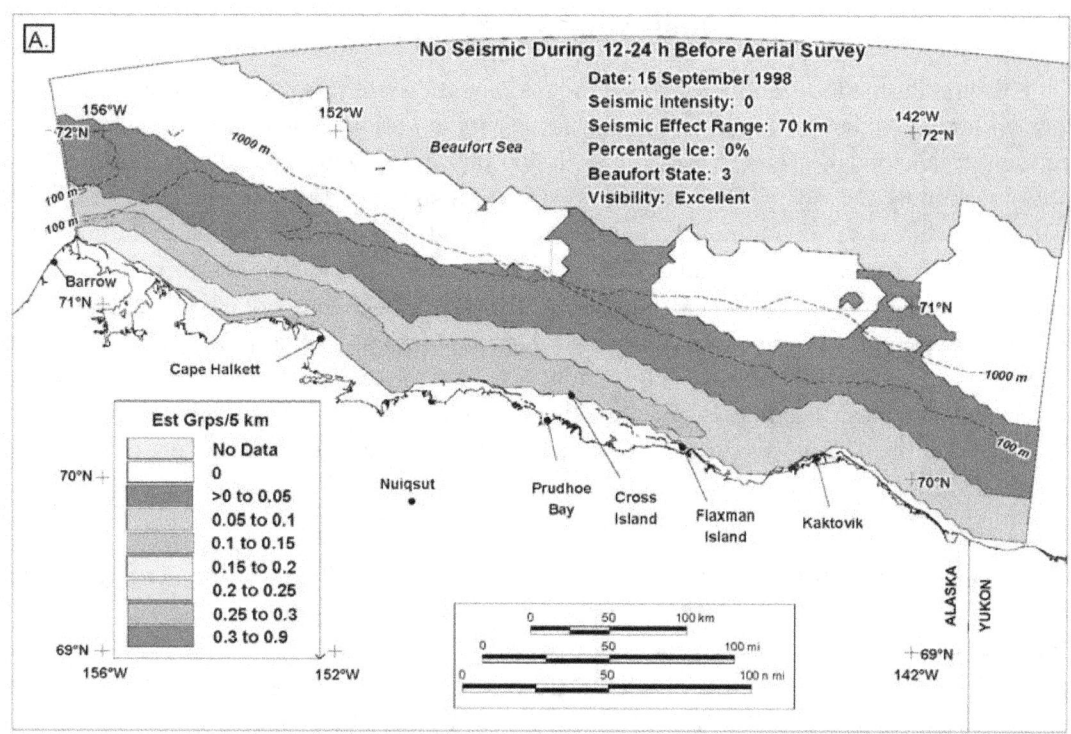

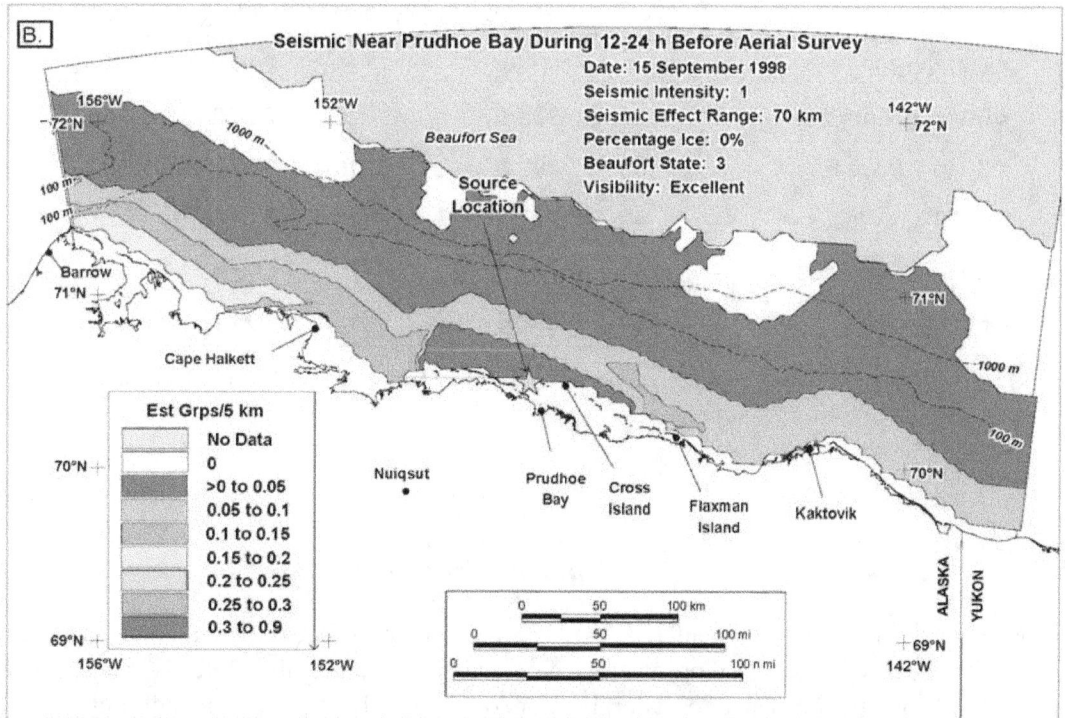

FIGURE 4. Distribution of expected number of bowhead whale sightings (per 5 km transect segment) in 1998 when **(A)** no seismic activity occurred 12-24 h before aerial surveys and when **(B)** a seismic source near Prudhoe Bay was active 12-24 h before aerial surveys. Expected numbers of sightings are based on the estimated coefficients of the Poisson regression model (12-24 h 'version') and the assumptions that the date was 15 Sep 1998, there was no ice, Beaufort state was 3, and visibility was excellent.

Analysis of Bowhead Headings

The circular randomization test was done to compare headings of traveling bowhead whales during periods with and without the presence of seismic activity at various distances east and west of the seismic operation (see Methods). The test was run with 50,000 randomizations, which is sufficient to determine P-values accurately (Manly 1997, Section 5.3). Table 8 shows the results obtained. The differences in mean heading during seismic minus the non-seismic periods are negative for the first two distance classes (30+ km east), but positive for all other classes, although only marginally so for whales >60 km west of the source. The differences for the individual distance classes are not significant at the 5 % level, although they are close to this for the first two distance classes. Nevertheless, the sum of the absolute differences is significant (P = 0.014). The conclusion from the test must therefore be that, overall, there is evidence that the mean heading is not the same for whales with and without the presence of seismic activity, but that the differences for the individual distance classes are not sufficient to give clear evidence of a mean difference for any particular class.

TABLE 8. Results from the circular randomization test on headings of "traveling" bowhead whales observed with and without the presence of seismic activity.

Distance Class Relative to the Seismic Source	Non-Seismic		Seismic			
	No. of Whales	Mean Heading	No. of Whales	Mean Heading	Difference	P-value
> 60 km East	4	15.0	6	275.8	-99.2	0.059
< 60 to 30 km East	11	333.5	20	288.2	-45.3	0.079
< 30 to > 0 km East	66	286.3	15	308.2	21.9	0.128
0 to 30 km West	49	292.6	16	312.6	19.9	0.151
> 30 to 60 km West	41	291.6	10	309.8	18.2	0.226
> 60 km West	21	297.6	15	296.4	-1.3	0.944
Sum of Absolute Differences					205.8	0.014

DISCUSSION

Natural Factors

Many natural or environmental factors are known or expected to influence the distribution of migrating bowhead whales, or the probability of detecting them, or both. Objectives 13 (in part), 15, and 16 address the potential influences of natural factors on the number of bowhead sightings.

Objective 13 was to quantify the probability of observing bowheads relative to percent ice cover, distance from shore, bottom slope, water depth, longitude, date within season, and year (along with some "Sightability" covariates). The preliminary Poisson models suggest that, after allowance for the effects of other covariates, distance from shore and water depth were significantly related to the number of bowhead sightings during at least one of the three years considered. In contrast, there were no statistically significant relationships between bowhead occurrence and any of the following: percent ice cover, bottom slope, date within season, and year. As noted in the "Results", for each covariate, the results are based on the overall multivariate models, and represent apparent effects after allowance for all other variables. Most previous studies have been based on simple bivariate relationships between bowhead occurrence and environmental, geographic, or temporal variables considered one at a time. Those bivariate relationships did not take account of possible confounding by other simultaneously-varying factors. As a result, it is not surprising that there would be some differences between the results of bivariate analyses described in earlier work as compared with our results concerning relationships after allowance for other factors.

Percent ice cover was not significantly related to the expected number of bowhead sightings in any of the three survey years considered here. Other studies, based on more years of data but not using multivariate methods, have found that bowhead whale distribution in the Alaskan Beaufort Sea is related to ice cover (Moore and DeMaster 1998; Moore 2000; Moore et al. 2000). Based on aerial survey data from 1982 to 1991, bowheads apparently tended to "select" open-water/light ice cover in late summer and autumn (Moore et al. 2000). However, bowheads are sometimes seen amidst the pack ice in autumn, and satellite-monitored bowheads (juveniles) are known to migrate through ice cover of 50 to >90 % during fall (Mate et al. 2000). Also, the bowhead migration corridor through the Alaskan Beaufort tends to be at significantly different distances from shore in different years, depending on the overall amount of pack ice present (Treacy 2002a). The corridor tends to be farthest offshore in heavy ice years, closest to shore in light ice years, and at intermediate distances in moderate ice years. During the three years considered in this study, there was almost no ice cover in 1997 and 1998, and (by our interpretation) 'moderate' ice cover in 1996. [1996 was classified as a "light ice year" by MMS.]

During aerial surveys for bowhead whales, the lateral distance where sighting probability is optimal declines with increasing ice cover (Thomas et al. 2002). It is probable that, during heavy ice conditions, a lower proportion of the bowheads present are detected by aerial observers. That could tend to confound the findings of Moore et al. (2000), which suggested a tendency to prefer open-water/light ice. In any case, the inclusion of more years of data in analyses similar to those done during this study would be helpful in refining the understanding of relationships between ice cover and the expected number of bowhead sightings. In particular, it would be helpful to include more data from years or times with substantial ice cover.

Distance from shore was significantly related to the expected number of bowhead sightings in 1997, and marginally so in 1998 as well (see Tables 6, 7). The models show that, in those years, more sightings occurred at intermediate distances from shore as compared with close to and far from shore. This pattern is evident from the positive coefficient associated with the linear "distance from shore" term combined with the negative coefficient associated with the quadratic term. These results from 1997-98 are consistent with what one would expect, given the known tendency for the bowhead migration corridor to be concentrated over the middle and outer continental shelf, at least in years with low to moderate ice cover (Treacy 2002a).

Bottom slope was not significantly related to the expected number of bowhead sightings and this covariate was excluded from the final models. However, the possibility of a relationship with bottom slope should be revisited in future analyses after revising the method for deriving bottom slope values. We calculated bottom slope for 200 x 200 m cells, but the available bathymetric data are much coarser-scale than that over most of the study area. In retrospect, more meaningful estimates of bottom slope probably could be obtained by considering the slope across a larger grid cell.

In some studies of other whale species, associations with bottom slope have been found (e.g., Kenney and Winn 1987; Cañadas et al. 2002). Associations with bottom slope may be less likely for bowheads during autumn migration than for other species that were feeding. However, bowheads often feed during autumn migration across the Alaskan Beaufort Sea (Richardson and Thomson [ed.] 2002; Treacy 2002b). Hence, it is possible that linkages between bottom slope and food availability to bowheads could result in correlations between bottom slope and probability of bowheads being present.

Water depth, at least in 1997, was negatively related to the expected number of bowhead sightings (Tables 6, 7). There were fewer bowhead sightings in deep than in shallow water, other factors being equal. This was to be expected based on previous studies, especially for years like 1996-98 when ice conditions were light to (at most) moderate. In such years, peak bowhead abundance would be expected to occur relatively close to shore and at relatively shallow water depths, and that was indeed observed in 1996-98 (Treacy 2002a). In fact, one might have expected a stronger and more consistent (across years) tendency for reduced sighting probability in deep water than was evident in our multivariate models, possibly coupled with a tendency for more sightings at intermediate than shallow depths. However, for the Alaskan Beaufort Sea, water depth is strongly correlated with distance from shore. We have not specifically investigated the effects of the intercorrelation of these two covariates on their respective bivariate vs. multivariate associations with bowhead sightings. However, it is to be expected that the way in which one of these closely-related covariates is incorporated into the model would affect how the other is represented in the model.

Date within season was not significantly (at the 5 % level) related to the expected number of bowhead sightings in any of the three survey years considered here. This was surprising, given the known tendency for bowhead migration across the Alaskan Beaufort Sea to peak during mid-September through early October, with lesser numbers during the earlier and later parts of the season. The lower-than-anticipated degree of association between bowhead sightings and date was presumably related at least in part to two things:

- The aerial surveys in 1996-98 did not begin before late August, and relatively little aerial survey work was done in mid-to-late October. If the surveys had been more evenly spaced across the full bowhead migration period in August through October, a stronger association with date probably would have been evident (e.g., Miller et al. 2002).

- MMS tends to concentrate their aerial survey work in the eastern and central part of the Alaskan Beaufort during the early part of the migration season, and in the central and western Alaskan Beaufort toward the end of the season. Given the westward progression of the migration, this survey pattern would tend to dampen out the seasonal trend in bowhead sighting rates.

Also, even though the associations between date and sighting rate were not significant, for 2 of the 3 years studied (1997 and 1998) the coefficients on the linear and quadratic functions of "date" were positive and negative, respectively. This pattern of coefficients is consistent with increasing sighting rates during the early part of the season, transitioning to decreasing rates during the latter part of the season.

Year was also not significantly related to the expected number of sightings. This suggests that, after accounting for other covariates, there was no overall difference in expected bowhead numbers from year to year within the 1996 to 1998 period. This result, along with the lack of significance for date within season, should be treated cautiously given the limited number of survey years included in the Phase I analyses.

Longitude was not significantly related to the expected number of bowhead sightings in any particular survey year. Given that migrating bowheads traverse the full longitudinal extent of the Alaskan Beaufort Sea during the course of the autumn migration, it is not surprising that, overall, there would be no longitude effect on sighting rate.

The interaction term for longitude vs. distance from shore was significantly related to bowhead sightings, at least in 1997. The negative coefficient (Tables 6 and 7) for this interaction suggests that, other factors being equal, more bowhead sightings tended to occur close to shore in the western portion of the study area in 1997.

Objective 15 concerned whether there was variation, over the duration of the migration season, in the typical distances offshore. Earlier work has suggested that distances from shore tend to be greater early in the migration season (August). However, in 1996-98, there were no aerial surveys until almost the end of August. Thus, one would not necessarily expect to see a tendency for distances from shore to decrease over the course of the season during those years. The possibility of such an effect was examined by considering the interaction term between date and distance from shore. The models suggest that bowhead sightings in 1996-98 were not significantly related (at the 5 % level) to this interaction term. However, in 1996, the association between the interaction term and bowhead sightings approached statistical significance ($P = 0.081$ or 0.074; Tables 6, 7). Analysis of more years of data would likely refine this relationship, as would the inclusion of data from early- and mid-August.

Objective 16 concerned whether the peak probability of observing bowheads occurs progressively later in the fall migration season with increasing longitude. After allowance for other variables, we found no statistical evidence that the peak number of bowhead sightings tends to occur progressively later in the season with increasing longitude. However, these results should be treated with caution given the preliminary nature of the models and the usual concerns about interpreting apparent relationships to single variables in isolation from others. The distribution patterns predicted by the model for various dates in the 1998 migration season (Fig. 2) indicate that, after allowing for all variables in the multivariate model, there was a tendency for the region with peak abundance to shift west over the season.

Sightability

Several sightability variables were anticipated to affect the number of bowhead whale sightings during aerial surveys. Objective 13 of this study was to quantify the number of bowhead sightings relative to sea state, visibility, survey altitude, aircraft type, and survey type (and other "natural" factors discussed above). The Poisson regression models suggested that, of these variables, only survey type was significantly (at the 5 % level) related to the number of bowhead sightings. However, the relationship to visibility was positive and very close to significant by this criterion.

The models indicated that significantly more bowhead sightings were recorded per sample unit during MMS vs. LGL surveys. There are several possible explanations for this finding. As mentioned previously, the covariates "survey type" and "aircraft type" are essentially the same variables given the consistent use of two different aircraft types by LGL and MMS during 1996-98. (Aircraft type was not included in the final models.) The Twin Otter aircraft used during MMS surveys in 1996-98 has a narrower zone of reduced visibility beneath the aircraft as compared with the Twin Commander aircraft used during LGL surveys (Thomas et al. 2002). Therefore, we might expect observers in Twin Otter aircraft, i.e., MMS surveys, to sight more bowheads than observers in Twin Commanders, i.e., LGL surveys. Also, for LGL surveys only the sightings recorded by the primary observers on the left and right sides of the aircraft were included. For MMS surveys, we included all sightings because it was not clear at the time of this analysis which MMS sightings were recorded by primary vs. other observers. This likely increased the sighting rate of bowheads during MMS surveys relative to LGL surveys. These two potential reasons for significant differences in the number of bowhead sightings are addressed below (see "Recommendations for Phase II"). A third potential explanation is that MMS surveys ranged over a broader geographical area than LGL surveys, and included areas in the western Alaskan Beaufort that LGL did not survey. Bowhead whales are sometimes especially abundant in parts of that area.

We were surprised that sea state and visibility were not significantly (at the 5 % level) related to the expected number of bowhead sightings, although the trends were in the expected directions and that for visibility was very close to significant at the 5 % level (Tables 6, 7). The data analyzed here included sightability conditions ranging from very poor (i.e., high sea states and low visibility) to good and excellent, so significant relationships of sighting rates to sea state and visibility were expected. Visibility, as influenced by haze, fog and precipitation, has obvious effects on the probability of detecting animals that are at the surface (Thomas et al. 2002). Increasing wave height ("sea state") also reduces the sightability of various species (Scott and Winn 1980; Holt 1987; Gunnlaugsson et al. 1988; DeMaster et al. 2001), including bowheads (Thomas et al. 2002). The weak relationships to these two sightability variables are surprising. This suggests that either the procedures for recording these two covariates or the Poisson regression models (or both) need further refinement.

Survey altitude was not significantly related to the expected number of bowhead sightings after allowing for other variables (including survey type). The nominal survey altitude for MMS surveys was 457 m and for LGL surveys it was 305 m. Thomas et al. (2002) found that, as one would expect, the higher the survey altitude, the wider the zone of restricted detectability beneath the aircraft. It is possible that there is some confounding in the models between the covariates survey type (=aircraft type for 1996-98) and altitude. The significant relationship to survey type (MMS vs. LGL) could be, in part, an aircraft altitude effect.

Human Activities

Seismic Surveys

Bowhead Sighting Probability.—"Objective 1" of the study was to quantify the probability of observing bowheads relative to distance and direction (E, W, N, S) from a seismic source, amount of exposure to sound pulses, and time since exposure (see Introduction). "Objective 3" was to assess whether the seismic effect, if any, is reduced or absent if there is a barrier island or shallow water between the airguns and the whale sighting.

With regard to *Objective 1*, the results of the analyses conducted in Phase I indicate that seismic activity within the general area reduced the number of bowhead whale groups expected to be sighted in a sample unit. We considered seismic activity during six time periods relative to the time of the aerial survey: 0-1, 1-2, 2-3, 3-6, 6-12, and 12-24 h before the survey; plus 0-3 h (combined) before the survey. It was found that the best model fits occurred when we considered seismic activity 0-1 h and 12-24 h before the aerial survey. Based on maps of sighting probability derived from the coefficients estimated by the Poisson model, the expected numbers of bowhead sightings were reduced near a seismic source operating in nearshore waters relative to an otherwise comparable situation when no airguns were operating. This distribution pattern was observed for both the 0-1 h and 12-24 h models, assuming a seismic survey at a representative location (near Prudhoe Bay) and date (15 Sep 1998).

With regard to *Objective 3*, the analysis did not show any appreciable improvement in the predictions of sighting probability when minimum water depth between the seismic vessel and observation area was taken into account. This was somewhat surprising, given earlier indications that the closest sightings of migrating bowheads to operating seismic vessels tended to occur in circumstances with shallow water (or gravel bars) between the vessel and the whales (Miller et al. 1999). The lack of clear evidence (from the Poisson regression model) for such an effect may be a result of low sample size in the most critical conditions. Alternatively, it may mean that the "minimum water depth" measure that we used was not a very good measure of the sound attenuating effect. Ideally, one would want to use a direct measure of sound attenuation along the path between the seismic vessel and the observation location as a predictor of the number of bowhead groups. In the absence of any direct measurement or comprehensive model for sound attenuation, we chose to use the use minimum water depth along the propagation path (over the range 2 to 20 m) as a surrogate measure. It would very likely be better to use a sound propagation model to predict sound attenuation along the propagation path, and use that prediction in lieu of the minimum water depth. However, that was outside the scope of this study, and to be done well would require synoptic data on bottom properties in regions where seismic surveys were done. Such data are not available.

Further investigation of the goodness-of-fit of the models, and associated model refinements, are required before specific conclusions can be drawn about the spatial scale, directional properties, and magnitude of seismic effects. While the results of analyses to date indicate that nearby seismic activity results in a reduction in bowhead numbers, probably both along the north-south axis and the east-west axis, the spatial extent of the effect cannot be determined with confidence from the model as it now exists. We made considerable efforts to optimize the form and coefficients of the model to obtain the best possible fit to the data, but it is quite likely that further adjustments are needed to obtain a realistic fit. For example, after trying other alternatives, the present model involves a quadratic fit to the east-west component of distance from the seismic source, combined with a separate quadratic fit to the north-south component of distance. There is also an assumption that the seismic effect does not extend beyond 70 km from the source. Use of the quadratic function of the east-west distance implies that the seismic effects to the east and west are mirror images of one another, which might not be correct. For example, one could hypothesize that the effect would extend farther west (downstream) than east (upstream) of the seismic vessel.

Some improvements to model fit might be achieved by additional analysis of the 1996-98 data used here, but it may be necessary to incorporate additional data (as planned for Phase II, if it proceeds) in order to develop a more realistic and informative model. The number of 5-km sample units in which bowhead whales were seen during the 1996-98 surveys was a very small proportion of the total sampling units, and also not especially large relative to the rather large number of potential covariates considered in the analysis. Thus, the analysis would benefit from the inclusion of additional data from a wider variety of circumstances. For example, seismic surveys during the bowhead migration seasons in 1996-98 were all fairly close to shore in relatively shallow water and in a relatively narrow range of longitudes (Richardson [ed.] 1997, 1998, 1999). Consideration of data from other years when seismic surveys occurred in other parts of the Alaskan Beaufort Sea should allow development of a more general, and probably better-fitting, model. Therefore, as expected, Objectives 1 and 3 need further consideration. Recommendations for additional analysis approaches to investigate seismic effects (and other human activities) on the expected number of bowhead sightings are provided in the section below "Recommendations for Phase II". In the meantime, results of the present Poisson regression analyses should be treated cautiously as there are several issues concerning the analysis approach that need to be addressed before one can be confident of some of the finer details of the fitted model.

Headings of Bowheads.—"Objective 2" concerned whether the distribution of headings for "traveling" bowheads is deflected from the typical WNW migratory direction at certain distances from the seismic vessel at times when the airguns are operating. Bowheads recorded as being engaged in activities other than "traveling" were not considered, as their headings would be influenced by other confounding factors such as feeding and social activities.

Overall, there was some evidence that the headings of traveling bowhead whales were significantly different during periods with vs. without seismic activity, but the evidence was not very convincing within any one specific distance and direction category relative to the seismic vessel. The categories were >60 km East, <60 to 30 km East, <30 to >0 km East, 0 to 30 km West, >30 to 60 km West, and >60 km West. Within each of these, a circular randomization test was applied. These tests indicated that the differences in mean bearings within the individual distance categories during seismic vs. no-seismic periods were not statistically significant. However, there were non-significant trends for the mean headings within 30 km to the east and 60 km to the west of the seismic vessel to be more to the northwest at times with seismic surveys (vs. WNW without seismic).

The randomization approach used here is more suitable for present purposes than the more classical methods applicable to circularly-distributed data (Batschelet 1981, Chapter 6; Fisher 1993, Chapter 5). The randomization method (a) makes no assumptions about the nature of the probability distribution of headings, (b) is relatively simple in concept, using test statistics that are the obvious ones of interest, and (c) allows testing for a significant difference both for the individual distance categories and for all distances combined.

This analysis should be revisited in future to include data from other years, thus increasing the sample size; to consider headings in different geographic areas relative to the industrial activity; and to investigate effects of other industrial activities not present in 1996-98 on headings. In the future, this test can be used not only to further address Objective 2, but also Objective 3 re sound attenuation by shallow waters, Objective 6 re drillship effects, and perhaps also Objective 9 re icebreaking effects (to the extent these can be discriminated from drillship effects).

Whaling Activity

"Objective 17" was to assess whether bowhead sighting probability tends to be reduced within whale hunting regions during the date range when hunting occurred within the region and year in question. The Poisson regression analysis indicated that subsistence hunting, as "quantified" in this study, did not significantly influence the number of bowhead sightings within a sampling unit. Only very limited data were available on specific locations and timing of whaling activities in 1996-98. Consequently, the results do not necessarily mean that there was no hunting effect. More specific data on the timing and locations of hunting are needed for a meaningful analysis. Recent MMS-supported work in conjunction with the hunters is starting to provide data at the necessary level of detail (Galginaitis 2002, 2003). However, such data are not available for the years up to 1998, which are the years for which information about other human activities has been compiled in the HAD.

Adequacy of Approach

There are a number of unresolved issues in the application of Poisson regression to the Phase I data, as discussed in the Methods and Results sections of this report. There are questions about the extent to which standard statistical theory can be relied upon for estimating variances and carrying out tests of significance. There are also questions about the assumptions made when allowing for the activity level of seismic sources, the minimum water depth between a seismic source and an observation area, the assumed range of influence for a seismic source, and the impact of serial correlation. (Recommendations for dealing with these questions are discussed below.) As standard statistical theory applies to large sample sizes, and the analysis in this study is on a very large sample of 5-km units of observation, it might seem surprising that there are questions regarding this theory. However, the problem is that the observed number of bowhead groups is zero for a very high proportion of the sample units. This may make the standard theory unreliable. In principle, these questions can be resolved. For example, with additional effort, simulation methods can be used to estimate variances and to carry out tests of significance. Also, the outcomes can be determined and compared when different assumptions are made about the effects of the seismic activity level, minimum water depth, range of influence of seismic surveys, etc. For some if not all of these extensions of approach, it would be beneficial to work with a larger number of bowhead sightings, i.e., with more years of data.

On a positive note, it has been possible to find models for the data that fit the observed numbers of whale groups quite well, and that—to a first approximation at least—give sensible estimates for seismic effects. Also, the models show that some of the covariates that were expected to influence the number of sightings of bowheads do indeed have effects of the anticipated nature. Given this, it is apparent that, as compared with bivariate analyses, multivariate models taking account of confounding influences can be expected to provide an improved basis for assessing the effects of human activity variables (or any specific natural factor) on bowhead sightings. Our view is, therefore, that the basic approach to data analysis is sound, but it requires further fine tuning before the output can be completely relied upon as a specific characterization of the influences of specific human activity, natural, or sightability factors.

Some of this fine tuning could be done based on further work with the 1996-98 data already analyzed, but additional improvements could be made by incorporating data from other years. Use of data from other years not only would increase sample size, but also would provide data from a greater variety of conditions. The latter would provide the basis for developing models that are less year-specific and more generally applicable.

Implications of Using Proprietary Data

The Human Activity Database (HAD) developed during an earlier project (Wainwright 2002) contains most of the human activity data used during the present analysis, and some of the data in the HAD are subject to confidentiality agreements between MMS and various providers of data. Seismic data, in particular, can have substantial commercial and competitive value. Some of that information was made available for purposes of the HAD and the present project on the condition that the original data would be kept confidential by MMS and the contractors. During the present study, the HAD has been accessible to or shared with only a small number of project participants who have signed Nondisclosure Agreements. Exchange of the proprietary data among project participants has been by secure e-mail between computers protected by firewalls, or by courier. These data have not been maintained on FTP sites or other facilities where they might be accessed by the public.

No raw data from the HAD are presented in this report. The proprietary data that were used in the analyses conducted during the present study were combined and manipulated to the extent that they are no longer recognizable or attributable to their original sources by a reader. The presentations of the results of the analyses would preclude a reader from identifying specific industrial sources in place or time.

As required by the contract terms, at the end of this project (or the end of Phase II if it proceeds), we will promptly upon the request of MMS return to MMS all of the information furnished by, or on behalf of MMS, without retaining copies of that information unless that is specifically authorized. Any analyses, compilations, studies, reports, or other documents that show proprietary information will be kept confidential and will not be used in any way, or will be destroyed upon the request of MMS.

Recommendations for Phase II

Overall, the results of Phase I are encouraging and we recommend that Phase II of this study proceed. Although several problems were encountered during Phase I, we learned from these problems and developed a suitable analysis approach for investigating how the distribution of bowhead whales has been jointly affected by human activities and natural factors. The Poisson regression approach allowed us to assess the influences of seismic activity on bowhead distribution while simultaneously allowing for the influences of (a) natural environmental factors on bowhead distribution, and (b) sightability factors on the likelihood of detecting a whale group that is present. However, there are several aspects of the study that can be improved upon and specific recommendations for Phase II are outlined below.

Data Structure

As discussed earlier, not all of the bowheads that are present are seen during aerial surveys. One of the reasons bowheads may be missed by observers is because of obstruction by parts of the aircraft structure (Thomas et al. 2002). Aircraft type affects the size of the zone directly below an aircraft where sightability is reduced. (The higher the altitude, the wider the zone.) Twin Otter aircraft, like those used during the MMS surveys, had a narrower zone of reduced sightability below the aircraft than did Twin Commanders like those used during LGL aerial surveys. In this study, although we included aircraft type as a covariate, our sample unit width (2.5 km on each side of the aircraft) was measured from the trackline, not from the outer edge of the zone of restricted detectability beneath the aircraft. For Phase II, we recommend investigating the possibility of excluding the zone of restricted detectability by using an aircraft-specific inner truncation distance. This would be more important for Phase II than for Phase I, as more aircraft types would be involved in the surveys conducted over the additional years.

During Phase I, only the sightings recorded by the primary observers on the left and right sides of the aircraft were included for LGL surveys. For MMS surveys, we included all sightings because it was not clear at the time of this study which sightings were recorded by primary vs. other observers. If Phase II proceeds, we recommend investigating the potential for using only those sightings recorded by primary observers during MMS surveys.

In future analyses, it may be appropriate to re-compute the bottom slope over a spatial scale other than the 200 x 200 m used in Phase I, and then reconsider whether bottom slope is a useful predictor of bowhead sightings.

Only very limited data were available on specific locations and timing of whaling activities in 1996-98. The decision to conduct a similar analysis for Phase II should depend upon the availability of more specific information about the timing and locations of hunting. If more specific information is available, the possible effects of nearby whaling on the probability of sighting bowheads could be tested more effectively. However, it is doubtful that sufficiently improved data on hunting activity will become available for the additional years in the 1990s likely to be used in Phase II analyses. Meaningful analysis of the influences of hunting on bowhead distribution will probably not be possible unless the analysis is extended to include more recent years for which specific data on the timing and locations of hunting are sometimes available (e.g., Galginaitis 2002, 2003).

Poisson Regression Approach

Initially, the expected analysis approach for this study was a logistic regression, which provides estimates of the probability of sighting bowhead whales in a sample unit given the influences of covariates (see Appendix A). After careful consideration, the procedure used for Phase I was Poisson regression, in which the dependent variable is the number of whale sightings in a sample unit. It is recommended that the Poisson regression approach should be used in Phase II.

Several recommendations concerning various aspects of future Poisson analyses were made in the Results section. These, plus some others, are listed below:

- Further investigation is required to assess the most appropriate way of estimating heterogeneity factors. It is recommended that the validity of using either the model deviance or the Pearson chi-squared estimates be examined by use of simulation, bootstrap, and randomization methods, depending upon the circumstances (Manly 1997). For example, to estimate a heterogeneity factor, many sets of data can be generated based on a fitted model but with the data following Poisson distributions. An estimate of the heterogeneity factor is then provided by the observed deviance for the fitted model divided by the mean deviance for the simulated sets of data. Alternatively, the Pearson chi-squared statistic for the observed data could be divided by the mean value of this statistic from the simulated sets of data.

- It was found that changing the maximum potential range of influence of seismic activity can produce quite variable and sometimes unrealistic estimates of seismic effects. For example, when the range of influence was unbounded, the models produced apparently unrealistic estimates of seismic effects at great distances. This was believed to be due to the clustering of distant whale groups either due to chance or due to concentrated feeding activity. Subsequent analyses in Phase I assumed a maximum distance for seismic effects of 100 km, 75 km, and finally 70 km. It is recognized that there is a subjective element in the decision to restrict the range of influence like this, but it does appear to produce patterns that are reasonable. This is an element of the data analysis that should be revisited in the future, not just for seismic activity but for other types of human activities like drilling, shallow-hazards surveys, etc.

- The selection of various time intervals for investigating effects of human activities should be further investigated. During Phase I, the time intervals considered for seismic effects were 0-1, 1-2, 2-3, 3-6, 6-12, and 12-24 h. Because these seismic covariates were highly correlated, this created problems in estimating coefficient values. As such, some time intervals were pooled but this did not improve model fit. Future analyses need to further investigate how time intervals are categorized and incorporated into the statistical models. The most appropriate intervals might not be the same for seismic surveys or drillships (both of which apparently can influence bowhead distribution over a substantial area, e.g., LGL and Greeneridge 1987; Davies 1997; Miller et al. 1999; Schick and Urban 2000) as for activities with smaller radii of influence.

- During Phase I, two primary approaches were used to scale the activity levels of a seismic source. Initially, the activity level θ of a seismic source was scaled so that it was at the standard level if there was an average of one shot every 20 seconds, and therefore 180 shots per hour, over the full interval length. If there was an average of 90 shots per hour, θ was 0.5, etc. The scaling was achieved by multiplying the values for all covariates that characterized seismic effects by θ. As an alternative to this scaling, seismic effects were left unscaled if θ exceeded 0.1, or otherwise the seismic effects were set to zero. The former treatment was used in the final models. Future analyses should revisit the question of how best to take into account varying activity levels for seismic surveys and other human activities. This will become especially critical when multiple human activities are potentially considered during Phase II.

- During Phase I, we attempted to address Objective 3, quantifying the presumed mitigating effect of sound attenuation by shallow water, by using a scaling based on the minimum water depth between an observed stretch of transect and a seismic source. This was investigated as an additional scaling applied after the θ scaling described above. As this minimum depth scaling failed to improve the fit of the model based on either the 0-1 hour seismic interval or the 12-24 hour seismic interval, its use was discontinued. This is another area that could be revisited in future analyses, possibly trying a range of water depth limits for the linear scaling effect. Also, something other than a linear effect over the specified range of minimum depths may be appropriate. As discussed earlier, it would be ideal if this factor could be a more direct measure of the anticipated sound attenuation between the sound source and the transect segment.

- During Phase I it was thought that quadratic functions were adequate to describe the data, or at least that cubic covariates provided no advantage over quadratic covariates. In any future analysis it would be desirable to consider alternatives to the quadratic formulation.

- In future analyses, it would be beneficial to use a systematic approach for considering which natural and sightability covariates should be included in the final regression models. During Phase I, no systematic attempt was made to see which, if any, of the covariates describing the distribution of whale groups in the absence of seismic activity could be removed from the model without appreciable deterioration in goodness-of-fit and predictive capacity.

- As a follow-up to the previous recommendation, it would be worthwhile to investigate in more detail the extent to which various covariates have different influences on numbers of bowhead sightings during different survey years. We allowed for the possibility that the relationships to several covariates would differ from year to year. For covariates where there is no year-to-year difference in effect, a simpler and possibly better model might be achievable if, after the lack of a year effect were recognized, the provision for year-specific differences were removed from the model.

- If Phase II proceeds, it is recommended that potential serial correlation problems be addressed as per the approach presented in Appendix D.

Objectives and Hypotheses

During Phase I, we attempted to address 7 of the 17 objectives/hypotheses presented in the Feasibility Study, specifically objectives 1, 2 and 3 concerning seismic effects, objectives 13, 15 and 16 concerning natural and sightability factors, and objective 17 concerning subsistence hunting effects. The remaining objectives/hypotheses (see Appendix B) could not be addressed during Phase I analysis based on the combined 1996-98 data. In these cases, the primary reason(s) for not addressing the objective in Phase I are that (a) a particular industrial activity did not occur during the years being analyzed, and/or (b) three years of data provide too few data to quantify effects. It is anticipated that including additional years of data (in Phase II) will allow us to better quantify effects of various natural and sightability covariates on the expected number of bowhead sightings. These improvements will be a result of the larger sample size and greater variety of circumstances in which the observations were obtained. Also, including additional years of data with varying types of human activities, including shallow-hazards surveys and drilling, as well as whaling and seismic surveys, will allow us to investigate potential effects of these additional activities on the expected number of bowhead sightings.

ACKNOWLEDGEMENTS

We thank Craig George of the North Slope Borough Department of Wildlife Management, Thomas Cook of Thomas Cook Consultants, and William Koski of LGL Ltd. for providing information on the timing and locations of the autumn hunts for bowheads conducted at Kaktovik, Cross Island, and Barrow. We are grateful to John Hall of COPAC, Mark Major of ConocoPhillips (formerly ARCO), Bob Griffeth (formerly with ARCO), and Jeremy Davies of the National Marine Mammal Laboratory, for the assistance they provided in our attempt to find a more detailed version of the 1993 COPAC dataset. We also thank BP Exploration (Alaska) Inc. and WesternGeco (formerly Western Geophysical) for use of data collected during aerial surveys conducted on their behalf, as well as the many MMS and LGL aerial surveyors and their pilots who collected the aerial survey datasets analyzed here. Peter Wainwright of LGL was primarily responsible for compiling the MMS-sponsored Human Activity Database that was a key starting point for this analysis; we also thank the many industry groups and individuals who made available the industrial activity information used here. Finally, at MMS we thank Steve Treacy for allowing us to use the MMS-BWASP aerial survey dataset; Warren Horowitz, who coordinated the compilation of the Human Activity Database; Michael Hargrove and Rhonda Fernandez, Contracting Officers for this analysis project; and Drs Charles Monnett, Cleveland Cowles and Jeffrey Gleason for their guidance and support.

The other authors acknowledge the major contribution of the late Gary W. Miller of LGL to this project. He was LGL's project manager for this contract. He had also been much involved in the original fieldwork that provided many of the industry-sponsored data used here.

LITERATURE CITED

Angliss, R.P., D.P. DeMaster and A.L. Lopez. 2001. Alaska marine mammal stock assessments, 2001. U.S. Dep. Comm., NOAA Tech. Memo. NMFS-AFSC-124. Nat. Mar. Fish. Serv. Seattle, WA. 206 p.

Batschelet, E. 1981. Circular Statistics in Biology. Academic Press, London, U.K. 371 p.

Cameron, A.C. and P.K. Trivedi. 1998. Regression Analysis of Count Data. Cambridge Univ. Press, Cambridge, U.K.

Cañadas, A., R. Sagarminaga and S. García-Tiscar. 2002. Cetacean distribution related with depth and slope in the Mediterranean waters off southern Spain. **Deep-Sea Res. I** 49:2053-2073.

Davies, J.R. 1997. The impact of an offshore drilling platform on the fall migration path of bowhead whales: a GIS-based assessment. M.S. thesis, Western Washington Univ., Bellingham, WA. 52 p.

DeMaster, D.P., L.F. Lowry, K.J. Frost and R.A. Bengtson. 2001. The effect of sea state on estimates of abundance for beluga whales (*Delphinapterus leucas*) in Norton Sound, Alaska. **Fish. Bull.** 99(1):197-201.

Fisher, N.I. 1993. Statistical Analysis of Circular Data. Cambridge Univ. Press, Cambridge, U.K.

Galginaitis, M. 2002. Annual assessment of subsistence bowhead whaling near Cross Island/Draft annual report for 2001. ANIMIDA Task Order 004. Rep. from Applied Sociocultural Res., Anchorage, AK, for LGL Alaska. Res. Assoc. Inc. and U.S. Minerals Manage. Serv., Anchorage, AK.

Galginaitis, M. 2003. Annual assessment of subsistence whaling near Cross Island/Draft annual report for 2002. ANIMIDA Task Order 004. Rep. from Applied Sociocultural Res., Anchorage, AK, for LGL Alaska Res. Assoc. and U.S. Minerals Manage. Serv., Anchorage, AK. 196 p

Galginaitis, M.S., and W. R. Koski. 2002. Kaktovikmiut whaling: Historical harvest and local knowledge of whale feeding behavior. p. 2-1 to 2-30 (Chap. 2) *In*: W.J. Richardson and D.H. Thomson (eds.), Bowhead whale feeding in the eastern Alaskan Beaufort Sea: update of scientific and traditional information. OCS Study MMS 2002-012; LGL Rep. TA2196-7. Rep. from LGL Ltd, King City, Ont., for U.S. Minerals Manage. Serv., Anchorage, AK, and Herndon, VA. Vol. I. 420 p. Available at http://www mms.gov/alaska/ref/Pubsreadingroom htm

Gunnlaugsson, T., J. Sigurjónsson and G.P. Donovan. 1988. Aerial survey of cetaceans in the coastal waters off Iceland, June-July 1986. **Rep. Int. Whal. Comm.** 38:489-500.

Hall, J.D., M.L. Gallagher, K.D. Brewer, P.R. Regos and P.E. Isert. 1994. ARCO Alaska, Inc. 1993 Kuvlum exploration area site specific monitoring program/Final report. Rep. from Coastal & Offshore Pacific Corp., Walnut Creek, CA, for ARCO Alaska Inc. [Anchorage, AK]. 219 p. + Data Appendix Vol. 1, 2.

Holt, R.S. 1987. Estimating density of dolphin schools in the Eastern Tropical Pacific Ocean by line transect methods. **Fish. Bull.** 85(3):419-434.

Kenney, R.D. and H.E. Winn. 1987. Cetacean biomass densities near submarine canyons compared to adjacent shelf/slope areas. **Cont. Shelf Res.** 7(2):107-114.

LGL Ltd. 2003. Study plan for analysis of covariance of human activities and sea ice in relation to fall migrations of bowhead whales, Phases I and II. LGL Rep. TA2799-1. Rep. from LGL Ltd., King City, Ont., and WEST Inc., Cheyenne, WY, for the U.S. Minerals Manage. Serv., Herndon, VA.

LGL and Greeneridge. 1987. Responses of bowhead whales to an offshore drilling operation in the Alaskan Beaufort Sea, autumn 1986. Rep. from LGL Ltd., King City, Ont., and Greeneridge Sciences Inc., Santa Barbara, CA, for Shell Western E & P Inc., Anchorage, AK. 371 p.

LGL and Greeneridge. 1996. Northstar marine mammal monitoring program, 1995: baseline surveys and retrospective analyses of marine mammal and ambient noise data from the central Alaskan Beaufort Sea. LGL Rep. TA2101-2. Rep. from LGL Ltd., King City, Ont., and Greeneridge Sciences Inc., Santa Barbara, CA, for BP Explor. (Alaska) Inc., Anchorage, AK. 104 p.

Ljungblad, D.K., S.E. Moore, J.T. Clarke and J.C. Bennett. 1988. Distribution, abundance, behavior and bioacoustics of endangered whales in the western Beaufort and northeastern Chukchi Seas, 1979-87. OCS Study MMS 87-0122. Rep. from Naval Ocean Systems Center and SEACO, San Diego, CA, for U.S. Minerals Manage. Serv., Anchorage, AK. 213 p. NTIS PB88-245584.

Manly, B.F.J. 1997. Randomization, Bootstrap and Monte Carlo Methods in Biology, 2nd Edit. Chapman & Hall, London, U.K. 281 p.

Manly, B.F.J. and M. Chotkowski. 2006. Two new methods for regime change analysis. **Arch. Hydrobiol.** 167(1-4):593-607.

Marko, J.R. 2001. Preparation of a sediment stratigraphy representative of the Alaskan North Slope. p. 70-91 *In:* P. Wainwright, GIS geospatial database of oil-industry and other human activity (1979 - 1999) in the Alaskan Beaufort Sea/Public report. Appendix 2. Rep. from LGL Ltd., Sidney, B.C., for U.S. Minerals Manage. Serv., Anchorage, AK. [Overall report date is 2002.]

MatLab. 2003. MatLab Version 6.5.1. The MathWorks Inc., Natick, MA.

Mate, B.R., G.K. Krutzikowsky and M.H. Winsor. 2000. Satellite-monitored movements of radio-tagged bowhead whales in the Beaufort and Chukchi seas during the late-summer feeding season and fall migration. **Can. J. Zool.** 78(7):1168-1181.

MathSoft. 2000. S-Plus 2000. Mathsoft Inc., Cambridge, Massachusetts, USA.

McCullagh, P. and J.A. Nelder. 1989. Generalized Linear Models, 2nd Edit. Chapman & Hall, London, U.K. 511 p.

Miller, G.W., R.E. Elliott, W.R. Koski and W.J. Richardson. 1997. Whales [1996] p. 5-1 to 5-115 *In:* W.J. Richardson (ed.), Northstar marine mammal monitoring program, 1996: marine mammal and acoustical monitoring of a seismic program in the Alaskan Beaufort Sea. LGL Rep. 2121-2. Rep. from LGL Ltd., King City, Ont., and Greeneridge Sciences Inc., Santa Barbara, CA, for BP Explor. (Alaska) Inc., Anchorage, AK, and Nat. Mar. Fish. Serv., Anchorage, AK, and Silver Spring, MD. 245 p.

Miller, G.W., R.E. Elliott and W.J. Richardson. 1998. Whales [1997]. p. 5-1 to 5-124 *In:* W.J. Richardson (ed.), Marine mammal and acoustical monitoring of BP Exploration (Alaska's) open-water seismic program in the Alaskan Beaufort Sea, 1997. LGL Rep. TA2150-3. Rep. from LGL Ltd., King City, Ont., and Greeneridge Sciences Inc., Santa Barbara, CA, for BP Explor. (Alaska) Inc., Anchorage, AK, and U.S. Nat. Mar. Fish. Serv., Anchorage, AK, and Silver Spring, MD. 318 p.

Miller, G.W., R.E. Elliott, W.R. Koski, V.D. Moulton and W.J. Richardson. 1999. Whales [1998]. p. 5-1 to 5-109 *In:* W.J. Richardson (ed.), Marine mammal and acoustical monitoring of Western Geophysical's open-water seismic program in the Alaskan Beaufort Sea, 1998. LGL Rep. TA2230-3. Rep. from LGL Ltd., King City, Ont., and Greeneridge Sciences Inc., Santa Barbara, CA, for Western Geophysical, Houston, TX, and U.S. Nat. Mar. Fish. Serv., Anchorage, AK, and Silver Spring, MD. 390 p.

Miller, G.W., R.E. Elliott, T.A. Thomas, V.D. Moulton and W.R. Koski. 2002. Distribution and numbers of bowhead whales in the eastern Alaskan Beaufort Sea during late summer and autumn, 1979-2000. p. 9-1 to 9-39 (Chap. 9) *In:* W.J. Richardson and D.H. Thomson (eds.), Bowhead whale feeding in the eastern Alaskan Beaufort Sea: update of scientific and traditional information, vol. 1. OCS Study MMS 2002-012; LGL Rep. TA2196-7. Rep. from LGL Ltd., King City, Ont., for U.S. Minerals Manage. Serv., Anchorage, AK, and Herndon, VA. 420 p. Available at http://www mms.gov/alaska/ref/Pubsreadingroom htm

Moore, S.E. 2000. Variability of cetacean distribution and habitat selection in the Alaskan Arctic, autumn 1982-91. **Arctic** 53(4):448-460.

Moore, S.E. and D.P. DeMaster. 1998. Cetacean habitats in the Alaskan Arctic. **J. Northw. Atl. Fish. Sci.** 22:55-69.

Moore, S.E., D.P. DeMaster and P.K. Dayton. 2000. Cetacean habitat selection in the Alaskan Arctic during summer and autumn. **Arctic** 53(4):432-447.

NAG. 2003. GenStat 7th Edit. Numerical Algorithms Group, Oxford, U.K.

Richardson, W.J. (ed.). 1997. Northstar marine mammal monitoring program, 1996: Marine mammal and acoustical monitoring of a seismic program in the Alaskan Beaufort Sea. LGL Rep. TA2121-2. Rep. from LGL Ltd., King City, Ont., and Greeneridge Sciences Inc., Santa Barbara, CA, for BP Explor. (Alaska) Inc., Anchorage, AK, and Nat. Mar. Fish. Serv., Anchorage, AK, and Silver Spring, MD. 245 p.

Richardson, W.J. (ed.). 1998. Marine mammal and acoustical monitoring of BPXA's seismic program in the Alaskan Beaufort Sea, 1997. LGL Rep. TA2150-3. Rep. from LGL Ltd., King City, Ont., and Greeneridge Sciences Inc., Santa Barbara, CA, for BP Explor. (Alaska) Inc., Anchorage, AK, and Nat. Mar. Fish. Serv., Anchorage, AK, and Silver Spring, MD. 318 p.

Richardson, W.J. (ed.). 1999. Marine mammal and acoustical monitoring of Western Geophysical's open-water seismic program in the Alaskan Beaufort Sea, 1998. LGL Rep. TA2230-3. Rep. from LGL Ltd., King City, Ont., and Greeneridge Sciences Inc., Santa Barbara, CA, for Western Geophysical, Houston, TX, and Nat. Mar. Fish. Serv., Anchorage, AK, and Silver Spring, MD. 390 p.

Richardson, W.J. and D.H. Thomson (eds.). 2002. Bowhead whale feeding in the eastern Alaskan Beaufort Sea: update of scientific and traditional information. OCS Study MMS 2002-012; LGL Rep. TA2196-7. Rep. from LGL Ltd., King City, Ont., for U.S. Minerals Manage. Serv., Anchorage, AK, and Herndon, VA. xliv + 697 p. 2 vol. Available at http://www mms.gov/alaska/ref/Pubsreadingroom.htm

Richardson, W.J., M.A. Fraker, B. Würsig and R.S. Wells. 1985. Behaviour of bowhead whales *Balaena mysticetus* summering in the Beaufort Sea: reactions to industrial activities. **Biol. Conserv.** 32(3):195-230.

Richardson, W.J., C.R. Greene Jr., J.S. Hanna, W.R. Koski, G.W. Miller, N.J. Patenaude and M.A. Smultea. 1995a. Acoustic effects of oil production activities on bowhead and white whales visible during spring migration near Pt. Barrow, Alaska—1991 and 1994 phases. OCS Study MMS 95-0051; LGL Rep. TA954. Rep. from LGL Ltd., King City, Ont., for U.S. Minerals Manage. Serv., Herndon, VA. 539 p. NTIS PB98-107667.

Richardson, W.J., C.R. Greene Jr., C.I. Malme and D.H. Thomson. 1995b. Marine mammals and noise. Academic Press, San Diego, CA. 576 p.

Richardson, W.J., G.W. Miller and C.R. Greene Jr. 1999. Displacement of migrating bowhead whales by sounds from seismic surveys in shallow waters of the Beaufort Sea. **J. Acoust. Soc. Am.** 106(4, Pt. 2):2281.

Richardson, W.J., B.F.J. Manly, G.W. Miller, W.C. Burgess, R.E. Elliott and P. Wainwright. 2001. Feasibility of using Human Activities Database and existing aerial survey data to analyze bowhead whale distribution in the Alaskan Beaufort Sea during autumn vs. human activities and sea ice. LGL Rep. EA1195-2. Rep. from LGL Ltd. (King City, Ont.), WEST Inc., and Greeneridge Sciences Inc. for Minerals Manage Serv., Anchorage, AK. 54 p. Included as Appendix A in this report.

SAS. 2003. SAS System for Windows, Release 8.2. SAS Institute, Cary, NC.

Schick, R.S. and D.L. Urban. 2000. Spatial components of bowhead whale (*Balaena mysticetus*) distribution in the Alaskan Beaufort Sea. **Can. J. Fish. Aquatic Sci.** 57(11):2193-2200.

Scott, G.P. and H.E. Winn. 1980. Comparative evaluation of aerial and shipboard sampling techniques for estimating the abundance of humpback whales (*Megaptera novaeangliae*). MMC-77/24. U.S. Mar. Mamm. Comm., Washington, DC. 96 p. NTIS PB81-109852.

Thomas, T.A., W.R. Koski, W.J. Richardson and B. Würsig. 1999. Bowhead distribution, numbers and activities. p. 71-155 (Chap. 3) *In:* W.J. Richardson and D. H. Thomson (eds.). Bowhead whale feeding in the Eastern Alaskan Beaufort Sea: Update of scientific and traditional information. Retrospective and 1998 results. LGL Rep. TA2196-2. Rep. from LGL Ltd., King City, Ont., and LGL Ecol. Res. Assoc., Bryan, TX, for the U.S. Minerals Manage. Serv., Herndon, VA. 366 p.

Thomas, T.A., W.R. Koski and W.J. Richardson. 2002. Correction factors to calculate bowhead whale numbers from aerial surveys of the Beaufort Sea. p. 15-1 to 15-28 (Chap. 15) *In:* W.J. Richardson and D.H. Thomson (eds.), Bowhead whale feeding in the eastern Alaskan Beaufort Sea: update of scientific and traditional information, vol. 1. OCS Study MMS 2002-012; LGL Rep. TA2196-7. Rep. from LGL Ltd., King City, Ont., for U.S. Minerals Manage. Serv., Anchorage, AK, and Herndon, VA. 420 p. Available at http://www.mms.gov/alaska/ref/Pubsreadingroom htm

Treacy, S.D. 1994. Aerial surveys of endangered whales in the Beaufort Sea, fall 1993. OCS Study MMS 94-0032. U.S. Minerals Manage. Serv., Anchorage, AK. 132 p.

Treacy, S.D. 1997. Aerial surveys of endangered whales in the Beaufort Sea, fall 1996. OCS Study MMS 97-0016. U.S. Minerals Manage. Serv., Anchorage, AK. 115 p.

Treacy, S.D. 1998. Aerial surveys of endangered whales in the Beaufort Sea, fall 1997. OCS Study MMS 98-0059. U.S. Minerals Manage. Serv., Anchorage, AK. 143 p.

Treacy, S.D. 2000. Aerial surveys of endangered whales in the Beaufort Sea, fall 1998-1999. OCS Study MMS 2000-066. U.S. Minerals Manage. Serv., Anchorage, AK. 135 p.

Treacy, S.D. 2002a. Aerial surveys of endangered whales in the Beaufort Sea, fall 2000. OCS Study MMS 2002-014. U.S. Minerals Manage. Serv., Anchorage, AK. 111 p.

Treacy, S.D. 2002b. Aerial surveys of endangered whales in the Beaufort Sea, fall 2001. OCS Study MMS 2002-061. U.S. Minerals Manage. Serv., Anchorage, AK. 117 p.

Wainwright, P. 2002. GIS geospatial database of oil-industry and other human activity (1979-1999) in the Alaskan Beaufort Sea/Public report. Rep. from LGL Ltd., Sidney, B.C., for U.S. Minerals Manage. Serv., Anchorage, AK. 91 p.

APPENDIX A

Feasibility of Using Human Activities Database and Existing Aerial Survey Data to Analyze Bowhead Whale Distribution in the Alaskan Beaufort Sea during Autumn *vs.* Human Activities and Sea Ice

by

W.J. Richardson [1], B.F.J. Manly [2], G.W. Miller [1],
W.C. Burgess [3], R.E. Elliott [1] and P. Wainwright [1]

[1] **LGL Ltd., environmental research associates**
22 Fisher St., POB 280, King City, Ont. L7B 1A6
phone: (905)-833-1244; *e-mail* wjr@lgl.com

[2] **Western EcoSystems Technology Inc.**
2003 Central Ave., Cheyenne, WY 82001

[3] **Greeneridge Sciences Inc.**
4512 Via Huerto, Santa Barbara, CA 93110

for

Minerals Management Service, Alaska OCS Region
949 East 36th Ave., Anchorage, AK 99508

MMS Contract 1435-01-98-CT-309156, mod. 3

LGL Report EA1195-2

18 May 2001

TABLE OF CONTENTS

INTRODUCTION

From September 1998 through March 2001, LGL Ltd. compiled a GIS database of offshore oil-industry and selected other human activities in the Alaskan Beaufort Sea for the years 1979 through 1998. This project was initiated and sponsored by the Minerals Management Service (MMS), Alaska OCS Region. The general objective was to compile a readily-accessible and quantitative Human Activities Database (HAD) that could be used as the basis for future analyses of the effects of those activities on whale migrations and other phenomena that might be influenced by human activities. A draft final report on the effort to compile the HAD, and on the status of the resulting database, has been submitted to MMS (Wainwright and Marko 2001).

Much information has been compiled into the HAD. However, as anticipated when work on the HAD was begun, it was not possible to obtain complete data on all of the human activities of interest. The data gaps are more pronounced for years prior to 1990 than for the more recent years. However, even for the 1990s, some information is missing from the HAD or is quite incomplete (e.g., records of icebreaking activity and shipping within the Alaskan Beaufort Sea). Some other types of information of potential importance in analyzing the relationships of whale distribution to human activities were purposefully excluded from the scope of the HAD by MMS (e.g., information about the timing and locations of subsistence hunts for bowheads).

MMS has, for some years, indicated that the HAD, when completed, would serve as one of the main starting points for a follow-on project entitled "Analysis of Covariance of Human Activities and Sea Ice in Relation to Fall Migrations of Bowhead Whales". The objectives of that study, as stated in MMS's most recent Alaska Regional Studies Plan (dated Jan. 2001, for FY 2002-2003) are as follows:

1. "Assess the comparability of bowhead whale data collected by site-specific and broad-area surveys and the feasibility of pooling these data to detect whale distributional shifts or behavioral changes up to 40 miles from noise sources."

2. "Obtain from available information appropriate measures of sea ice for covariant analysis with whale distribution data."

3. "Present preliminary tests and findings, define biases and assumptions, and recommend appropriate statistical procedures (e.g., analysis of covariance, regression techniques, K-S tests, spatial analysis, computer modeling) to a Scientific Review Board."

4. "Apply applicable procedures to test hypotheses on relationships of the timing, location, and activity status of oil-industry/human activity and the distribution and behavior of bowhead whales (1979-1998)."

The latest MMS Regional Studies Plan goes on to say that the "Methods" for the planned study would be as follows:

"This study will utilize existing data in the recently developed MMS database for Beaufort Sea human activity and data in the MMS Bowhead Whale Aerial Survey Project database. [As noted in objective (1), above, MMS also intends that site-specific survey results will also be used.] It will consider positions and daily activity status of each drilling platform, helicopter, icebreaker, and other support vessels. It will adopt similar measures between years to facilitate inter-year comparisons and trend analysis. It will control for presence of commercial vessels, subsistence hunting, and low-flying aircraft. It will evaluate site-specific and wide-area data from MMS- and oil-industry-funded surveys of the fall distribution of bowhead whales (1979-1998) for applicability and pooled analysis. Using appropriate inferential statistical procedures, it will then test hypotheses for significant relationships of human activities and bowhead distribution and evaluate power of tests…"

The HAD, as it presently exists, does not include all of the human activity data that MMS had originally hoped to include, and it does not include an acoustical database or acoustical modeling capability. Some of the "missing" data are types of information that MMS had anticipated using in the planned analysis of covariance of human activities and sea ice vs. fall migrations of bowhead whales. Hence, MMS has requested that LGL include, in the final report on the compilation of the HAD, an assessment of the feasibility of going ahead with at least some parts of the planned "analysis of covariance". This document provides that feasibility analysis.

SCOPE AND APPROACH

MMS posed 11 questions that were to be addressed during this "feasibility analysis". These are listed below in the order given by MMS:

1. Assess the quality and quantity of the … HAD … and determine its usefulness, along with MMS BWASP, NOSC, site-specific survey databases, and available ice data, for addressing the objectives of MMS's planned study entitled "Analysis of Covariance of Human Activities and Sea Ice in Relation to Fall Migrations of the Bowhead Whale".

2. Develop specific hypothesis of statistical analysis that could be tested relative to effects of oil-and-gas-related activities on bowhead whales using HAD against BWASP, NOSC, and other aerial survey databases.

3. Evaluate the feasibility of using the HAD to detect multiple, combined, and/or cumulative effects of industrial activity on the movement and behavior of the bowhead whale (as represented in BWASP or other available bowhead aerial survey data). Specifically address need for acoustic model identified in current contract.

4. Describe the recommended statistical procedures and illustrate the type of product such analyses would produce.

5. Provide descriptive statistics and maps developed from the HAD for seismic and other industrial activities during late summer and autumn from 1990 to 1999.

6. Determine the quality and quantity of the icebreaker data and their reliability/suitability for enhancing statistical comparisons relative to drilling noise.

7. Determine the need, cost, and feasibility of collecting selected additional icebreaker data at the resolution needed for making meaningful statistical comparisons.

8. Evaluate the possibility of using all data including those data sets prior to 1990.

9. Recommend whether adequate information is available to proceed with the goals and objectives of the proposed new study ["Phase II"].

10. Recommend any modification of the current database structure, ArcView shape files, DBF files, and data documentation.

11. Recommend how drilling, ice-breaker, geohazard, and CDP seismic data could be collected by industry in a more useful format for estimating any effects from acoustic disturbances in the future.

Of these questions, numbers (1) and (9) concern the overall feasibility of moving ahead with at least some parts of the "Analysis of Covariance of Human Activities and Sea Ice in Relation to Fall Migrations of Bowhead Whales". The other nine questions are more specific, and the answers to most of those specific questions form the basis for answering questions (1) and (9) about the overall feasibility of the planned analysis. Therefore, the following feasibility analysis addresses the nine specific questions first, and then addresses the overall feasibility. Also, as part of the overall feasibility assessment near the end of this document, we review (briefly) the specific statements of objectives and methods listed by MMS in the FY 2002-2003 Regional Study Plan, as quoted in the "Introduction" above.

LGL was assisted in the preparation of this analysis by Dr. Bryan F.J. Manly, statistician with WEST Inc., and Drs. William C. Burgess and Charles R. Greene Jr., physical acousticians with Greene-ridge Sciences Inc.:

- Dr. Manly is an authority on the statistical analysis of data on wildlife distribution and many related topics. Dr. Manly's comments concerning the feasibility of MMS's planned "Analysis of covariance..." are included verbatim in Annex 1, and are summarized in various parts of this report.

- Drs. Burgess and Greene have measured many types of industrial sounds in the Beaufort Sea, have studied the factors affecting the propagation of those sounds, and have developed propagation models applicable to specific situations. Their comments on the feasibility of developing a procedure for estimating the received levels of all types of man-made sounds (combined) as received at a particular location are included in the section responding to question (3).

It is anticipated that this "feasibility analysis" document will be incorporated into the final version of the overall report on the compilation of the HAD.

SPECIFIC QUESTIONS

Nine of the 11 questions posed by MMS are specific in nature, and they are addressed here. Questions (1) and (9) relate to the overall feasibility of the planned "Analysis of covariance...". They are addressed in a subsequent section.

Question (2): Specific Hypotheses

Develop specific hypothesis of statistical analysis that could be tested relative to effects of oil-and-gas-related activities on bowhead whales using HAD against BWASP, NOSC, and other aerial survey databases.

In this section, we suggest some testable hypotheses concerning the effects of marine seismic exploration, offshore drillsites, and ice (in conjunction with other environmental factors) on the distribution of bowhead whales in the Alaskan Beaufort Sea in late summer and autumn. Although no statistical power analyses have been done, the hypotheses suggested below are considered to be potentially testable given the types and quantities of data that are available either now or with only a modest additional effort. (Subsequent sections of this Feasibility Analysis discuss many aspects of the available data.)

Much is already known about the influences of seismic exploration, drillships, ice, and other factors on the likelihood of seeing bowhead whales at specific locations. We know that these factors all do influence the distribution of bowhead whales. Therefore, it can be argued that it is not meaningful to formulate questions about these influences as conventional "null vs. alternate" hypotheses. In many cases, previous studies have already convincingly rejected the null hypothesis. In these cases, the primary reason for conducting additional analyses is to better quantify the magnitude, geographic extent, and duration of effects that are already known to exist, taking account of more data than in past studies, and allowing for the influences of confounding factors to a greater extent than in the past. However, for other factors, the influence (if any) on the probability of sighting bowhead whales is uncertain, and the "null vs. alternate hypothesis" formulation is meaningful.

In the list of hypotheses, the following points should be kept in mind:

- We suggest the possible wording of the alternate hypothesis but (for brevity) do not write out the corresponding null hypothesis;

- Hypotheses marked "*" are ones where the null hypothesis has already been rejected convincingly. In these cases, the primary purposes for considering these human-activity or natural factors in future analyses are (a) to better quantify the known effects, and (b) to take those effects into account when attempting to quantify the effects of other factors.

- What we now know about the influences of seismic exploration, drillships, ice, etc., on the distribution of bowhead whales in the Alaskan Beaufort Sea during late summer and fall has come largely from previous analyses of some of the same data that are now planned for inclusion in the "Analysis of covariance...". Therefore, the planned tests of hypotheses will not be independent of previous tests of similar hypotheses. However, the planned tests will be more powerful because more data will be included, and more of the potentially confounding factors will be taken into account.

- We expect that the primary method for testing these hypotheses will be logistic regression, as discussed under Question (4) and in Annex 1. That technique will allow the confounding influences of other human-activity and natural factors to be taken into account when testing each of the specific hypotheses listed below.

- All hypotheses suggested below relate specifically to bowhead whales in the Alaskan Beaufort Sea during late summer and autumn. The influences of human-activity and natural factors in other areas and seasons, when bowheads are often engaged in different activities, may differ.

- Hypotheses concerning disturbance effects are worded in terms of distance from the source of disturbance. They could, in theory, be reworded in terms of received sound levels. However, many of the necessary acoustic data are not available at the present time. Also, there are merits in expressing the results in terms of easy-to-visualize distances rather than sound levels. The response to Question (3), below, provides further discussion of these points.

- The specific wording of these hypotheses should be re-considered during the early stages of the "Analysis of covariance…" and refined as appropriate.

Hypotheses re Influences of Seismic and Shallow-Hazards Surveys

1. Seismic surveys result in reduced numbers of bowhead sightings in the region from x km inshore to x km offshore of the seismic vessel at times when the airguns are operating.* [It is assumed that the effects of water depth and distance from shore are accounted for by covariates.]

2. Seismic surveys result in reduced numbers of bowhead sightings in the region within y km east of the seismic vessel at times when the airguns are operating.*

3. Seismic surveys result in reduced numbers of bowhead sightings in the region within z km west of the seismic vessel at times when the airguns are operating.*

Note: Hypotheses 1, 2, and 3 have not been distinguished during previous hypothesis-tests. However, it is clear from previous work (Miller et al. 1999) that the null hypothesis can be rejected in each case.

4. The reduction in number of bowhead sightings near a seismic vessel persists for t hours following the cessation of airgun operations.*

5. The distribution of headings for "traveling" bowheads is affected at distances up to w km east of the seismic vessel at times when the airguns are operating. [Bowheads recorded as being engaged in activities other than "traveling" should not be considered.]

6. Operating airguns have reduced or no effect on x, y, z, t, and w if there is a barrier island or shallow water between the airguns and the whales. (*) [This hypotheses has not been tested formally in previous studies, but there is evidence that it is true – see Miller et al. (1999).]

7. Shallow-hazards and similar surveys employing single-airgun and/or mid-frequency pulsed sources (e.g., sparkers, boomers, sub-bottom profilers) result in reduced numbers of bowhead sightings in the region within v km of the survey vessel at times when one or more of these sources are operating.

Hypotheses re Influences of Drilling and Related Activities

8. Drillships result in reduced numbers of bowhead sightings in the region from x km inshore to x km offshore, and in the region from y km east to z km west, of the drillship.* [This summary statement represents three different hypotheses, pertaining to x, y, and z.]

9. The distribution of headings for "traveling" bowheads is affected at distances up to w km east of the drillship.

10. The distances within which numbers are reduced or headings are affected (x, y, z and w in the preceding two hypotheses) are larger when icebreaking is underway than at times without ice-breaking. [See Question (7), later, for discussion of possible refinements to this hypothesis.]

Note: Available data from the Alaskan Beaufort Sea show that the number of bowhead sightings near drillships is reduced (LGL and Greeneridge 1987; Hall et al. 1994; Davies 1997; Schick and Urban 2000). However, it is uncertain whether there will be sufficient data to determine whether x, y, and z differ from one another, or whether headings of traveling whales are demonstrably deflected east of the drillship, or whether the reaction distances depend on the occurrence of icebreaking.[1] The extent to which these specific determinations can be made from existing data may depend on whether sufficient information about covariates (especially seismic and icebreaking) can be assembled for 1986 to allow use of the drillship monitoring data collected that year. These topics are discussed further under Questions (6-8), below.

11. Caisson-based drilling operations result in reduced numbers of bowhead sightings within v km of the caisson.

12. Drilling operations on gravel islands (artificial or natural), aside from those in lagoons, result in reduced numbers of bowhead sightings within u km of the island. [There may be too few days with drilling on gravel islands during the whale migration period for this hypothesis to be tested meaningfully; this needs to be checked.]

Note: Up to the present time, there has been no hydrocarbon production from the Beaufort Sea aside from the Endicott Development, which is in a lagoon distant from waters used by bowhead whales. Therefore, it will not be possible to use existing data to test hypotheses concerning the influence of production activities on bowhead whales. Such hypotheses could be appropriate in future years after hydrocarbon production begins at one or more sites in the Beaufort Sea *per se*.

Simultaneous Industrial Activities Nearby

13. Proximity to two (or more) active seismic vessels and/or drillships results in a greater reduction in the probability of a bowhead sighting than expected based on simple addition of the effects of the individual activities; this reduction in sighting probability is greatest in the area between the two (or more) vessels.

---

[1] There are indications that bowheads may tend to stay farther from drillships operating in the Alaskan Beaufort Sea in autumn (often with active icebreaking) as compared with the distances of bowheads from drillships in the Canadian Beaufort Sea in summer (usually without icebreaking) (*cf.* Richardson et al. 1990, 1995b).

Note: The wording of the preceding hypothesis needs further consideration when formulating the multivariate statistical model to be used in testing the statistical significance of individual factors.

Hypotheses re Ice and Other Natural Factors

14. Sighting probability is (a) related to percent ice cover, (b) negatively related to sea state, and (c) positively related to visibility. [Three separate hypotheses. Before proceeding with analyses, it needs to be decided whether the direction of the ice effect in (a) should be predicted.] *

15. Whale density (and thus sighting probability) depend on (i) date within the season, (j) distance from shore, and (k) water depth, probably in a non-linear manner in each case. [Three separate hypotheses.] *

16. The preferred distance from shore (or preferred water depth) varies with (q) percent ice cover, and (r) date within season. [Two separate hypotheses.] *

17. Peak whale density occurs progressively later in the season with increasing longitude.

Note: Effects of ice cover, sea state, and visibility on bowhead sighting probability, as listed under hypothesis (14), are being investigated as part of the MMS-funded bowhead feeding study (see Thomas et al. 2000 for preliminary results). The final results from that study are expected to be available in late 2001.

Effects of date, distance from shore, water depth, longitude, and various interactions thereof have been investigated in several previous analyses of the aerial survey data that have been done by NOSC, MMS, S.E. Moore, etc. However, those studies have not attempted to take account of a wide variety of factors (natural and industrial) simultaneously, as contemplated here. Also, most previous analyses of natural factors affecting bowhead density have been based on the MMS area-wide surveys and have not used the results of industry-funded site-specific surveys. The approach suggested here can use the data from both types of studies [see Annex 1 and "Question (4), Statistical Procedures"].

Other Factors

Hypotheses concerning the potential effects of other factors such as vessel traffic, subsistence hunting, and aircraft overflights could be formulated. However, for reasons discussed later in this document, data on all of these human activities are seriously incomplete. Also, it is doubtful that straight-line aircraft overflights have much effect on bowhead distribution. It may be possible to incorporate covariates into the multivariate analyses to allow for some fraction of the confounding effect of factors that are only partially documented. However, the available data are not well suited for proper tests of the influence of these factors on probability of finding bowheads at any given location.

Question (3): Cumulative Effects & Acoustic Model

Evaluate the feasibility of using the HAD to detect multiple, combined, and/or cumulative effects of industrial activity on the movement and behavior of the bowhead whale (as represented in BWASP or other available bowhead aerial survey data). Specifically address need for acoustic model identified in current contract.

Multiple, Combined and Cumulative Effects

The first sentence of this question is closely related to Question (2), on specific hypotheses, and Question (4), on statistical procedures.

We envisage fitting multivariate statistical models to the historical aerial survey and human activity data in order to simultaneously assess the influences of several industrial and natural factors on the probability of detecting bowheads at a given location during aerial surveys. We envisage two categories of models.

- One type of model would consider surveys conducted near one type of industrial activity (e.g., seismic vessel or drillship), and would be primarily designed to assess the specific hypotheses pertaining to the effects of that activity. However, this type of model would include covariates that would "allow for" other human activities that happened to be occurring nearby, and for natural factors that influence the probability of seeing a bowhead (ice, visibility, distance from shore, water depth, etc.)

- The other type of model would consider aerial survey and human activity data on an area-wide basis, possibly over the entire Alaskan Beaufort Sea. The terms in the model would be structured to allow for all hypotheses identified above under Question (2), above.

The rationale for these two approaches is discussed in Annex 1.

One form of cumulative impact would occur if two or more major human activities in close proximity have more effect than the simple sum of their individual effects. This possibility has been explicitly identified as hypothesis (13) in the above list. The multivariate statistical models fitted to the whale survey results and HAD can be structured to include one or more terms that specifically test for this possibility. The models can be set up to determine whether, after allowance for the closest industrial operation of each type, there is any detectable further influence from the presence of more than one such activity nearby. As a further refinement, it will probably be appropriate to set up the model to test the hypothesis that, if two (or more) activities are nearby, they cause a greater reduction in sighting probability if they are on widely separated bearings (e.g., close to 180° apart) than if they are on similar bearings.

Single vs. Multiple Measures of Noise Exposure

A possible way to analyze the combined effects of multiple industrial activities on bowhead whales would be to estimate, for each location where aerial surveys are conducted, the overall received level from all sources of industrial sounds. This "total sound level" could then be related to the occurrence or number of bowheads. One major problem with this approach is the fact that, as yet, there is no model that can be used to predict acoustic propagation loss in the shallow waters of the Beaufort Sea with any degree of confidence (see next subsection). If and when such a model becomes available, the total amount of sound expected at any location from all industrial sources near that location could be determined by adding up the predicted received levels on an energy basis. The resulting overall predicted sound level might be used as one of the predictor variables when fitting a logistic regression (or some other) model to the whale sighting data.

However, even if the overall level of industrial sound could be estimated reliably, this single-variable approach is probably not the best way to predict the net acoustic influence on whale occurrence.

There is evidence that bowhead (and other) whales have differing sensitivities to sounds of different types (Richardson and Malme 1993; Richardson et al. 1995b). For example, bowheads and other whales tend to be less tolerant of increasing or variable sounds than of steady sounds, and they tend to be more responsive to mobile sources that are heading directly toward the whales than to those passing tangentially. They also tend to react to lower levels of continuous sounds than of pulsed sounds. They may be especially responsive when two or more sources of disturbance are present in quite different directions, tending to "box in" the animals, than when the same sources are in approximately the same direction. Therefore, the overall level of sound received from all industrial sources in the area is probably not the best way to represent the various sources of disturbance.

A better prediction of whale reactions may be obtained by treating the different sources separately. This could be done on the basis of several predictor variables, each representing the received level of a particular category of industrial sounds (if a suitable acoustic model is available). Alternatively, it could be done on the basis of several predictor variables each representing the distance to the closest industrial activity of a particular type. In the latter formulation, it may be appropriate to include interaction or other terms to take account of water depth between the source and receiver. As noted in the previous subsection, it may also be useful to include one or more terms representing the angular spread of bearings to nearby sources. This could allow for the possibility of greater responsiveness when there are industrial activities in a variety of directions – the possible "boxing in" effect.

Acoustic Model

The second part of question (3) was a request to address the need for the acoustic model identified in the original contract. The database was to include two acoustical components. One of these was to document the measured levels and spectral characteristics of sounds from the types of industrial sources occurring in the Alaskan Beaufort Sea. The other component was to be a sound propagation model suitable for calculating received levels at any specified location in the Beaufort Sea (e.g., a location where whales were or were not sighted), given the locations of various industrial sources with known acoustic output. These two acoustic components have not been included in the database. This was largely a result of difficulties in accessing data on source-spectra on a timely basis. However, another reason has been concern about the imprecise estimates of received levels that would inevitably result from the estimation process as originally envisaged.

Source Levels.—Variability in source levels accounts for some of the expected imprecision in received level estimates:

- *Variability between sources*: There is substantial variability between different sound sources of a given general type (e.g., one icebreaking supply ship or one airgun array vs. another). Not all of the individual sources have been measured, and specific information on the type of source (e.g., airgun array configuration) is sometimes not available. Hence, acoustic data from a supposedly "representative" source of a given general type would often have to be used in lieu of missing data about the specific source. This would result in imprecision in estimates of source (and thus received) levels.

- *Variability over time for a single source*: Equally important, there can be much variability in the sounds emitted by a given industrial activity at different times, depending on its specific configuration and mode of operation. We frequently do not have detailed records of the specific configuration or activities of a given source at particular times. Thus, there would be imprecision in estimates of the source level for a given industrial activity at particular times even if we did have information about its source levels when it was engaged in different activities.

Propagation.—Uncertainty in sound propagation phenomena is an even more serious contributor to uncertainty in received sound levels. Recent detailed studies of received sound levels from airgun arrays operating in the Alaskan Beaufort Sea provide good examples of variability (e.g., Greene et al. 1998; Burgess and Greene 1999; Greene and Burgess 2000). Received levels at a given distance commonly vary by ±10 dB, and sometimes by as much as ±15 dB. Burgess and Greene (1999, p. 3-17*ff*) showed that the presence of relic permafrost in the seafloor could have a dramatic effect on received sound levels.

We undertook, as part of this feasibility analysis, to evaluate the possibility of implementing an effective generalized propagation model applicable to any combination of source and receiver locations in the Alaskan Beaufort Sea. The main question to be addressed concerns the accuracy that can be expected from such a model given what is known about • the variability of sound propagation in the Beaufort Sea, and • subsea permafrost and other bottom properties. As part of the main HAD project, Arctic Sciences Ltd. (ASL) reviewed and summarized the available data on bottom properties (Marko 2001). The review by Marko (2001) confirmed that the data on bottom properties are incomplete, and that their influences on propagation are uncertain.

After examining the review by Marko (2001), Dr. W.C. Burgess of Greeneridge Sciences Inc. has provided the following commentary regarding the accuracy with which received levels could be predicted based on source level data (when available) and a state-of-the-art propagation model:

Introduction.—One of the goals of MMS is to assess the effects of geophysical prospecting and resource extraction on nearby wildlife. In the specific case of the bowhead whale, MMS has conducted aerial surveys for over twenty years to monitor abundance and distribution in regions of the Beaufort Sea potentially affected by sounds from offshore industrial activity. In some years, additional aerial surveys have been conducted for industry. When combined with acoustic stimulus information, the distributional data from these surveys could reveal the presence or absence of noise effects on bowhead migration.

Unfortunately, an accurate synoptic characterization of industrial acoustic stimuli experienced by bowhead whales has remained out of reach. The only two ways to characterize this sound field, measurement and modeling, have both proved difficult to implement over a large scale in the arctic environment. Large-scale measurement programs face a host of obstacles associated with weather, ice, logistics, and recording equipment. Modeling efforts have been stymied by the paucity of seafloor geoacoustic data with which to characterize propagation in near-shore waters, as well as limited information on industrial-sound source strengths and radiation patterns. Without sufficient measurements or modeling of industrial acoustic stimuli experienced by bowhead whales, no investigation of acoustic effects on bowhead behavior can be complete.

Progress.—ASL recently surveyed the available literature on the stratigraphy of the Alaskan North Slope and offered a general geoacoustic model for large-scale propagation modeling (Marko 2001). These parameters, when combined with industrial source characteristics and bathymetric data, would be important components of a propagation model to predict acoustic stimuli encountered by migrating bowhead whales. Simple propagation models have already been applied to short paths (1-6 km) in the Alaskan Beaufort Sea with reasonable success (Burgess and Greene 1999; Burgess and Lawson 2001).

The geoacoustic model offered is, however, far from perfect. Marko (2001) points out that the stratigraphic surveys on which the report is based tended to focus on small and often non-overlapping subsets of the offshore region and that the geological interpretations derived by different authors have differed. Marko also notes that attempts to generalize propagation conditions suffer from the sporadic presence of strong reflectors and from occasional modification of layer structure by tectonic activity. These inhomogeneities, while present generally near shore and in patches, nevertheless have the power to alter acoustic propagation significantly. Many of these inhomogeneities are relic permafrost.

Discussion.—Because the geoacoustic model offered by Marko (2001) incorporates extensive and acknowledged limitations, its utility in predicting the sound exposure of migrating whales becomes questionable. The model would almost certainly be inadequate to predict sound exposure for a given individual at a given location. The model's shortcomings may be of less concern, however, when examining sound exposure from a statistical point of view. This could be especially true in regions lacking strong reflectors, such as relic permafrost and boulders. Unfortunately, Marko (2001) found reflectors of one kind or another to be present throughout much of the area where at least limited geoacoustic data were available. A further limitation is that geoacoustic data are unavailable for a substantial part of the Alaskan Beaufort Sea. This is shown in Figures A3-1 to A3-4 in Marko (2001), where the stratigraphy is shown as unknown, speculative, or extrapolated in a high proportion of the area of interest.

More than any other obstacle, inhomogeneities in the near-shore seafloor would reduce confidence in acoustic exposure predictions based only on near-source measurements, bathymetry, and Marko's (2001) geoacoustic model. Once sound from an industrial source propagated beyond the inhomogeneities, the geoacoustic model might be more reliable, but even a relatively small inhomogeneity located near the sound source could alter received levels in the bowhead migration corridor by several decibels.

Another potential problem with a model to predict received sound levels concerns very low frequencies. Studies of airgun pulses received at 10–40 km ranges (Burgess and Greene 1999) documented the efficient propagation, apparently through the seafloor and not the water, of frequencies between 5 and 25 Hz. In some cases at longer ranges, this "ground wave" arrived at the receiver with greater strength than the water wave. Ground waves depend more heavily on sediment structure than water waves, and may prove more difficult to model. Nevertheless, if concern over acoustic exposure extends to such low frequencies, as it does for a baleen whale like the bowhead, ground waves cannot be excluded from consideration when preparing propagation models.

Conclusion.—Sporadic inhomogeneities, including discontinuous relic permafrost, are known to exist in nearshore seafloor sediments in the Beaufort Sea. The sound from a given nearshore industrial source could therefore propagate over an unknown configuration of such inhomogeneities before reaching either a location of interest (e.g. bowhead whale) or an area of more uniform and predictable propagation conditions. As a result, sound levels in the bowhead migration corridor resulting from specific nearshore industrial sources will tend to depend heavily on the location of those sources relative to nearby seafloor inhomogeneities. Sound propagation predictions based on Marko's (2001) general geoacoustic map will only be reliable for sources located away from seafloor inhomogeneities, or for sources whose sound field has been measured at longer ranges so as to incorporate the effects of any inhomogeneities on the propagation paths of interest.

Thus, in predicting propagation loss between specific industrial sources and specific distant locations in the Beaufort Sea, any possible propagation model will have considerable uncertainties. These are associated mainly with the incomplete data on subsea permafrost and other bottom properties. This uncertainty must be combined with the substantial uncertainties in the source levels and spectra for particular sources on past occasions when their specific configuration and mode of operation were often not documented. Therefore, we conclude that a prediction of the overall received sound level at a given location and time may not be much better than "distances from sound sources", combined with data on water depths along the path from source to receiver, in predicting the effects on bowhead whales.

This situation is expected to change if and when more comprehensive data on subsea parameters relevant to acoustic propagation become available. At that time, we expect it will become useful to build source level data into the HAD, and to link an acoustic propagation model with the HAD. These tasks could be done in a preliminary way now. However, the value of the resulting received-level estimates for purposes of analyzing whale distribution would be questionable until sub-bottom parameters are better documented.

A further benefit of analyzing whale distribution primarily in terms of distances from various industrial activities (rather than approximate sound levels) is the fact that managers and subsistence users are ultimately interested in the distances over which disturbance effects occur. Statistical models based on distance will be easier to understand. Given the inherent complexity of multivariate statistical models, there is merit in avoiding unnecessarily abstract approaches.

Question (4): Statistical Procedures

Describe the recommended statistical procedures and illustrate the type of product such analyses would produce.

It is clear that the "analysis of covariance..." planned by MMS requires a multivariate approach, given the many factors known or suspected to influence the distribution and sighting probability of bowhead whales. A multivariate approach will allow many of the hypotheses suggested above to be tested simultaneously, including allowance for otherwise confounding factors. However, because of the complexity of the questions and of the datasets, including the incomplete data on certain factors of interest, it is also clear that a number of different (but related) analyses will need to be run.

Different subsets of the data would be included in different analyses. For example, analyses concerned primarily with the influences of ice and other natural factors probably should use all systematic aerial survey results that are available, going back to the early 1980s and perhaps to 1979. However, some important industrial activity data are not available for the 1980s [see Question (8), later]. Analyses focussing primarily on industrial effects will probably need to be restricted to data collected since 1990, or possibly 1986 plus the 1990s for drillship effects.

In addressing industrial effects, we envisage two categories of multivariate models, as noted under Question (3). • One type of model would consider surveys conducted near a specific type of industrial activity (e.g., seismic vessel or drillship), and would be primarily designed to assess the specific hypotheses pertaining to the effects of that activity. However, this type of model would include covariates that would "allow for" other human activities that happened to be occurring nearby, and for natural factors that influence the probability of seeing a bowhead. • The other type of model would consider aerial survey and human activity data on an area-wide basis. The terms in the model would be structured to allow for many if not all of the hypotheses identified above under Question (2), above.

The available data represent uncontrolled observations at a variety of places and times. The data have not been collected in a form amenable to a highly structured analysis such as conventional analysis of variance or covariance. If the data were organized into a multidimensional matrix with the various industrial activity and natural factors as the dimensions of the matrix, there would be wide variation in the number of observations in the various cells of the matrix, and many cells would be empty.

Although this type of dataset is not amenable to conventional analysis of variance or covariance, multivariate models can be fitted by techniques such as logistic regression, log-linear modeling (=Poisson regression), and Mantel matrix randomization tests (Manly 1992, 1997). These methods can be applied to data of the types available here, and can provide hypothesis tests. Each of these approaches has been applied to bowhead distributional data in at least one study. Davies (1997) applied logistic regression to some of the bowhead vs. drillship data from 1993. Schick and Urban (2000) applied the Mantel approach to the same data. Miller et al. (1999) used a simple form of log-linear modeling in analyzing the bowhead vs. seismic data from 1996-98. The selection ratio method used by Moore et al. (2000) and Moore (2000) is another possible approach.

Annex 1, by Dr. B.F.J. Manly, reviews the potential applicability of each of these approaches to the planned "Analysis of covariance…". Annex 1 concludes that logistic regression is very likely the most appropriate approach. This conclusion applies in analyzing either • the data collected near a particular type of industrial activity (where that activity is the primary focus of the analysis) or • the area-wide data that are subject to the influences of a wider range of industrial and natural factors. Logistic regression is a standard type of analysis for data of this type (Section 8.8 in Manly 1992).

Annex 1 also notes that other approaches could be preferable in certain specific situations:

- In the unexpected event that it is fairly common for more than one group of bowheads to be sighted in a given transect segment, then the log-linear (=Poisson regression) approach may be preferable to logistic regression. Poisson regression is applicable to count data, whereas logistic regression considers only presence or absence. Otherwise the two approaches are fairly similar. We have recently applied Poisson regression in an analysis of industrial and natural factors affecting seal sightings during aerial surveys in the Prudhoe Bay area (Moulton et al. 2001).

- In the event that there is strong spatial and temporal autocorrelation in the bowhead sighting data, then amendments to the logistic or Poisson regression approaches will be needed. Alternatively, a partial Mantel test similar to that of Schick and Urban (2000) might perhaps be useful. However, there are serious limitations in applying the Mantel approach to a dataset with the size and complexity of the one at hand. An analysis by Davies (1997) indicated that, at least for the subset of the 1993 bowhead data that he analyzed, autocorrelation was not a problem. If it is, then adjustments to the logistic or Poisson regression approach would appear to be a better solution than the partial Mantel test. Annex 1 gives more details.

The selection ratio method used by Moore et al. (2000) and Moore (2000) is far less flexible than logistic regression. As applied by Moore, it uses MMS data only, and also only addresses the effects of the natural factors of ice, distance from shore, and season on whale sightings.

In conclusion, logistic regression appears to be the main analysis of choice for both site-specific and area-wide analyses. The product of such analyses is a logistic regression equation. Each term of the equation represents one of the hypothesized relationships between bowhead whales and an industrial or natural factor. A test of statistical significance is provided for each of these terms (i.e., for each hypothesis). The logistic regression equation gives the estimated probability that an aerial survey would detect a whale in a sample unit with specified values of the industrial and natural factors. This probability can be used to produce a map showing the relative preference of whales for different types of unit (as defined by environmental and human activity variables). The equation and map could provide an objective basis for estimating zones of influence of different human activities on whale distribution. This, in turn, could provide one basis for estimating "take by harassment", and for estimating the potential scale of effects on the availability of bowhead whales to subsistence hunters. The logistic regression equation is in fact a resource selection probability function as discussed by Manly et al. (1993).

Question (5): Descriptive Statistics and Maps

Provide descriptive statistics and maps developed from the HAD for seismic and other industrial activities during late summer and autumn from 1990 to 1999.

Descriptive statistics for CDP seismic surveys, geohazard surveys, and drilling operations conducted from 1 Sept. to 20 Oct. in 1990-98 are tabulated, by year, in Table A-1.

Figures B-1 to B-44, in Appendix 5 of the draft final report, mapped available industry data of several types on a year-by-year basis for the 1 Sept. to 20 Oct. periods of 1979 to 1998. Types of industrial activities that were mapped consisted of CDP seismic surveys, geohazard and seafloor surveys, drilling and icebreaking activities, and "other human activities" (mainly the MMS aerial survey tracklines).

Question (6): Icebreaker Data in HAD

Determine the quality and quantity of the icebreaker data and their reliability/suitability for enhancing statistical comparisons relative to drilling noise.

Icebreaking by the oil industry has been conducted primarily in support of drillship operations. The limited data on icebreakers and supply vessels in the existing human activities database consist primarily of vessel sightings during site-specific aerial surveys for marine mammals near those drillships. These data are very incomplete:

- In some years (1988, 1989) there were no site-specific aerial surveys around certain drillship operations that were supported by icebreakers, and thus there are no (or at most few) aircraft-based records of vessel locations.

TABLE A-1. Summary statistics for drilling operations, CDP seismic surveys, and geohazard surveys, by year, for the 1 Sept. - 20 Oct. periods of 1990-98.

Year	SoundTypeID	Activity	Platform	Hours	Total Hours
Drilling Operations					
1990	Fireweed #1				
1990	80	Actively drilling	SSDC	9.75	
1990	81	Cleaning	SSDC	4.00	
1990	84	Stand by	SSDC	11.25	
1990	85	Tripping	SSDC	17.00	42.00
1991	Galahad #1				
1991	17	Abandonment	Explorer II	10.50	
1991	18	Actively drilling	Explorer II	336.00	
1991	19	Cleaning	Explorer II	124.50	
1991	21	Logging	Explorer II	153.00	
1991	22	Pre drilling activities	Explorer II	53.00	
1991	24	Tripping	Explorer II	26.00	
1991	25	WOI	Explorer II	3.50	
1991	62	Active	Explorer II	24.00	730.50
1992	Kuvlum #1				
1992	65	Abandonment	Kulluk	48.50	
1992	67	Actively drilling	Kulluk	139.50	
1992	68	Pre drilling activities	Kulluk	111.50	
1992	69	WOI	Kulluk	301.50	
1992	86	Cleaning	Kulluk	12.50	
1992	87	Tripping	Kulluk	216.00	
1992	88	Logging	Kulluk	197.00	
1992	89	Stand by	Kulluk	41.00	1067.50
1993	Wild Weasel *				
1993	67	Actively drilling	Kulluk	359.00	
1993	86	Cleaning	Kulluk	67.00	
1993	87	Tripping	Kulluk	47.00	
1993	88	Logging	Kulluk	17.00	
1993	89	Stand by	Kulluk	86.50	576.50

CDP Surveys					
	length (km)	shotpoints	lines	lines w/o shotpoints	permits
1990	5757.0	93052	605	0	90-18, 90-15, 90-06, 90-05
1991	94.4	3600	11	0	91-03
1993	464.2	15747	43	0	93-08, 93-07
1996	1137.2	25524	186	0	96-03
1997	585.8	25547	97	0	97-04
1998	2177.1	44560	568	0	98-05
Geohazard Surveys					
1992	1213.1	0	110	110	Kuvlum

* For 1993, drillship records now in the HAD are known to be incomplete (see "Kuvlum III" in Table A-2).

- For years and drillsites where there were aerial surveys, the aerial surveys were limited to days with suitable weather. Icebreaking also occurred on some poor-weather days and at night when there were no aerial surveys.

- In general, even on days with aerial surveys, the aircraft was present in a given area for only one small part of the day. The aerial observers could (at best) note the presence and locations of icebreakers and other ships only during that short interval of time.

- In some years (e.g., 1991, 1993), icebreaker and ship sightings were recorded by aerial surveyors and/or by shipboard personnel but were not in a form that was easily loaded into the database. In some cases, ship sighting data are available in technical reports but are not in the HAD.

It is especially useful to consider the status of the icebreaker data for each year in the 1990s, assuming that those are the years most likely to be included in any future analysis of whale distribution relative to industrial activities [see Question (8), below]:

- In 1991, the drillship *Explorer II* operated at the Galahad site offshore of Camden Bay, and was supported by four icebreakers. No icebreaker data are included in the HAD for 1991, although some records of icebreaker activity are included in the report by Gallagher et al. (1992). In 1991, there was heavy ice around the drillship during early autumn, and thus extensive icebreaking activity around the drillship.

- In 1992, the floating drilling platform *Kulluk* operated at the Kuvlum #1 site offshore of Camden Bay, and was supported by three icebreakers that were involved in ice management and one vessel that was on standby. Icebreaker sightings during the aerial surveys of Brewer et al. (1993) are included in the HAD and are mapped in Figures A-33 and B-24 of Wainwright and Marko (2001). In 1992, there was moderate-to-heavy ice around the drillship during early autumn, and thus substantial icebreaking around the drillship.

- In 1993, the floating drilling platform *Kulluk* was used consecutively at three drillsites offshore from Camden Bay (Hall et al. 1994). Of these three, only one (Wild Weasel) is included in the HAD at present. (The others were Kuvlum #2 and Kuvlum #3.) No icebreaker sightings during aerial surveys are mapped in Figures A-34 and B-25 in Wainwright and Marko (2001) although the drilling operations were usually supported by three icebreakers (Hall et al. 1994). In 1993, there was no ice around the drillship during early autumn, and thus no icebreaking around the drillship. Some information about the icebreaker operations can be found in Tables 18-21 of Hall et al. (1994) based on observations by shipboard observers. However, those data are not in a format that could have been loaded into the HAD easily.

- In 1990 and from 1994 to date, there were no drillship operations in the Alaskan Beaufort Sea, and thus no icebreaking in support of drillship operations.

In general, the data in the HAD on locations and activities of icebreakers (and of supply ships with limited icebreaking capability) are incomplete and unreliable, and unsuitable for use in statistical analyses. This is true for 1991-1993 as well as for prior years when drillships were used. Using the HAD it is possible to distinguish various types of drilling operations (artificial islands, caissons, and drillships). Of these, only drillships are normally supported by icebreaking. However, from the HAD alone, it is not possible to differentiate between drillships without icebreaker support (if this ever occurred), drillship operations with icebreaker support but no data on the icebreakers, and drillship operations for which ice-breaker support was sometimes noted during by aerial or shipboard observers but those notes were not entered into the database.

Also, the aerial sightings of icebreakers, when they do exist and when they are represented in the HAD, do not indicate the activity of the icebreaker. Thus, it would not be possible to separate idling or transiting icebreakers from those involved in active icebreaking activities. Active icebreaking produces considerably more noise and more potential for disturbance of marine mammals (Richardson et al. 1995b, p. 117*ff*). If icebreaker information is to be used in analyses of whale distribution, it will be important to know (and to take account of) the activity of the icebreaker(s) – i.e., whether they were actively icebreak-ing at or shortly before the time in question.

Question (7): Additional Icebreaker Data

Determine the need, cost, and feasibility of collecting selected additional icebreaker data at the resolution needed for making meaningful statistical comparisons.

Need

Additional data on icebreaking in past years would be very desirable, as icebreaking is a noisy activity that may have a notable effect on underwater sounds, and on bowhead whale distribution, out to a substantial distance from the icebreaker (Richardson et al. 1995a,b). In the absence of fairly specific information about the locations and times when icebreaking is underway, one of the more important industry influences on underwater sounds and on whale distribution could not be taken into account.

Most icebreaking by industry has been around drillships. (Here we consider the floating drilling platform *Kulluk* to be a drillship). It will be most important to have information about icebreaking when analyzing whale distribution around drillships, or when conducting any broader analysis of whale distri-bution in which drillships are one of the factors. Data on icebreaking activities would allow times with no icebreaking to be separated from times with icebreaking. That, as a minimum, would be an important variable to include in any analysis of bowhead distribution (or other parameter) vs. industrial activities (see Hypothesis 10 under Question (2), above).

It would be preferable to consider something more specific than a categorical "icebreaking pres-ent/absent" variable in the analysis. With sufficient data on icebreaking activities, the amount of ice-breaking in some time interval considered relevant to the present distribution of bowhead whales could be quantified for use in the analysis. For example, a measure of the amount of icebreaking near a specified drillsite within a several hour period preceding the time of an aerial survey for whales could be a valuable parameter. As a further level of refinement, the specific locations of icebreaking relative to the drillsite could also be useful. For example, we hypothesize that the distance east of the drillsite at which westbound bowheads begin to show avoidance depends on the location of the icebreaking relative to the drillship (e.g., to the east vs. west). If the location of icebreaking were known consistently, it would be desirable to build this into an analysis of bowhead distribution around the drillsites. For purposes of these more refined analyses, it would be necessary to know not only the numbers of icebreakers present at the drillsite each day, but also their specific locations and activities on an hour by hour basis.

Feasibility

1990s.—During the 1990-2000 period, autumn drillship operations that were supported by icebreakers occurred in 1991, 1992 and 1993, as summarized in Table A-2. Site-specific monitoring reports prepared by COPAC (Coastal & Offshore Pacific Corp.) for those three years provide considerable information about the operations of these icebreakers. "Surface Observations" were usually conducted from a vessel (drillship or icebreaker) at the drillsite. These observations consisted of up to 12 observation periods per day, lasting a minimum of 15 minutes/hour, during daylight hours. Observations printed in Appendix 6 of Gallagher et al. (1992), Appendix 2 of Brewer et al. (1993), and Data Appendix Volume 1 of Hall et al. (1994) summarize the status of the drilling platform, seismic vessels associated with the drilling operation, ice management and supply fleet, weather conditions, and marine mammal sightings. These data were not available in digital form for inclusion in the human activities database.

These records indicate, separately for each icebreaker, whether or not icebreaking occurred during each observation period. Thus, the presence or absence of icebreaking activity was sampled (generally at least 15 minutes/hour) during daylight hours. In some of these years (e.g. 1992-93), detailed information concerning the location (range and bearing from drillship), speed, and activity (icebreaking or not) are presented in tabular format for each vessel for each hourly surface observation period (Brewer et al. 1993; Hall et al. 1994). Some hourly observations were not conducted, or have missing data. For example, in 1991, information is reported for 280 (93%) of a possible 300 hourly observation periods during daylight hours in the 12 Sept. - 12 Oct. period (Gallagher et al. 1992). It should be possible to interpolate for at least some of the missing periods, based on the hourly records of ice conditions and the records of icebreaker activities before and after the missing observations. Also, there are Tables that summarize daily vessel activity. Thus, if an icebreaker did not break ice during the course of an entire day, then this should be evident from those records.

The vessel-based observations of icebreaker activities were generally limited to about a 12-hour period each day, usually during daylight hours from about 07:00 until 18:00. This period encompassed the great majority of the hours when aerial surveys were done both by MMS and by industry-sponsored surveyors. Thus, some information about icebreaking should be available for the great majority of the hours for which there are aerial-survey data on bowhead distribution.

In general, there is considerable information about icebreaker activities in technical reports, appendices, and data files for the three years (1991-1993) when drillships were active in the Alaskan Beaufort Sea during the 1990s. These data were not in a form that could have been loaded easily into the HAD. However, it should be feasible to determine whether or not icebreaking was occurring during any particular autumn aerial survey during those years. We estimate that it would take about 10 days of someone's time, including support from a GIS/data specialist, to determine the appropriate format, extract the data from the various technical reports, and add them to the HAD. These data should be adequate for categorizing presence/absence of icebreaking activities around a given drillship during aerial surveys for bowheads.

The data might not be adequate if the statistical approach required taking into account icebreaker activities for many hours prior to the time in question. For example, it might be decided that the best measure of icebreaking activity at the time of a given bowhead sighting was the activity of icebreakers during the 6 hours or perhaps even 12 hours prior to that sighting. If so, then the absence of hourly surface observations of vessel activity during nighttime periods would represent an important data gap. If

TABLE A-2. Alaskan Beaufort Sea drillsites supported by icebreaking vessels, Sept. - Nov. 1990 - 1998.

Year	Prospect	Location	Drilling Unit	Water Depth (m)	Dates	Ice Conditions	Icebreakers	Ice-breaker Class	Length (m)	Comments
1991	Galahad	Camden Bay	Explorer II	54	7 Sep - 12 Oct	Heavy; ice management 80% of time	Kigoriak	4	91	
							Arctic Ivik	2	67	
							Supplier I	2	58	
							Supplier II	2	58	
1992	Kuvlum I	Camden Bay	CDU Kulluk	34	1Sep - 22 Oct	Moderate to Heavy, Kulluk frequently forced offsite for ice.	Kigoriak	4	91	
							Kalv k	4	88	
							Miscaroo	4	79	
							Arctic Ivik	2	67	23-25 Sep only
							Supplier I	2	58	Did not break ice
1993	Kuvlum III	Camden Bay	CDU Kulluk	39	1 Sep - 5 Oct	None	Kigoriak	4	91	Departed 1 Sep, did not return
							Kalv k	4	88	Did not break ice
							Ikaluk	4	79	Did not break ice
							Miscaroo	4	79	Did not break ice
							Supplier II	2	58	Did not break ice
"	Wild Weasel	Camden Bay	CDU Kulluk	23	6 Oct - 11 Nov	None	Kalv k	4	88	Did not break ice
							Ikaluk	4	79	Did not break ice
							Miscaroo	4	79	Did not break ice
							Supplier II	2	58	Did not break ice

hourly data were required during nighttime periods, then it would be necessary to identify the vessels involved, locate and obtain access to their logbooks, and go through those logbooks manually, transcribing the data on ship location and activity at frequent intervals. This laborious process could probably be restricted to the icebreaking vessels listed in Table A-2 for the years 1991 and 1992, as there was no need for icebreaking during 1993 (see below).

During the three years in the 1990s with icebreaker-supported drilling operations (1991-93), the ice conditions varied considerably. In 1993, there was no ice in the drilling area after 31 Aug. and drilling operations were able to continue until 11 Nov. (Hall et al. 1994). Although icebreakers were present throughout the Sept.–Nov. operations period, icebreaking was not required. Thus, the noisiest aspects of icebreaker operations did not occur during the autumn of 1993. Considering their limited operations, the icebreakers present at the drillsites in 1993 were probably not substantially different, from an acoustical perspective, than the supply ships at drillsites without icebreaker support.

Much heavier ice conditions prevailed in 1991 and 1992. An operations summary for the Galahad site in 1991, included as Table A-2 in Gallagher et al. (1992), indicated that ice management activities occurred 80% of the time at the Galahad site. Moderate to heavy ice conditions also occurred at the Kuvlum I site in 1992. Thus, the missing icebreaker data for nighttime operations during the 1991-92 period would be vessel positions and activities for the six different icebreakers listed for those years in Table A-2. Although it would be a lower priority to obtain access to the logbooks of vessels present near the drillship in 1993 (when there was no ice), many of the same support vessels present in 1991-92 were also present at the drillsites in 1993. Thus, if it were considered necessary to find and review the logbooks for 1991-92, it would involve relatively little additional effort to obtain comparable data for 1993.

We have not made a systematic attempt to locate the relevant logbooks as part of this feasibility analysis. However, ship logbooks are normally retained either aboard the ship or in the hands of the ship's owner. The relevant vessels have not operated in the Beaufort Sea for several years, but (with some effort) they and their logbooks could very likely be located. The icebreaking supply ship *Arctic Ivik*, for example, is presently owned by the Chouest organization based in Louisiana, and has been converted to a seismic survey ship named the *Snapper*, operated by WesternGeco. The *Snapper* (=*Arctic Ivik*) is scheduled to return to the Canadian Beaufort Sea during the summer of 2001.

1980s.—Icebreaker data from the 1980s as well as the 1990s would, in theory, be useful. Drillship operations occurred in the Alaskan Beaufort Sea in 1985 and 1986 (conventional drillship) and in 1988 and 1989 (*Kulluk* floating drilling platform). However, as discussed under Question (8), other important sources of data are incomplete and unavailable for the 1980s. Therefore, we have restricted the preceding paragraphs to the period from 1990 to 1998, for which the existing industrial activity database is reasonably complete, aside from data on icebreaking.

Site-specific monitoring studies were done by LGL during the 1985 and 1986 drilling projects, and reports on the results are available (McLaren et al. 1986; LGL and Greeneridge 1987). The only specific information about daily icebreaker operations that appears in these reports involves mapped sightings of vessels during aerial surveys. (In 1986, in particular, there were many such sightings, which are included in the HAD and summarized in Figure B-20 of Wainwright and Marko 2001.) There was no site-specific monitoring during the 1988-89 drillship programs at the Belcher site.

If it were useful to compile specific data on icebreaking for the 1980s, and especially for 1988-89, it would probably be necessary to identify the relevant ships, find and access their logbooks, and go through those logbooks manually, transcribing data about ship location and activity. It is uncertain what fraction of these old (12-16 years) records could be found, or how complete they would be if found. During the 1980s, we compiled related types of industrial activity data for the Canadian Beaufort Sea (Richardson et al. 1985a, 1987; Brouwer et al. 1988). Those efforts were difficult enough even though they were done when the records were still readily accessible. The situation is more difficult in the present situation, when the records are (at best) widely dispersed. Given the incompleteness of information on some other important industrial activities during the 1980s [see Question (8)], it does not seem useful to expend a great deal of effort to compile icebreaker data for the 1980s.

One exception that might be considered is to attempt to access and compile the icebreaker logs for the autumn of 1986. This would be worthwhile if the seismic surveys near the drillship during that period can also be compiled. For purposes of analyzing drillship effects, if would be very valuable if those 1986 icebreaker and seismic data could be acquired. This would allow another important season of data to be used in detailed analyses of drillship effects [see Question (8), below].

Cost

As noted above, we estimate that it would take about 10 days of someone's time, including support from a GIS/data specialist, to extract icebreaker data from the various technical reports for 1991-93 and to add them to the HAD.

We have not attempted to estimate the cost to locate and access logbooks from all the relevant icebreakers and icebreaking supply ships, i.e. those that supported drillship operations in the Alaskan Beaufort Sea during the 1991-93 (or 1991-92 as a minimum). The cost to do this would depend strongly on how long it takes to locate the logbooks, and where they are located. To determine their locations could take considerable effort in itself. If, after reviewing this document, MMS wants us to go ahead with a search for the relevant logbooks, we can do so. We do not recommend undertaking such an effort for the icebreakers and other support vessels that were used during drillship operations in the 1980s.

Question (8): Pre-1990 Data

Evaluate the possibility of using all data including those data sets prior to 1990.

The main issues with respect to completeness of the industrial activity data in the HAD are incomplete data (i) on icebreaker and some other shipping activities, and (ii) on seismic surveys. Data on aerial surveys over the Beaufort Sea are also recognized as incomplete, especially for the 1980s, but this is considered to be a less serious data gap as overflights probably have no significant effect on distribution of bowhead whales. The lack of data in the HAD concerning subsistence hunting activities is also a concern.

Icebreaker Data

Regarding icebreaker and related shipping data in years before (and since) 1990, the possibility of obtaining a useable dataset through additional data compilation efforts directed at the late summer/autumn period has been discussed under Question (7), above. See that section for a discussion of the anticipated difficulties in completing that task. It might be possible, with much effort, to obtain a substantial proportion of the icebreaker data for years before as well as since 1990, but this cannot be confirmed until the logbooks are located. The high level of effort that would be required to locate and extract the data on icebreaker activity in the 1980s may not be justified, given that other key types of data (especially on seismic surveys) are likely to remain incomplete the period prior to 1990. However, if seismic data can be compiled for the Flaxman Island/Camden Bay area during the autumn of 1986, when a drillship was operating there (see below), then it would also be worth determining whether the icebreaker data for that area and season could be compiled.

Seismic Data

We have already spent considerable time and funding attempting to compile seismic data sets for years prior to 1990. We have confirmed that, for all years prior to 1990, there were seismic activities under state permits for which the specific data were not accessible. MMS has some additional data sets in its vault that were not compiled. However, it appears that many of these data sets lack specific information about the dates and times when the seismic work was done at individual shotpoints. That makes the data of little value for the planned analysis of covariance. Given the important influence that seismic surveys can have on bowhead distribution (Miller et al. 1999), the lack of adequate data on the seismic work during the 1980s makes it doubtful that the data from the 1980s can be used in any analysis requiring use of industrial activity data.

To illustrate how many seismic data were unavailable in the years prior to 1990, it is instructive to look at the situation for 1985, a year that we have investigated in detail. Seismic permit data from the MMS Field Operations Vault (FOV) in Anchorage indicate that seven seismic programs were conducted that year in the Alaskan Beaufort Sea. A summary table in Appendix 2 of Wainwright and Marko (2001) shows that, of seven permitted projects in 1985, • complete data (including date and time) were available for three programs, • partial data (date and time for start and end of each seismic line) were available for one program, and • no dates or times were available for three programs. Thus, complete data were available for only 3 of 7 (43%) of the known seismic programs. In addition, the State permits issued for that year include an open water program that may be additional to the seven programs documented (in part) in the data in the MMS Field Operations Vault. Thus, in this sample year, the HAD contains adequate data for less than half of the known seismic programs. In contrast, for the period 1990 to 1999, the available data were considered adequate for all seismic programs and all but one geohazard program (see Appendix 2 in Wainwright and Marko 2001).

Implications for Analyses of Seismic Effects.—If these data gaps for the 1980s cannot be filled, there would be significant limitations in any analysis of the effects of seismic surveys on whale distribution in the 1980s. Seismic surveys are known to have a strong effect on the distribution of migrating bowheads at distances out to at least 20-30 km (11-16 n.mi.), with some probable effect to 35-40 km (19-22 n.mi.) (Miller et al. 1999). Thus, even in a "site-specific" analysis of seismic effects, it is necessary to consider the survey results out to a radius well in excess of 40 km in order to compare the results within vs. beyond the zone of influence. The study area should extend at least 60 km (32 n.mi.) in each direction from the seismic vessel, and preferably farther. The movements of some seismic vessels during the 1980s are documented, and it would be possible to look at whale distribution relative to those specific vessels. However, given the amount of seismic survey activity in the Alaskan Beaufort Sea at many times in the 1980s, there is a substantial probability that one or more additional seismic boats were operating at undocumented locations within 60 km of any given seismic boat. There is the further problem that, even for the "documented" boats, the HAD contains no records of some of the airgun shots. The inability to allow for these undocumented shots, and for the presence of other undocumented seismic boats, would substantially confound the results of analyses of whale distribution relative to boats whose shots were partially documented.

Some shots that were not used in the geophysical dataset (i.e., during testing, along lines that were subsequently re-shot, and during line changes) are not represented in the data provided to MMS. This problem very likely occurs for the early 1990s as well as in the 1980s. (For the late 1990s, complete records of all shots are available.) Thus, even if the remaining seismic data in the MMS vault were compiled, and if the missing date/time information were somehow obtained, there would be some missing data about seismic activities for every year prior to 1990, and probably some missing data for the early 1990s as well. The undocumented shots are a much smaller problem than the absence of data from entire seismic programs in the years prior to 1990. For example, in 1998, seismic testing and ramp-ups (seismic categories that would not normally be documented in seismic end-of-year reports) represented 10% (71 of 711 hours) of the seismic operations during the late July-mid October period (from Table A-4.4 in Lawson and Moulton 1999). Corresponding percentages for 1996 and 1997 were 13% and 12%.[2] The ramp-up technique was not standard practice in the Beaufort Sea before 1996, so the proportion of undocumented shots was probably lower then. Also, the potentially-undocumented types of seismic operations are frequently interspersed with seismic production. Hence, the lack of data for these types of non-standard seismic shots is not a major issue – it is of much less concern than the lack of data on some entire seismic programs.

Confounding of Analyses of Other Industrial Effects.—Undocumented seismic programs would also confound analyses of the effects of other human activities on bowhead distribution. For example, in 1986 there is considerable information about whale distribution and behavior near the drillship *Explorer II* operating at the Corona (offshore Camden Bay) and Hammerhead (north of Flaxman Island) drillsites (LGL and Greeneridge 1997). Corona operated from late July to 17 Sept. The drillship then moved to Hammerhead where it operated from 18 Sept. to 10 Oct. These operations also involved use of icebreakers and icebreaking supply ships (see Fig. A-27 and B-20 in Wainwright and Marko 2001). There was a concurrent seismic program involving a single vessel that operated in a large area. This area sometimes included the study area used for systematic aerial surveys designed to assess the effects of drilling operations on bowhead migration (Davis 1987). During acoustic monitoring studies at the drillsites, seismic pulses were received 8% of the time at Corona, and 46% of the time at Hammerhead (Greene 1987). The received levels of these seismic impulses ranged from "...weak, buried in the background noise, to very strong, corresponding to passages of the survey vessel close to the hydrophones" (Greene 1987). The HAD contains no data concerning the seismic program that was conducted concurrently with, and close to, these drilling projects. Thus, an analysis of bowhead whale distribution in relation to human activities as presently documented in the HAD would risk finding "effects" from the Corona and Hammerhead drilling operations that might actually represent, in part, a response by bowheads to seismic activity that is not documented in the HAD.

Similarly, in 1985 the drillship *Explorer II* and various support vessels also operated at the Hammerhead and Corona sites (McLaren et al. 1986). For 1985 (unlike 1986), extensive seismic surveys

[2] The 1996 and 1997 percentages do not consider times when a single airgun was in use. Those single-gun operations were specific to the Ocean Bottom Cable method used from 1996 onward, and were not representative of operations in earlier years. The 1996-97 data are also from Lawson and Moulton (1999, Table 4.4).

have been documented in the HAD (see Fig. A-4 and B-4 in Wainwright and Marko 2001). However, the dates when many of these lines were shot are not available (see "Date Ambiguous" lines on Fig. B-4). This makes the seismic survey dataset for 1985 unusable for purposes of the planned "Analysis of covariance...". Acoustic monitoring at Hammerhead showed that pulsed noise from several different seismic and shallow-hazards survey vessels was detectable in the water near Hammerhead during Sept. 1985 (McLaren et al. 1986, p. 35). For example, of 176 hourly sound measurements near Hammerhead, 102 (58%) included audible seismic pulses.

Low Altitude Aircraft Flights

The HAD does not, at present, document all of the low altitude aerial survey flights, especially for years prior to 1990.

For years both before and since 1990, the HAD contains the flightlines for the MMS or NOSC aircraft (Turbo Goose or Twin Otter) that was responsible for systematic surveys of whales. However, in some late summer/autumn seasons before 1990, the NOSC/MMS project involved use of one or two additional aircraft – another Turbo Goose and (in 1983-84) a Twin Otter (Reeves et al. 1983, 1984; Ljungblad et al. 1984, 1985, 1988). These additional aircraft were used to document bowhead distribution and behavior in response to seismic and other industry activities in some years. Flightlines for the 2nd and 3rd aircraft do not appear to be included in the flightline dataset provided by MMS for inclusion in the HAD. We understand that the flightlines for the 2nd and 3rd aircraft were often logged automatically from the on-board navigation system, but the resultant data files have not been used very extensively or recently. Obtaining the flightlines from the 2nd and 3rd aircraft involved in the NOSC/MMS work during the early 1980s might be difficult.

Also, most industry-funded site-specific aerial surveys for marine mammals during the entire 1979-98 period are not, at present, included in the HAD and are not mapped in Figures A-36 through A-55, or in Figures B-26 through B-44 of Wainwright and Marko (2001). Most of these data are available in digital form and could be added to the HAD with little additional effort.

Data concerning offshore helicopter flights during the late summer/autumn period, mostly in support of drillships and drilling platforms, are not included in the HAD, and data documenting these flights are generally not available. This is true for both the 1980s and 1990s. Helicopter sounds are somewhat stronger and more complex (more tones) than those of fixed wing survey aircraft (Chapter 6 *in* Richardson et al. 1995b). Thus, the lack of data on helicopter overflights could be considered to be more serious than the lack of complete data on fixed-wing survey activities.

However, the underwater sounds from a passing fixed-wing survey aircraft or helicopter are of short duration. More often than not, bowhead whales show no obvious reaction to a passing aircraft or helicopter, even when it is as low as 500 ft (150 m) above the water (Richardson et al. 1985b, 1995a,b). When bowheads do react to a single straight-line overflight, these reactions are usually limited to a single hasty dive or other brief reaction. Although local avoidance reactions can occur in response to prolonged circling or hovering by aircraft, there is no evidence and no likelihood that infrequent straight-line overflights affect the distribution of bowheads. Therefore, we believe that the lack of a complete record of aircraft and helicopter overflights is not a serious data gap. We do not believe that it should be a priority to consider aircraft overflights as one of the "covariates" in the planned "Analysis of covariance...", or to add additional aircraft overflight data to the HAD.

Subsistence Activities

The HAD does not contain any information about subsistence hunting activities. This topic is discussed under Question (11), below.

Conclusion

The lack of adequate seismic data for the pre-1990 period is a serious data gap in the HAD. That data gap will make it difficult to use the HAD for the intended "Analysis of covariance..." for years before 1990. A concerted effort to obtain more seismic data for those years would probably result in some additions to the HAD. However, it is unlikely that enough additional data on seismic activities would result to substantially change the outlook for the use of the 1979-89 data in statistical analyses of the effects of human activities on bowhead distribution. In the absence of adequate data on seismic surveys during the 1980s, it does not seem useful to attempt to compile detailed data on icebreaker activities or low-altitude aircraft overflights during those years.

The one possible exception could be 1986, when there are potentially valuable aerial survey data on bowheads around a drillship engaged in drilling. It would be worth a focussed effort to document the seismic program(s) occurring in the Flaxman Island/Camden Bay area where the drillship was operating. If those seismic data (including specific dates and times) could be obtained, then the 1986 aerial survey data from that area (both site-specific and MMS) could be used in site-specific multivariate analyses of bowhead distribution near drillships, augmenting the data of that type available from the early 1990s. If these 1986 seismic data can be obtained, it would also be worthwhile to obtain the 1986 icebreaker data from the same area.

Thus, we recommend the following:

- Most of the detailed analyses of bowhead distribution relative to human activities should be restricted to the years from 1990 onward.

- One exception would be to include 1986 results from the Flaxman Isl./Camden Bay area in site-specific analyses of whale distribution relative to drillships (and covariates) if a focused effort to document seismic surveys and icebreaker activity in that region during 1986 is successful.

- Area-wide analyses of whale distribution relative to natural factors can use data from all years, both before and since 1990. These natural factors include year, date-in-season, ice conditions, water depth, distance from shore, and one or more measures of sightability. It would be useful to take account of drillship activities in these analyses, as these are known for all years, and appear to have a significant influence on bowhead distribution. Some other industrial covariates that are well documented for the 1980s as well as the 1990s could also be used. This approach for analyzing influences of ice and other natural factors requires an assumption that, on an area-wide scale, the effects of human activities excluded from the analysis, especially seismic surveys, are sufficiently localized to allow meaningful analyses of natural influences without considering the undocumented industrial activities as covariates. That assumption is probably justified for area-wide analyses.

Question (10): Database Structure

Recommend any modification of the current database structure, ArcView shape files, DBF files, and data documentation.

The existing database structure appears to be appropriate. However, it would be useful to include additional fields (variable length text) that provide descriptions of the meanings/scope of the classifications used in the database, particularly

- the activity and sub-activity classification;

- the equipment classification; and

- the parameter classification for environmental observations.

Consideration should be given to expanding the structure of the "Sources" table to be more consistent with conventions for bibliographic databases, e.g., separate fields for authors, title, date, etc. The current structure was adopted to provide compatibility with the G-WIS database structure.

Consideration should be given to migration of the Visual Foxpro database structure to Microsoft Access to provide compatibility with ArcView 8.1. This recently released version of ArcView supports the Microsoft Access format and provides a built-in metadata management system. In contrast, Visual Foxpro is only supported through ODBC, without the metadata system, and tables with memo fields (variable length text) are not supported. ArcView 3.2 and earlier versions do not support Visual Foxpro tables.

It will be useful to re-examine the database structure early in Phase II, after the statistical analyses have been designed, and again near the end of Phase II when the analyses have been completed. Before the analyses begin, some changes in the database are likely to be needed in order to incorporate or to transform specific variables needed in the analyses. After the analyses are completed, there will be a good basis for recommending further changes based on the experience gained in relating the HAD to bowhead survey data, taking account of the requirements of the specific statistical approaches that have been developed.

Question (11): Future Data Collection; Ice and Weather Data

Recommend how drilling, ice-breaker, geohazard, and CDP seismic data could be collected by industry in a more useful format for estimating any effects from acoustic disturbances in the future.

During the compilation of human activity data, difficulties were encountered because of the problems with the completeness and/or availability of some types of data. This section describes the difficulties encountered and presents recommendations where possible.

In addition, the final three subsections discuss the adequacy of available data on • subsistence hunting, • ice conditions, and • weather conditions for purposes of MMS's planned "analysis of covariance…". Also included are recommendations for organizing the available historical data of those types and for collection of those types of data in future.

Drilling

Problems.—Industry has been required to submit daily reports of drilling activity. The records submitted to MMS were complete and adequate to describe the drilling activity. However, activities related to drilling, such as supply vessel and helicopter movements in support of drilling operations, are generally not identified. Also, preparatory activities occurring far in advance of drilling (e.g., construction of gravel islands) are generally not documented on a day-by-day basis. For purposes of analyzing industry influences on bowhead whales, it is the activities in late summer and autumn (e.g. 15 Aug. – 31 Oct.) that are important; missing information about those activities is a problem. For other purposes, missing information about activities in other seasons might also be a problem.

Recommendations.—If MMS wishes to have records of industrial activities year around, then all activities during the construction, commissioning, crewing, drilling and decommissioning of all offshore drilling platforms, including natural islands, artificial islands, ice platforms, caissons, and drillships, should be documented. At the least, these details should be documented for the 15 Aug. to 31 Oct. period. The date and time that each activity begins and ends should be noted, and the activity underway should be logged at some standard and frequent interval (e.g., 3 hours). Any specific activity during these phases that could generate appreciable underwater sound should be documented and distinguished (e.g., dumping fill, excavating, laying armor, pile driving, various phases of drilling, etc). When there are potentially noisy activities whose sounds have not previously been documented in detail, the characteristics of the underwater sound (and, in winter, vibrations) from that activity should be determined quantitatively.

Shipping and Icebreaking

Problems.—Numerous types of vessel traffic occur in the Alaskan Beaufort Sea. These include supply vessel movements in support of drilling operations (see above), sea lift operations in support of coastal communities, as well as passages of cruise ships, Coast Guard, military, and research vessels. None of these activities are presently documented by MMS or in the database. Locations of vessels recorded during aerial surveys for marine mammals have been included in the HAD when available in an easily accessible format. However, this information is very incomplete, to the point that it is of little if any value in its present form.

Information on ice-breaking activity was difficult to compile but is important because of the high noise levels associated with active icebreaking. Industry is not required to submit reports about icebreaking except in unusual circumstances such as spills or obvious impacts on marine life. The information of interest is recorded in detailed monitoring reports in some cases [see Questions (6) and (7), above]. However, more often the only available data are in ship logs. Ship logs are required to remain on the vessel or (for older logs) in the possession of the vessel owner. They are not formatted to facilitate compilation, and may not always include information with the spatial and temporal resolution that would be desirable for purposes of analyzing whale distribution relative to icebreaker activities. Therefore, the level of effort to obtain desired data from logbooks (either historical or future) would be high, and even then there is no guarantee that all of the desired information could be extracted.

Recommendations.—For ice-breaking and other large support vessels operating in support of activities permitted by MMS, consideration should be given to requiring industry to submit either copies of ship logs or (preferably) digital data summarizing the vessel movements and activities. One option would be to require the installation of Vessel Tracking System (VTS) recorders on large vessels, and sub-mission of the resulting digital data on ship movements. VTS recorders are relatively inexpensive "black-boxes" that incorporate GPS receivers and log vessel activity. A common application is the monitoring of fishing vessel activity. Use of a system such as VTS would involve a modest start-up cost and little ongoing operational cost. Therefore, it should not be an onerous requirement. The cost of installation and operation of a VTS system is likely to be notably less than conventional data compilation. If bowhead whales are the only concern, these requirements could be restricted to the 15 Aug. to 31 Oct. period.

It would very likely be more difficult to acquire VTS or other relevant data on ship activities from commercial vessels engaged in activities not directly permitted by MMS, e.g. some sea lift operations, coastal barge traffic, and tourism; or from military, Coast Guard, or non-U.S. ships. Before implementing some data collection system applicable to oil industry vessels, it would be appropriate to assess whether the planned system would cover a sufficiently high proportion of the vessel traffic in the Alaskan Beau-fort Sea to be worthwhile.

Geohazard and CDP Seismic Data:

Problems.—Industry has been required to submit digital data describing geohazard and CDP seismic surveys conducted under federal permits to MMS. These data were primarily for geological assessment. Industry has considerable discretion in the format for data submission, and as a result many of the seismic data are inadequate for purposes of analyzing industry effects on marine mammals.

- Frequently, the submitted data provide locations of shotpoints, but not time and date. Date and time information is essential for purposes of relating marine mammal distribution to the occurrence of seismic surveys. Date and time were not recorded in the accessible records for many of the seismic projects conducted during the 1980s. This is the principal reason why, in our opinion, the human activity data from the 1980s are not suitable for use in analyzing marine mammal distribution relative to the HAD.

- The general practice appears to be to exclude seismic shots that do not meet specifications, and to exclude shots fired off the pre-planned lines and during testing of equipment. This practice continues to the present. In some projects, including some recent projects, the excluded shot-points can constitute a substantial proportion of the total. From the perspective of disturbance to marine mammals, those "excluded" shotpoints are little if any different from the included shot-points. During recent seismic operations conducted under the provisions of Incidental Harass-ment Authorizations issued by NMFS (e.g., Miller et al. 1999), all shots have been documented. For some years, it has been possible (with industry permission) to include these alternative and more complete shotpoint datasets in the HAD. However, these types of more complete data are not available for years prior to 1996.

- CDP seismic data submitted by industry to MMS are confidential and may not be used in a publicly accessible database without industry approval. Although some such approvals have been obtained, many of the data remain confidential.

- Some projects are conducted entirely in state waters. Those projects may not require federal permits, and in that case MMS may have no record of the project. We have not been successful in obtaining data on seismic projects conducted under state permits.

Recommendations.—Consideration should be given to requiring industry to submit digital data documenting seismic surveys in ESRI shapefile format in geographic coordinates (NAD83 datum). The ESRI shapefile format is a published standard supported by many GIS and CAD programs. Source code (in C) for creating shapefiles is publicly available on the Internet. Therefore, it should not be onerous for industry to submit data in this format.

Dates, times (in GMT), and locations should be documented for all airgun shots. For purposes of fine-scale analysis, it is important that there be no confusion as to whether times are recorded in GMT, local daylight, or local standard time.

MMS should consider requiring that data be submitted documenting all airgun shots, including shots during testing, ramp-ups, and line changes, and off-specification and off-line shots. Data concerning these "non-production" airgun discharges typically have not been submitted.

If possible, airgun depth and water depth at every shotpoint should be logged to aid in calculating the likely received sound levels at locations some distance from the seismic vessel. Additional types of data have been logged automatically during some recent seismic programs, including the specific airguns that fired during each shot, and (at 2-min intervals) the positions of all vessels involved in the project. The latter data files of ship positions also include the vessel speed, heading, and water depth for each record.

Arrangements should be established to ensure that seismic and geohazard surveys in state as well as federal waters are documented in the same manner as those in federal waters.

If bowhead whales are the only concern, these requirements could be restricted to the 15 Aug. to 31 Oct. period.

Subsistence Hunting

Problems.—The January 2001 description of the proposed "Analysis of covariance…" study indicates that the study will control for subsistence hunting. The current human activity database contains no data concerning subsistence hunting activities. Although MMS has indicated (in describing the HAD) that it would include information about subsistence hunting, assembly of such data was not part of the present project. Bowhead whales are known to show avoidance reactions to approaching powerboats such as are used for the autumn bowhead hunt. Any analysis that is designed to identify and quantify the simultaneous effects of a variety of human activities on the distribution and movements of bowhead whales should take account of subsistence hunting as one of those activities.

Whaling crews from three communities (Kaktovik, Nuiqsut/Cross Island, and Barrow) hunt bowheads in the Beaufort Sea during autumn. Although the dates when bowheads are landed by each community are well documented, we are not aware of any publicly available data concerning the specific dates when the autumn hunts have begun and ended each year. The hunt begins an unspecified time before the first whale is landed, and (in some years) continues after the last whale is landed. We also are not aware of any systematic records of the dates (within the hunting season) when whalers were at sea hunting for whales vs. ashore. In years when an industry/whaler coordination center is in place at Prudhoe Bay during the autumn hunt, much of this information is available there in near-real-time for the Nuiqsut/Cross Island and the Kaktovik hunts. However, we have (during other projects) not had much success in obtaining useful information from that source after-the-fact. In recent years, the locations where bowheads are struck are frequently documented by the hunters through use of GPS. However, the routes followed while searching for whales are not documented. The search can range over a wide area. The value of acquiring such information has been discussed at various meetings, but insofar as we are aware, no specific project is yet in place to obtain these data.

Recommendations.—It is suggested that MMS's sociocultural specialists coordinate with the Alaska Eskimo Whaling Commission (AEWC) regarding the value of collecting more specific information about past and future hunts, and incorporating that information into the human activity database. It is recognized that there will be concerns about the purposes of this data collection effort, and that it will not be a simple or quick matter to obtain agreement to proceed.

For past years, AEWC records no doubt contain some information about the timing of the hunts at some or all Beaufort Sea communities in the various years. We have not attempted to determine how complete this information is. It is unlikely that there are consistent records of the specific days when the hunters were at sea in prior years. MMS sociocultural specialists might wish to explore with the AEWC the possibilities for assembling relevant data from AEWC records. If available, Minutes of meetings of the Kaktovik, Nuiqsut, and Barrow Whaling Captains Associations may also contain relevant information, e.g. about the date when the autumn hunt was scheduled to start in specific years. The North Slope Borough Dept of Wildlife Management maintains a database documenting the dates when harvested bowheads were landed, and many types of biological information about the individual harvested whales. For some years, the basic harvest information has been published in papers in the *Report of the International Whaling Commission*.

For the future, information about the areas traversed by the whaling boats could be logged automatically (if the hunters agreed to cooperate) through use of GPS-based Vessel Traffic System (VTS) recorders of the type mentioned under "Shipping and Icebreaking", above.

Ice Data

Background and Problems.—There are three primary sources of data on ice conditions in the Beaufort Sea. These range from assessments with little temporal or spatial detail that cover a very broad geographical area, to very detailed information that typically covers only a small area on a given date. The broadest and least detailed ice assessments are categorizations of a given year as "light", "medium" or "heavy" ice years. These assessments have been made by MMS or its contractors for each year from 1979 to date. During the 20-year period 1979-98, 13 years were classed as "light" ice conditions, 3 were classed as "moderate", and 4 were considered "heavy". These assessments are based on the distance between Pt. Barrow, AK, and the five-tenths ice concentration as determined from ice imagery for 15 Sept. (Treacy 2000).

The second source of ice data is MMS's weekly summaries of ice conditions, which are based on the Beaufort Sea Ice Analysis provided by the National Ice Center in Suitland, MD. The Beaufort Sea Ice Analysis shows average ice concentrations over the prior 2- to 3-day period based on various types of satellite imagery and other sources. In the most recent years, these sources have included visual, infrared, and synthetic-aperture-radar satellite imagery, combined with ice observations from occasional reconnaissance flights, ships and shore, along with ice observations during MMS aerial surveys for whales (Treacy 2000). In earlier years (e.g. Treacy 1988) the satellite imagery was less sophisticated and the overall resolution of ice conditions was probably lower than in recent years. The weekly sea ice conditions for the study area have been compiled by MMS into a GIS format for each year in the 1979-98 period, and are available from MMS for inclusion in the HAD. They are currently in a raster format with a specific map projection that would require conversion when imported into the HAD. These weekly data have the advantages of considerable detail and broad coverage (entire Alaskan Beaufort Sea). However, their resolution is coarse both spatially and temporally — especially in the context of site-specific studies and near-daily aerial surveys.

The third and most detailed source of ice information is the ice observations made during aerial surveys for marine mammals. These data are specific to the aerial surveys that document bowhead distribution, and therefore should be available for all areas surveyed and all bowhead sightings. They are geographically precise, as data on ice conditions are recorded either at frequent regular intervals along every transect (typically every 2 minutes $\cong$ 7 km during LGL surveys), or whenever changes in ice conditions are noted (MMS and COPAC surveys). In some survey protocols, ice conditions are also recorded at every bowhead sighting location. For recent years, and some earlier studies, these ice data are recorded in digital formats, varying somewhat depending on which group conducted the survey. For some earlier years, again depending on the source of the data, the data are presently available only as summary tables in printed reports (although LGL is in the process of digitizing some of this information for another project). The data on ice conditions from all the aerial survey data to be considered in the "Analysis of covariance..." would need to be converted into a standard format.

Recommendations.—The most appropriate ice data for use in statistical analyses of bowhead sighting data will vary depending on the objectives, scope and scale of the analysis. Very broad-scale analyses that examine locations of bowhead migration corridors across the entire study area in different years, similar to analyses already done by MMS, may benefit from using some combination of the yearly "light, moderate, heavy" classifications and the weekly average ice conditions. However, both site-specific analyses and area-wide analyses based on multivariate statistical approaches would benefit greatly from use of the ice data collected during aerial surveys. These ice data are available for the specific locations and times where whale survey data are available. It would probably be useful to make provision to use all three types of ice data in analyses, thereby maintaining the flexibility to use the level of detail most appropriate for a given analysis. In some analyses it may be useful to include all three types of ice data as covariates.

We recommend that the weekly average data be incorporated in the HAD, which will require transformation of the present projection. In addition, ice data acquired during whale surveys need to be converted to a standard format and made available for use in statistical analyses. This would take an estimated 15 days of effort by a GIS/data specialist. To accomplish this, they could either be kept as part of the whale survey dataset or incorporated into the HAD. The former (keep in whale survey dataset) might be more efficient if these ice data are to be used only for purposes of analyzing marine mammal data acquired via aerial surveys. The latter (incorporation into the HAD) would be desirable if there is any intention to use the ice data from the whale surveys for purposes other than analyzing the whale data.

Although some minor improvements in collection of ice data could be recommended for the future, the most important recommendation is to ensure that future data are consistent with past data.

Meteorological Data

Background and Problems.—Weather conditions and "sightability" (sea state, visibility, etc.) have a large influence on the probability that aerial surveyors will detect bowhead whales that are at the surface near the trackline (Thomas et al. 2000). It is important that this confounding influence be taken into account when analyzing bowhead sightings relative to industrial activities.

Data from all weather stations near the Alaskan Beaufort Sea, including coastal weather stations as well as temporary weather stations associated with offshore industry sites, have been compiled and loaded into the HAD. These data are limited in that they represent primarily coastal weather conditions from relatively few locations. They probably do not provide a good record of offshore weather conditions across the entire study area.

An additional source of data, not currently in the HAD, is weather observations recorded during aerial surveys. These data include information about sea state, glare, visibility and sometimes a combination of factors termed sightability. Sightability is a partly subjective variable that records the observer's judgement concerning the overall probability of sighting bowheads that are present at the surface. As with aerial survey data concerning ice conditions, these data exist in varying digital and non-digital formats. For some earlier years (again depending on who conducted the surveys), the data may only be available as summary tables in printed reports. LGL is presently digitizing some of this information for another project.

During some aerial surveys, other weather variables have been recorded, including wind speed (estimated) and temperature at survey altitude and/or upon takeoff or landing, cloud cover, etc. However, these variables are not consistently available and will be of varying accuracy. These data are undoubtedly less useful for present purposes than the data on sea state, visibility, and sightability, which have an important influence on the probability of sighting a bowhead that is present at the surface near the trackline.

Recommendations.—The weather conditions that would affect the probability of sighting bowheads (sea state, visibility, glare, and sightability) should be standardized for all of the bowhead whale aerial survey datasets that are to be included in "Analysis of covariance...". This would take an estimated 15 days of effort by a GIS/data specialist. The standardized data could either be kept with the aerial survey datasets or incorporated in the HAD. As for ice data, the latter would be appropriate if there is any expectation that these data would be useful for some purpose other than analysis of the whale survey data.

Different aerial survey groups who have operated in the Alaskan Beaufort Sea have used differing procedures for recording sea state, visibility, glare, and sightability (and also ice conditions). The resultant data can be converted to more-or-less consistent scales for purposes of analyzing existing historical data. However, it is recommended that, as part of the standardization process, specific recommendations be formulated regarding the manner in which future aerial surveyors should record these sightability parameters in the field. The recommendations should incorporate the maximum possible consistency with previous procedures but should also recommend a standard procedure in situations where varying procedures have been used during past surveys.

OVERALL ASSESSMENT OF FEASIBILITY

Comments on MMS Objectives and Suggested Methods

MMS Objectives

The "Analysis of covariance..." that MMS has planned as a follow-on to the compilation of the human activities database has four specific objectives, according to the project description in MMS's most recent Alaska Annual Studies Plan (dated Jan. 2001, for FY 2002-2003). Those objectives, with our general comments on their feasibility, are as follows:

(1) "Assess the comparability of bowhead whale data collected by site-specific and broad-area surveys and the feasibility of pooling these data to detect whale distributional shifts or behavioral changes up to 40 miles from noise sources."

This objective for the "analysis of covariance" has, for the most part, been met by the present feasibility analysis.

Although there have been differences in some data recording procedures during MMS/NOSC broad-area surveys vs. industry-sponsored site-specific surveys, the data are sufficiently comparable to allow pooling. Some information that was coded in different ways by different projects have already (for purposes of previous projects) been converted by LGL into standardized formats. Some industry-sponsored site-specific survey data – especially the supplementary information on sighting conditions and ice – have not been available to LGL in digital form. We are in the process of digitizing much of that information as part of another project (Table A-3). Additional effort will be required to complete the assembly of the industry-sponsored site-specific data in a digital form consistent with the MMS dataset.

As discussed in previous sections and in Annex 1, it is feasible to combine the broad-area and site-specific data in order to achieve more comprehensive site-specific analyses and more comprehensive broad-area analyses. In the latter case, the highly uneven survey coverage that results from combining the two types of data will cause some complications in the analysis. However, Annex 1 has identified an approach that can cope with those complications while taking advantage of the extra sample size achievable by combining the two types of data. This approach involves treating each day's surveying in a given site-specific survey area or MMS survey block as a unit.

The approach recommended in this document here has been formulated to analyze distributional data and data on the headings of traveling bowhead whales, as documented during systematic aerial surveys ("transect" sightings). Sightings during reconnaissance and other non-systematic flights should not be included. We have not given any specific consideration to analysis of the "whale activities" recorded during systematic surveys, given the difficulties in recording whale activity meaningfully during straight-line surveys [but see comments about Objective (4), below].

One set of site-specific data that does not appear to be readily available is the information acquired in the early-to-mid 1980s by NOSC for MMS during small-scale grid surveys around industry sites.

TABLE A-3. Site-specific aerial survey projects, Alaskan Beaufort Sea, late summer and autumn: status of data.

| | | | | Status of Data* | | | | | |
Year	Prospect	Region	Description	Sightings	Effort (Flight Lines)	Ice & Sightability	Reference	Surveyors	Proponent
1982	Seal Isl.	Prudhoe	Island Construction	E	E	E	1	LGL	Shell
1984	Seal Isl.	Prudhoe	Island Drilling	E	E	E	2	LGL	Shell
1985	Sandpiper Isl.	Prudhoe	Island Standby	E	E	E	3	LGL	Shell
1985	Hammerhead and Corona	Flaxman	Drillship Standby	P	P	P	4	LGL	UNOCAL
1985	-	Kaktovik	Bowhead Feeding	E	E	E	5	LGL	MMS
1986	-	Kaktovik	Bowhead Feeding	E	E	E	5	LGL	MMS
1986	Corona	Camden B.	Drillship	E	E	E	6	LGL	SWEPI
1986	Hammerhead	Flaxman	Drillship	P	P	P	6	LGL	SWEPI
1991	Cabot	Pt. Barrow	Caisson Drilling	E	P	P	7	COPAC	ARCO
1991	Galahad	Camden B.	Drillship	E	D	D	8	COPAC	AMOCO
1992	Kuvlum I	Camden B.	Drillship	E	D	D	9	COPAC	ARCO
1993	Kuvlum II, III; Wild Weasel	Camden B.	Drillship	E	D	D	10	COPAC	ARCO
1995	Northstar	Prudhoe	Baseline	E	E	E	11	LGL	BPXA
1996	Northstar	Prudhoe	Seismic	E	E	E	12	LGL	BPXA
1997	Northstar	Prudhoe	Seismic	E	E	E	13	LGL	BPXA
1998	Northstar and Liberty Areas	Prudhoe	Seismic	E	E	E	14	LGL	Western Geo
1998	-	Kaktovik	Bowhead Feeding	E	E	E	15	LGL	MMS
1999	-	Kaktovik	Bowhead Feeding	E	E	E	15	LGL	MMS
2000	-	Kaktovik	Bowhead Feeding	E	E	D	15	LGL	MMS

E = electronics; D = being digitized now; P = on paper

1. Hickie & Davis (1983)
2. Davis et al. (1985)
3. Johnson et al. (1986)
4. McLaren et al. (1986)
5. Richardson (ed., 1987)
6. LGL & Greenridge (1987)
7. Gallagher et al. (1992a)
8. Gallagher et al. (1992b)
9. Brewer et al. (1993)
10. Hall et al. (1994)
11. LGL & Greenridge (1996)
12. Miller et al. (1997)
13. Miller et al. (1998)
14. Miller et al. (1999)
15. LGL (in prep.)

Reports were prepared summarizing some of these data on a day by day basis (e.g., Ljungblad et al. 1984). However, we believe that data of this type were also obtained in 1984, and we are not aware of a report on those data. We understand that the MMS/NOSC site-specific datasets may not have been converted to the format presently used by MMS for aerial survey data. We do not know whether these data are accessible or useful. The status of these data should be checked to ensure that a valuable source of information is not overlooked. However, in assessing the feasibility of the planned project, we have assumed that these data would not be used.

(2) "Obtain from available information appropriate measures of sea ice for covariant analysis with whale distribution data."

Information about ice will be important for the planned "Analysis of covariance...". As discussed under Question (10), above, three types of information on ice conditions are available. One is very general – categorization of each year as "light", "moderate" or "heavy". The 2nd involves weekly summary maps of ice cover. The 3rd is the very specific information on ice cover along the aerial survey lines at the times they were surveyed. All three types of information could be useful in the planned "Analysis of covariance...". The weekly maps, now available in digital form at MMS, need to be loaded into the HAD, which will require a conversion of their projection. The ice observations acquired during aerial surveys are not all in consistent form, and some of those from site-specific surveys are not available in digital form. Although LGL has been gradually assembling those data in GIS form during previous and ongoing projects, additional effort will be required to complete this effort during the early stages of the "Analysis of covariance...".

As discussed earlier in this report, there is also a need to assemble additional data on some other variables, e.g. icebreaking during years with drillship operations [see Questions (6) and (7)]; seismic surveys in the Flaxman Isl./Camden Bay area during 1986 [see Question (8)]. This will need to be done during early stages of the "Analysis of covariance..." if it is not done in the final stages of the present project on compiling the human activity database.

(3) "Present preliminary tests and findings, define biases and assumptions, and recommend appropriate statistical procedures (e.g., analysis of covariance, regression techniques, K-S tests, spatial analysis, computer modeling) to a Scientific Review Board."

This feasibility analysis has already gone part of the way toward addressing this objective. This report has identified a list of provisional hypotheses, and a statistical approach that appears to be practical for testing those hypotheses.

Some of the hypotheses listed above in response to Question (2) need refinements of the wording. This should be done early during the "Analysis of covariance...". Some specific questions about the wording are identified in the list of provisional hypotheses.

The most suitable statistical approach will very likely be logistical regression. As discussed in Annex 1, some initial analysis is needed to work out the details of this analysis. One question to be resolved will be to define the most appropriate size of the sampling units into which the transect data should be divided. Also, there will be a need to confirm that some key assumptions of the suggested logistical regression approach are met, e.g. few sampling units with more than one bowhead sighting per sampling unit; spatial autocorrelation sufficiently limited to allow compensation with the logistical regression context. Some alternative analysis approaches have been identified for use in any special situations where these assumptions are violated, i.e. log-linear (=Poisson) regression if there are many cases with more than one sighting per sampling unit; Mantel matrix-randomization tests if too much spatial autocorrelation.

Considerable planning and thought will be required in deciding how best to address each hypothesis. This will need to be done during early stages of the "Analysis of covariance…". Some questions will be best addressed by analyses that concentrate on the data collected near industrial sites of a particular type. (MMS as well as industry-sponsored aerial survey data can be used in these analyses.) Other questions can best be addressed by analyses of area-wide data, again incorporating both MMS area-wide and industry-sponsored site-specific data. The specific formulation of the multivariate models to be used in each analysis will require careful planning. Some of the variables representing human activities and natural factors will require transformations and allowance for potential non-linear relationships. Some interaction terms will be required to test for hypothesized differences in bowhead relationships to one variable depending on another variable. Two examples of probable interactions are distance from drillship vs. presence/absence of active icebreaking, and distance from shore vs. date in season.

We concur that it would be desirable, after completion of these preliminary steps of the "Analysis of covariance…", that the results of the preliminary work and the plans for the main analyses be written up in an interim report. That report should be reviewed by MMS and by a Scientific Review Board including specialists in a variety of relevant disciplines. Reviewers should include persons knowledgeable about industrial activities, bowhead whales, and subsistence hunting in the Alaskan Beaufort Sea; the influences of anthropogenic and natural factors on whale distribution; and statistical procedures appropriate for analysis of the interrelationships of those types of data.

(4) "Apply applicable procedures to test hypotheses on relationships of the timing, location, and activity status of oil-industry/human activity and the distribution and behavior of bowhead whales (1979-1998)."

The procedures and datasets suggested in this feasibility analysis are suitable to address factors affecting the distribution of bowhead whales.

No detailed data on bowhead behavior are available from systematic aerial surveys. However, some data on whale headings and general activities of whales are usually recorded when bowheads are seen. Table A-1 *in* Treacy (2000) lists the type of whale activities and behaviors that are recorded when noted during MMS aerial surveys. Related (but not identical) categories have been used during some of the site-specific aerial surveys. Some of the proposed hypotheses address the influences of seismic surveys and drillships industrial activities on the headings of traveling bowhead – see Hypotheses 5, 6, and 9 under Question (2). No specific analyses of whale activity have been suggested in earlier parts of this document, given the difficulties in recording whale activity reliably during straight-line aerial surveys. However, it would certainly be possible to conduct multivariate analyses to assess the factors (anthropogenic and natural) associated with recorded occurrences of feeding, mating, cow-calf pairs, etc. The level of effort that is to be placed on this should be resolved early in the planned "Analysis of covariance…".

Methods Suggested by MMS

The latest Alaska Annual Studies Plan (for FY 2002 – 2003) also includes a paragraph summarizing the anticipated "Methods" for the planned "Analysis of covariance…". This paragraph is listed in its entirety in the "Introduction" to this report. Here we repeat the paragraph sentence-by-sentence (in italics), with comments on some of the statements made by MMS.

(1) "This study will utilize existing data in the recently developed MMS database for Beaufort Sea human activity and data in the MMS Bowhead Whale Aerial Survey Project database."

As noted in MMS's objective (1) and in a later sentence in the "Methods" paragraph, MMS has indicated that it also intends that site-specific aerial survey results will also be used. The use of those data is one of the main reasons for going ahead with "Analysis of covariance…". There has been no previous comprehensive analysis of the combined area-wide and site-specific aerial survey datasets. The site-specific results are of special value in addressing industry effects, as they provide a large increment in sample size in areas around some important types of industrial activities including seismic vessels and drillships.

(2) "It will consider positions and daily activity status of each drilling platform, helicopter, icebreaker, and other support vessels."

Data on drilling operations of various types (drillships, caissons, island-based rigs) are available in the HAD, with only a few exceptions.

Data on helicopter traffic are missing, as are some data for low-altitude survey aircraft, as discussed under Question (8). Helicopter data are not available. Missing data on industry-sponsored low-altitude aerial surveys for whales will more-or-less automatically become available when the sighting and effort data are assembled for use in the the "Analysis of covariance…". Some or all data from NOSC/MMS site-specific and reconnaissance surveys in the early-mid 1980s *may* be available, but have not been used recently would probably require significant effort to edit and incorporate. As noted under Question (8), we do not believe it is a high priority to incorporate or analyze the flightline data as there is little likelihood that whale distribution is affected by straight-line aircraft overflights.

The icebreaker data in the HAD are very incomplete and of poor quality – see responses to Questions (6) and (7). For the 1990s, significant additional data are available in technical reports and these need to be incorporated into the HAD. It may be desirable to seek more detailed data from icebreaker logbooks, but that would be a major undertaking. For the 1980s, it is suggested that data on icebreaking in 1986 should be acquired if possible, especially if equally-important and now-missing seismic data for that area and time can be acquired. Those 1986 icebreaker and seismic data, if available, would allow the analysis of an important set of data on whale occurrence near a drillship operation during 1986.

Few data are available in the HAD on other vessels, either those involved oil industry operations or those engaged in other activities. It is probably not practical to acquire a comprehensive retrospective dataset on vessel movements.

Seismic vessels are not mentioned in this sentence from MMS's paragraph on suggested Methods. Operating seismic vessels are one of the types of industrial activity known to have a substantial effect on the distribution of migrating bowheads. Seismic vessels are one of the main factors that must be considered in the "Analysis of covariance...". Given the lack of adequate documentation about the locations, dates and times of seismic surveys during the 1980s, we suggest that most data from the 1980s will not be useable for the analysis of bowhead distribution relative to human activities. However, we recommend that a concerted effort be made to document the seismic work done around the drillship that operated in 1986. If successful, that would allow use of the 1986 data, in conjunction with data from the early 1990s, in analyses of drillship effects on bowheads.

(3) " It will adopt similar measures between years to facilitate inter-year comparisons and trend analysis."

The suggested analysis approach provides for across-year integration of data, which is an essential component of the planned "Analysis of covariance...".

(4) "It will control for presence of commercial vessels, subsistence hunting, and low-flying aircraft."

As noted above in the comments on "Methods" sentence (2), the available data on commercial vessels and low-flying aircraft (especially helicopters) are very incomplete. Data on some specialized commercial vessels, specifically seismic boats and drillships, are available for at least some years. Other data, e.g. basic data on icebreaking in the early 1990s and on industry-sponsored aerial surveys, could be added to the HAD with relatively little effort. However, the available data do not adequately represent the amounts and locations of routine vessel traffic, helicopter traffic, or NOSC/MMS site-specific and reconnaissance flights in the early-mid 1980s. As previously discussed, we do not consider the lack of detailed data on these aircraft activities to be an important data gap. The lack of data on general vessel movements is of more concern given the known disturbance reactions of bowheads to boats and ships (Richardson et al. 1985b; Richardson and Malme 1993). However, we are confident that meaningful analysis of the influences of other important anthropogenic and natural factors, including seismic surveys, drillships, icebreaking, ice, water depth, date in season, etc., can be done without allowing for the localized effects of vessels.

Inclusion of data on subsistence activities in the HAD was not within the scope of the project under which the HAD was developed. The desirability and possibilities of acquiring relevant data for past and/or future years are discussed under Question (11). The planned "Analysis of covariance..." can go forward without information about day-by-day hunting activities. However, the analysis would be improved if that type of information were available for past years.

(5) It will evaluate site-specific and wide-area data from MMS- and oil-industry-funded surveys of the fall distribution of bowhead whales (1979-1998) for applicability and pooled analysis.

The present feasibility analysis has already addressed this point. We conclude that these two types of aerial survey data can and should be combined for use in the "Analysis of covariance...".

(6) Using appropriate inferential statistical procedures, it will then test hypotheses for significant relationships of human activities and bowhead distribution and evaluate power of tests..."

In our response to Question (2), we have suggested a series of hypotheses concerning various factors (industrial and natural) that may affect bowhead distribution and also bowhead headings. A statistical approach that will be effective in testing those hypotheses is described in the response to Question (4), with additional background information and details in Annex 1, "Statistical Considerations". Logistic regression is the recommended approach.

In a logistic regression context, the power to detect an effect of specified size given a particular set of data can be estimated. However, this is ***not*** a simple or straightforward calculation. A simulation approach is required. Power calculations would be needed if the analysis fails to reject some of the important null hypotheses. In that instance, it will be important to know whether it is likely that the null hypothesis could have been rejected it were false. It has already been shown that several industrial activity and natural environmental factors have significant influences on bowhead distribution. Therefore, we are confident that several of the null hypotheses concerning the effects of drillships, seismic vessels, ice, distance from shore, date-in-season, etc., will be rejected. For those hypotheses, statistical power will not be a major issue. Power calculations should concentrate on other potential predictors that do not seem to have any strong influence on bowhead distribution.

Overall Assessment

Questions (1) and (9), as posed by MMS, were as follows:

Assess the quality and quantity of the ... HAD ... and determine its usefulness, along with MMS BWASP, NOSC, site-specific survey databases, and available ice data, for addressing the objectives of MMS's planned study entitled "Analysis of Covariance of Human Activities and Sea Ice in Relation to Fall Migrations of the Bowhead Whale"

Recommend whether adequate information is available to proceed with the goals and objectives of the proposed new study ["Phase II"].

These two questions, taken together, summarize the overall objectives of the Feasibility Analysis.

As documented in this report and in Wainwright and Marko (2001), the HAD now contains many of the data needed for the "Analysis of covariance...". Some additional needed data can be added with little effort (e.g., basic icebreaking data for the 1990s). However, some important data on human activities are not readily available, especially for the 1980s. The incomplete icebreaker and limited seismic data for the 1980s are particular problems, to the point that we reluctantly recommend that most of the data from the 1980s not be used in the main analyses of industry effects. The data from the 1980s (as well as the 1990s) can be used for multivariate analyses of ice and other natural environmental effects. Also, we suggest that additional effort be devoted to locating adequate icebreaker and seismic data for the Flaxman Isl./Camden Bay area in the late summer and autumn of 1986. If those industry data can be acquired, that would allow data on whale distribution around drillship operations in that area and season to be included in the analysis of industrial effects. Available ice data are suitable for the intended analyses, although some work will be necessary to organize and standardize them.

Table A-4 summarizes our recommendations on these and other topics, including cross references to the locations in the report where the various recommendations are discussed.

The results from the existing wide-area and site-specific aerial surveys for bowhead whales can be combined for purposes of analyzing bowhead distribution and headings relative to industrial and natural factors. By doing so, the sample sizes will be much increased relative to those available from either type of survey individually. This will increase statistical power, and will allow meaningful testing of a wider variety of hypotheses, with allowance for a larger number of potential covariates, than would otherwise be possible. Appropriate statistical techniques are available, and it will be possible (although not simple) to calculate the statistical power of the hypothesis tests that are done.

We conclude that adequate information is available, or can be made available with a practical amount of additional effort, to proceed with the goals and objectives of the proposed new study. There are some limitations, especially the fact that industrial activity data from the 1980s are too incomplete to allow use of most of the aerial survey data from the 1980s in analyses of industrial effects. Even so, there are very good prospects for significant advances in knowledge. These advances in knowledge of factors affecting bowhead whale distribution and headings will result from applying more comprehensive analysis approaches than used previously to larger quantities survey data than have been analyzed in previous studies.

TABLE A-4. Summary of recommendations made in the present "Feasibility Study".

Question Number	Existing or Future Data?		Recommendation
2	Existing	1	Reconsider the specific wording of suggested hypotheses during early stages of Phase II.
2	Future	2	Add hypotheses concerning hydrocarbon production when data become available.
2, 8	Existing	3	Assemble data concerning 1986 seismic activity to allow use of drillship monitoring data.
3	Future	4	Build source level data into HAD and link an acoustic propagation model with the HAD, if and when sub-bottom parameters are better documented.
7	Existing	5	Determine whether icebreaking was occurring during each aerial survey in during 1991-93.
7, 8	Existing	6	Access and compile icebreaker logbooks for autumn 1986, especially if seismic data can also be acquired for that period.
8	Existing	7	Restrict most detailed analyses of bowhead distribution relative to human activities to years from 1990 onward.
8	Existing	8	Area wide analyses of whale distribution relative to natural factors can use data from all years.
10	Existing	9	Include additional fields in database structure for activity and sub-activity classification, the equipment classification, and the parameter classification for environmental observations.
10	Existing	10	Consider expanding the structure of the "Sources" table to be consistent with bibliographic databases.
10	Existing	11	Consider changing Visual Foxpro database structure to Microsoft Access to provide compatibility with ArcView 8.1.
10	Existing	12	Re-examine the database structure early in Phase II after the statistical analyses have been designed, and again later when the analyses have been completed.
11	Future	13	Document all activities associated with drilling, including construction, commissioning, crewing, drilling, and decommissioning of all drilling platforms (at least for 15 Aug.-31 Oct. period.
11	Future	14	Have icebreaking and large support vessels operating in support of MMS-permitted activities submit copies of shiplogs or (preferably) digital data summarizing vessel movements and activities.
11	Future	15	Consider installation of Vessel Tracking System (VTS) recorders on icebreaking and large support vessels operating in support of MMS-permitted activities.
11	Future	16	Consider requiring industry to submit digital data documenting seismic surveys in ESRI shapefile format in geographic coordinates (NAD83 datum).
11	Future	17	Dates, times (in GMT) and locations should be documented for all airgun shots.
11	Future	18	Consider requiring that seismic data be submitted documenting all airgun shots, including non-production shots.
11	Future	19	Consider requesting that airgun depth and water depth at every shotpoint be logged.
11	Future	20	Arrange for access to documentation of seismic and geohazard surveys in state waters in the same format as for federal waters.
11	Future	21	If bowhead whales are the only concern, these requirements could be restricted to the 15 Aug.-31 Oct. period.
11	Future	22	MMS's socioeconomic specialists could coordinate with the AEWC regarding collection of specific information about past and future bowhead hunts.
11	Future	23	Consider possibility of logging subsistence hunting vessels automatically with GPS based VTS recorders.
11	Existing	24	Incorporate weekly average ice data into HAD.
11	Existing	25	Convert ice data acquired during aerial surveys into standard format and make available for use in statistical analyses.
11	Future	26	Ensure that future ice condition data are consistent with past data.
11	Existing	27	Sightability data recorded during aerial surveys should be standardized for all datasets to be used in "Analysis of covariance...".
11	Future	28	Formulate specific recommendations concerning the manner in which future aerial surveyors should record sightability parameters during surveys.

ACKNOWLEDGEMENTS

We thank Dr. Charles R. Greene Jr. of Greeneridge Sciences for input on Question (3). We also thank the many individuals, corporations, and agencies that assisted in various ways in the compilation of the Human Activities Database on which this assessment is based. We acknowledge the many aerial surveyors and pilots, and their sponsoring agencies and companies, who were responsible for collecting the aerial survey datasets that are referenced here. Finally, we thank MMS, and especially Steve Treacy, for allowing us to use the MMS-BWASP aerial survey dataset in various projects over the past few years. In addition to benefiting those projects, access to that dataset has greatly increased our familiarity with one of the key datasets that will be needed for the "Analysis of covariance...". That familiarity has been invaluable in formulating the assessment and recommendations included in this document.

LITERATURE CITED

Brewer, K.D., M.L. Gallagher, P.R. Regos, P.E. Isert and J.D. Hall. 1993. ARCO Alaska, Inc. Kuvlum #1 exploration prospect/Site specific monitoring program final report. Rep. from Coastal & Offshore Pacific Corp., Walnut Creek, CA, for ARCO Alaska Inc., Anchorage, AK. 80 p.

Brouwer, P., J.W. McDonald, W.J. Richardson and R.A. Davis. 1988. Arctic industrial activities compilation-- Volume 3/Canadian Beaufort Sea: seismic and sounding surveys, vessel movements, helicopter traffic and site-specific activities 1980 to 1986. Can. Data Rep. Hydrog. Ocean Sci. 32. Can. Dep. Fish. & Oceans, Sidney, B.C. 170 p.

Burgess, W.C. and J.W. Lawson. 2001. Marine mammal and acoustic monitoring of Western Geophysical's shallow-hazards survey in the Alaskan Beaufort Sea, summer 2000. p. C-1 to C-28 *In:* W.J. Richardson (ed.), Marine mammal and acoustical monitoring of Western Geophysical's open-water seismic program in the Alaskan Beaufort Sea, 2000. LGL Rep. TA2503 (Appendix C in LGL Rep. TA2424-4). Rep. from LGL Ltd., King City, Ont., and Greeneridge Sciences Inc., Santa Barbara, CA, for WesternGeco LLC, Anchorage, AK, and Nat. Mar. Fish. Serv., Anchorage, AK, and Silver Spring, MD. 133 p.

Burgess, W.C. and C.R. Greene Jr., with R. Norman and R.W. Blaylock. 1999. Physical acoustics measurements. p. 3-1 to 3-65 *In:* W.J. Richardson (ed.), Marine mammal and acoustical monitoring of Western Geophysical's open-water seismic program in the Alaskan Beaufort Sea, 1998. LGL Rep. TA2230-3. Rep. from LGL Ltd., King City, Ont., and Greeneridge Sciences Inc., Santa Barbara, CA, for Western Geophysical, Houston, TX, and U.S. Nat. Mar. Fish. Serv., Anchorage, AK, and Silver Spring, MD. 390 p.

Davies, J.R. 1997. The impact of an offshore drilling platform on the fall migration path of bowhead whales: a GIS-based assessment. M.S. thesis, Western Washington Univ., Bellingham, WA. 52 p.

Davis, R.A. 1987. Integration and summary report. (Chap. 1, 51 p.) *In:* LGL and Greeneridge (1987), Responses of bowhead whales to an offshore drilling operation in the Alaskan Beaufort Sea, autumn 1986. Rep. from LGL Ltd., King City, Ont., and Greeneridge Sciences Inc., Santa Barbara, CA, for Shell Western E & P Inc., Anchorage, AK. 371 p.

Davis, R.A., C.R. Greene and P.L. McLaren. 1985. Studies of the potential for drilling activities on Seal Island to influence fall migration of bowhead whales through Alaskan nearshore waters. Rep. from LGL Ltd., King City, Ont., for Shell Western E & P Inc., Anchorage, AK. 70 p.

Fraker, M.A., D.K. Ljungblad, W.J. Richardson and D.R. Van Schoik. 1985. Bowhead whale behavior in relation to seismic exploration, Alaskan Beaufort Sea, autumn 1981. OCS Study MMS 85-0077. Rep. from LGL Ecol. Res. Assoc. Inc., Bryan, TX, and Naval Ocean Systems Center, San Diego, CA, for U.S. Minerals Manage. Serv., Reston, VA. 40 p. NTIS PB87-157442.

Gallagher, M.L., K.D. Brewer and J.D. Hall. 1992a. ARCO Alaska, Inc. Cabot prospect/Site specific monitoring plan/Final report. Rep. from Coastal & Offshore Pacific Corp., Walnut Creek, CA, for ARCO Alaska Inc. [Anchorage, AK]. 78 p. + App.

Gallagher, M.L., K.D. Brewer and J.D. Hall. 1992b. Amoco Production Company Galahad exploration prospect / Site specific monitoring plan/Final report. Rep. from Coastal & Offshore Pacific Corp., Walnut Creek, CA [for Amoco Prod. Co., Anchorage, AK]. 44 p. + App.

Greene, C.R. 1987. Acoustic studies of underwater noise and localization of whale calls. (Chap. 2, 128 p.) *In:* LGL and Greeneridge (1987), Responses of bowhead whales to an offshore drilling operation in the Alaskan Beaufort Sea, autumn 1986. Rep. from LGL Ltd., King City, Ont., and Greeneridge Sciences Inc., Santa Barbara, CA, for Shell Western E & P Inc., Anchorage, AK. 371 p.

Greene, C.R., Jr., R. Norman and J.S. Hanna, with R.W. Blaylock. 1998. Physical acoustics measurements [1997]. p. 3-1 to 3-66 *In:* W.J. Richardson (ed.), Marine mammal and acoustical monitoring of BP Exploration (Alaska's) open-water seismic program in the Alaskan Beaufort Sea, 1997. LGL Rep. TA2150-3. Rep. from LGL Ltd., King City, Ont., and Greeneridge Sciences Inc., Santa Barbara, CA, for BP Explor. (Alaska) Inc., Anchorage, AK, and U.S. Nat. Mar. Fish. Serv., Anchorage, AK, and Silver Spring, MD. 318 p.

Greene, C.R., Jr., and W.C. Burgess, with R. Norman and R.W. Blaylock. 2000. Physical acoustics measurements, 1999. p. 3-1 to 3-45 *In:* W.J. Richardson (ed.), Marine mammal and acoustical monitoring of Western Geophysical's open-water seismic program in the Alaskan Beaufort Sea, 1999. LGL Rep. TA2313-4. Rep. from LGL Ltd., King City, Ont., and Greeneridge Sciences Inc., Santa Barbara, CA, for Western Geophysical, Houston, TX, and U.S. Nat. Mar. Fish. Serv., Anchorage, AK, and Silver Spring, MD. 155 p.

Hall, J.D., M.L. Gallagher, K.D. Brewer, P.R. Regos and P.E. Isert. 1994. ARCO Alaska, Inc. 1993 Kuvlum exploration area site specific monitoring program/Final report. Rep. from Coastal & Offshore Pacific Corp., Walnut Creek, CA, for ARCO Alaska Inc. [Anchorage, AK]. 219 p. + Data Appendix Vol. 1, 2.

Hickie, J. and R.A. Davis. 1983. Distribution and movements of bowhead whales and other marine mammals in the Prudhoe Bay region, Alaska 26 September to 13 October 1982. p. 84-117 *In:* B.J. Gallaway (ed.), Biological studies and monitoring at Seal Island, Beaufort Sea, Alaska 1982. Rep. from LGL Ecol. Res. Assoc. Inc., Bryan, TX, for Shell Oil Co., Houston, TX. 150 p.

Johnson, S.R., C.R. Greene, R.A. Davis and W.J. Richardson. 1986. Bowhead whales and underwater noise near the Sandpiper Island drillsite, Alaskan Beaufort Sea, autumn 1985. Rep. from LGL Ltd., King City, Ont., for Shell Western E & P Inc., Anchorage, AK. 130 p.

Lawson, J.W. and V.D. Moulton. 1999. Seals [1998]. p. 4-1 to 4-69 *In:* W.J. Richardson (ed.), Marine mammal and acoustical monitoring of Western Geophysical's open-water seismic program in the Alaskan Beaufort Sea, 1998. LGL Rep. TA2230-3. Rep. from LGL Ltd., King City, Ont., and Greeneridge Sciences Inc., Santa Barbara, CA, for Western Geophysical, Houston, TX, and U.S. Nat. Mar. Fish. Serv., Anchorage, AK, and Silver Spring, MD. 390 p.

LGL and Greeneridge. 1987. Responses of bowhead whales to an offshore drilling operation in the Alaskan Beaufort Sea, autumn 1986. Rep. from LGL Ltd., King City, Ont., and Greeneridge Sciences Inc., Santa Barbara, CA, for Shell Western E & P Inc., Anchorage, AK. 371 p.

LGL and Greeneridge. 1996. Northstar marine mammal monitoring program, 1995: baseline surveys and retrospective analyses of marine mammal and ambient noise data from the central Alaskan Beaufort Sea. LGL Rep. TA2101-2. Rep. from LGL Ltd., King City, Ont., and Greeneridge Sciences Inc., Santa Barbara, CA, for BP Explor. (Alaska) Inc., Anchorage, AK. 104 p.

Ljungblad, D.K., B. Würsig, R.R. Reeves, J.T. Clarke and C.R. Greene Jr. 1984. Fall 1983 Beaufort Sea seismic monitoring and bowhead whale behavior studies. Interagency Agreem. 14-12-0001-29064. Rep. for U.S. Minerals Manage. Serv., Anchorage, AK. 180 p. NTIS PB86-196912.

Ljungblad, D.K., B. Würsig, S.L. Swartz and J.M. Keene. 1985. Observations on the behavior of bowhead whales (*Balaena mysticetus*) in the presence of operating seismic exploration vessels in the Alaskan Beaufort Sea. OCS Study MMS 85-0076. Rep. from SEACO Inc., San Diego, CA, for U.S. Minerals Manage. Serv., Anchorage, AK. 78 p. NTIS PB87-129318.

Ljungblad, D.K., B. Würsig, S.L. Swartz and J.M. Keene. 1988. Observations on the behavioral responses of bowhead whales (*Balaena mysticetus*) to active geophysical vessels in the Alaskan Beaufort Sea. **Arctic** 41(3):183-194.

Manly, B.F.J. 1992. The design and analysis of research studies. Cambridge Univ. Press, Cambridge, U.K.

Manly, B.F.J. 1997. Randomization, bootstrap and Monte Carlo methods in biology, 2nd Edit. Chapman and Hall, London, U.K.

Manly, B.F.J., L.L. McDonald and D.L. Thomas. 1993. Resource selection by animals: Statistical design and analysis for field studies. Chapman and Hall, London, U.K.

Marko, J. 2001. Preparation of a sediment stratigraphy representative of the Alaskan North Slope. Appendix 3 *In:* P. Wainwright and J. Marko (2001), GIS geospatial database of oil-industry and other human activity (1979 - 1999) in the Alaskan Beaufort Sea. Rep. from LGL Ltd., Sidney, B.C., for U.S. Minerals Manage. Serv., Anchorage, AK. Var. pag. Draft.

McLaren, P.L., C.R. Greene, W.J. Richardson and R.A. Davis. 1986. Bowhead whales and underwater noise near a drillship operation in the Alaskan Beaufort Sea, 1985. Rep. from LGL Ltd., King City, Ont., and Greeneridge Sciences Inc., Santa Barbara, CA, for UNOCAL Corp., Anchorage, AK. 137 p.

Miller, G.W., R.E. Elliott, W.R. Koski and W.J. Richardson. 1997. Whales [1996] p. 5-1 to 5-115 *In:* W.J. Richardson (ed.), Northstar marine mammal monitoring program, 1996: marine mammal and acoustical monitoring of a seismic program in the Alaskan Beaufort Sea. LGL Rep. 2121-2. Rep. from LGL Ltd., King City, Ont., and Greeneridge Sciences Inc., Santa Barbara, CA, for BP Explor. (Alaska) Inc., Anchorage, AK, and Nat. Mar. Fish. Serv., Anchorage, AK, and Silver Spring, MD. 245 p.

Miller, G.W., R.E. Elliott and W.J. Richardson. 1998. Whale [1997]. p. 5-1 to 5-124 *In:* W.J. Richardson (ed.), Marine mammal and acoustical monitoring of BP Exploration (Alaska's) open-water seismic program in the Alaskan Beaufort Sea, 1997. LGL Rep. TA2150-3. Rep. from LGL Ltd., King City, Ont., and Greeneridge Sciences Inc., Santa Barbara, CA, for BP Explor. (Alaska) Inc., Anchorage, AK, and U.S. Nat. Mar. Fish. Serv., Anchorage, AK, and Silver Spring, MD. 318 p.

Miller, G.W., R.E. Elliott, W.R. Koski, V.D. Moulton and W.J. Richardson. 1999. Whales [1998]. p. 5-1 to 5-109 *In:* W.J. Richardson (ed.), Marine mammal and acoustical monitoring of Western Geophysical's open-water seismic program in the Alaskan Beaufort Sea, 1998. LGL Rep. TA2230-3. Rep. from LGL Ltd., King City, Ont., and Greeneridge Sciences Inc., Santa Barbara, CA, for Western Geophysical, Houston, TX, and U.S. Nat. Mar. Fish. Serv., Anchorage, AK, and Silver Spring, MD. 390 p.

Moore, S.E. 2000. Variability of cetacean distribution and habitat selection in the Alaskan Arctic, autumn 1982-91. **Arctic** 53(4):448-460.

Moore, S.E., D.P. DeMaster and P.K. Dayton. 2000. Cetacean habitat selection in the Alaskan Arctic during summer and autumn. **Arctic** 53(4):432-447.

Moulton, V.D., R.E. Elliott, T.L. McDonald and W.J. Richardson. 2001. Fixed-wing aerial surveys of seals near BP's Northstar and Liberty sites in 2000 (and in 1997-2000 combined). p. 5-1 to 5-66 *In:* W.J. Richardson and M.T. Williams (eds.), Monitoring of industrial sounds, seals, and whale calls during construction of BP's Northstar Oil Development, Alaskan Beaufort Sea, 2000. [Draft, April 2001.] LGL Rep. TA2428-3. Rep. from LGL Ltd., King City, Ont., and Greeneridge Sciences Inc., Santa Barbara, CA, for BP Explor. (Alaska) Inc., Anchorage, AK, and Nat. Mar. Fish. Serv., Anchorage, AK, and Silver Spring, MD.

Reeves, R., D.K. Ljungblad and J.T. Clarke. 1983. Report on studies to monitor the interaction between offshore geophysical exploration activities and bowhead whales in the Alaskan Beaufort Sea, fall 1982. Rep. from Hubbs-Sea World Res. Inst., San Diego, CA, for U.S. Minerals Manage. Serv., Anchorage, AK. 38 + appendices p. NTIS PB86-168903.

Reeves, R.R., D.K. Ljungblad and J.T. Clarke. 1984. Bowhead whales and acoustic seismic surveys in the Beaufort Sea. **Polar Rec.** 22(138):271-280.

Richardson, W.J. (ed.). 1987. Importance of the eastern Alaskan Beaufort Sea to feeding bowhead whales, 1985-86. OCS Study MMS 87-0037. Rep. from LGL Ecol. Res. Assoc. Inc., Bryan, TX, for U.S. Minerals Manage. Serv., Reston, VA. 547 p. NTIS PB88-150271.

Richardson, W.J. and C.I. Malme. 1993. Man-made noise and behavioral responses. p. 631-700 *In:* J.J. Burns, J.J. Montague and C.J. Cowles (eds.), The bowhead whale. Spec. Publ. 2. Soc. Mar. Mamm., Lawrence, KS. 787 p.

Richardson, W.J., R.A. Davis, C.R. Evans and P. Norton. 1985a. Distribution of bowheads and industrial activity, 1980-84. p. 255-306 *In:* W.J. Richardson (ed.), Behavior, disturbance responses and distribution of bowhead whales *Balaena mysticetus* in the eastern Beaufort Sea, 1980-84. OCS Study MMS 85-0034. Rep. from LGL Ecol. Res. Assoc. Inc., Bryan, TX, for U.S. Minerals Manage. Serv., Reston, VA. 306 p. NTIS PB87-124376.

Richardson, W.J., M.A. Fraker, B. Würsig and R.S. Wells. 1985b. Behaviour of bowhead whales *Balaena mysticetus* summering in the Beaufort Sea: reactions to industrial activities. **Biol. Conserv.** 32(3):195-230.

Richardson, W.J., R.A. Davis, C.R. Evans, D.K. Ljungblad and P. Norton. 1987. Summer distribution of bowhead whales, *Balaena mysticetus*, relative to oil industry activities in the Canadian Beaufort Sea, 1980-84. **Arctic** 40(2):93-104.

Richardson, W.J., B. Würsig and C.R. Greene Jr. 1990. Reactions of bowhead whales, *Balaena mysticetus*, to drilling and dredging noise in the Canadian Beaufort Sea. **Mar. Environ. Res.** 29(2):135-160.

Richardson, W.J., C.R. Greene Jr., J.S. Hanna, W.R. Koski, G.W. Miller, N.J. Patenaude and M.A. Smultea, with R. Blaylock, R. Elliott and B. Würsig. 1995a. Acoustic effects of oil production activities on bowhead and white whales visible during spring migration near Pt. Barrow, Alaska--1991 and 1994 phases. OCS Study MMS 95-0051; LGL Rep. TA954. Rep. from LGL Ltd., King City, Ont., for U.S. Minerals Manage. Serv., Herndon, VA. 539 p. NTIS PB98-107667.

Richardson, W.J., C.R. Greene Jr., C.I. Malme and D.H. Thomson. 1995b. Marine mammals and noise. Academic Press, San Diego, CA. 576 p.

Schick, R.S. and D.L. Urban. 2000. Spatial components of bowhead whale (*Balaena mysticetus*) distribution in the Alaskan Beaufort Sea. **Can. J. Fish. Aquatic Sci.** 57(11):2193-2200.

Thomas, T.A., W.R. Koski and W.J. Richardson. 2000. Correction factors to calculate bowhead whale numbers from aerial surveys of the Beaufort Sea. (Chap. 16, 13 p.) *In:* W.J. Richardson and D.H. Thomson (eds.), Bowhead whale feeding in the eastern Alaskan Beaufort Sea: update of scientific and traditional information: Results of studies conducted in year 3. Draft. LGL Rep. TA2196-5. Rep. from LGL Ltd., King City, Ont., for U.S. Minerals Manage. Serv., Herndon, VA.

Treacy, S.D. 1988. Aerial surveys of endangered whales in the Beaufort Sea, fall 1987. OCS Study MMS 88-0030. U.S. Minerals Manage. Serv., Anchorage, AK. 142 p. NTIS PB89-168785.

Treacy, S.D. 2000. Aerial surveys of endangered whales in the Beaufort Sea, fall 1998-1999. OCS Study MMS 2000-066. U.S. Minerals Manage. Serv., Anchorage, AK. 135 p.

Wainwright, P. and J. Marko. 2001. GIS geospatial database of oil-industry and other human activity (1979 - 1999) in the Alaskan Beaufort Sea. Rep. from LGL Ltd., Sidney, B.C., for U.S. Minerals Manage. Serv., Anchorage, AK. Var. pag. Draft.

ANNEX 1: STATISTICAL CONSIDERATIONS, by B.F.J. MANLY, WEST INC.

Notes on the Feasibility of Using the Human Activity Database and Other Data for Addressing the Objectives in the Mineral Management Service's Planned Study "Analysis of Covariance of Human Activities and Sea Ice in Relation to Fall Migrations of the Bowhead Whale"

Bryan F.J. Manly
Western EcoSystems Technology Inc.

Data Sets Available

The Human Activities Database (HAD) and other sources contain information on the following variables that are relevant to the proposed study:

- seismic survey locations for 1981-99, with reliable activity dates for 1990-99 (some pre-1990 data not loaded into HAD);

- geohazard and seafloor survey locations for 1980-97, with reliable activity dates for 1983 and 1989-99;

- drilling and ice-breaking locations for 1981-97, with reliable drilling dates for most years but very incomplete ice-breaking dates;

- flight lines, dates, and whale observation locations for Minerals Management Service (MMS) fall aerial surveys of the Beaufort Sea for the years 1979-2000 are mostly available from sources other than the HAD;

- flight lines, dates, and whale observation locations for aerial surveys used to monitor about ten industry activities, e.g. the Coastal Offshore and Pacific Corporation (COPAC) survey of the effects of a conical drilling unit at the Kuvlum #3 site from 31 August to 5 October 1993, are mostly available from sources other than the HAD;

- ice cover data from weekly surveys estimated for all map locations are available digitally from the MMS, with maps in the annual MMS aerial survey reports;

- ice cover as recorded from aerial surveys;

- bathymetric data for all map locations; and

- weather information from coastal stations.

Site-Specific Studies

Site-specific studies such as the COPAC survey of the effects of a conical drilling unit at the Kuvlum #3 site in 1993 provide one obvious approach for studying the effects of human activities on bowhead whale movements.

The data from the COPAC study have been analyzed by Davies (1997) by estimating the probability of observing one or more bowhead whales in 1 km^2 sample units during aerial surveys, as a function of the water depth, the distance from shore, and the distance from the drilling unit. There were 17,472 such sample units, consisting of those within 3 km of 12 fixed flight lines that were flown repeatedly while the drilling unit was in operation. Of these units, there were 118 with a recorded detection of one or more whales. It was assumed that the probability of a detection in each sample unit is well approximated by a logistic regression function of the form

$$p(x_1, x_2, ..., x_p) = \exp(\beta_0 + \beta_1 x_1 + ... + \beta_p x_p)/[1 + \exp(\beta_0 + \beta_1 x_1 + ... + \beta_p x_p)], \qquad (1)$$

where x_1 to x_p are values of explanatory variables such as the water depth, and the β values are coefficients to be estimated from the data. Logistic regression is a standard type of analysis for data of this type (Manly, 1992, Section 8.8).

Davies concluded that the probability of a detection was a function of the distance from the drilling unit and the interaction between this distance and the water depth. Although there might be some minor concerns about details of the analysis (such as including the product of the distance to the drilling unit and the depth in the final equation without including depth as a separate term), the basic approach is sound and could be used with other site-specific studies.

The COPAC data were reanalyzed by Schick and Urban (2000) but using only the results from the six aerial flight lines closest to the drilling unit, with 56 recorded detections of whales. They first tested whether the whales were randomly located in the area surveyed by comparing the mean values for the water depth, the distance to the shore, and the distance to the drilling unit for the 56 whale locations with the mean values for many samples of 56 randomly located possible locations, using a randomization test (Manly, 1997). They did not obtain significant differences overall, but did for each variable when the analysis was conducted only on locations within 30 km of the drilling unit. This analysis is reasonable except that they chose to use one sided-tests after seeing which directions would give the most significant results, which is strictly speaking not valid.

Schick and Urban also used Mantel matrix randomization tests (Manly, 1997) to test whether the locations with whale detections were more similar than expected for randomly selected sites in terms of the water depth, the distance to the shore, and the distance to the drilling unit, taking into account spatial correlation. Mantel tests are based on distance matrices. For example Schick and Urban constructed one matrix ("distance to rig") in which the element in the ith row and j^{th} column was the absolute difference between the distance to the drilling unit for sampled site i and the distance to the drilling unit for sampled site j. Another matrix ("whales") is such that the element in row i and column j is 0 if sampled sites i and j are similar in terms of whale detection and a 1 if they are different (i.e., one site has a whale detection and another does not).   Given the whale and distance to rig matrices, the Mantel randomization test considers whether these matrices seem to be associated, i.e. it answers the question: do sites at similar distances from the drilling unit tend to be similar in terms of whale detection and and non-detection?

An extension to the simple Mantel test is the partial Mantel test, which attempts to determine whether two matrices are significantly related after allowing for the values in a third matrix. For example, Schick and Urban calculated another matrix ("space") in which the element in row i and column j is the spatial distance between sampled sites i and j. They were then able to ask the question: do sites at similar distances from the drilling unit tend to be similar in terms of whale detection and non-detection, after taking into account the fact that — if two sites are close together — then this in itself may lead to some similarity in terms of whale detection or non-detection, and will certainly lead to a strong similarity in terms of the distance to the rig?

While the Mantel tests used by Schick and Urban are certainly valid, there are several reasons why they do not really seem to be appropriate for whale distribution studies in general:

- the output from a Mantel test (a significant result or not) is far less informative than what is obtained from an approach like the logistic regression analysis of Davies (1997);

- the Mantel test is also far less flexible than conventional regression methods in terms of assessing the effects of many factors (such as the sample time and location) on whale distributions;

- the Mantel test is only really justified if spatial correlation is a serious problem, but the small number of whale sightings plus the tests for spatial correlation carried out by Davies (1997) suggest that this is not the case; and

- there are limitations on the number of sampling sites that can be handled at one time using a distance matrix approach.

The last point may be rather crucial in practice. Schick and Urban never say what their sample unit was, but it may be the 1 km^2 areas used by Davies (1997) because there are the same number of whale detections. In that case there are approximately 1,200 of these units with the COPAC data, and hence the matrices to be tested had about this number of rows and columns, with the data for all sample times combined. It is not difficult to imagine that a study taking the sample time into account, with a larger study area, might have 10,000 sample units, and matrices with 100 million elements to be randomized. Even with today's fast computers this would seem to make the Mantel test approach impossible unless the size of the sample units was increased considerably.   However, increasing the size of sample units could introduce problems because of the loss of spatial resolution when trying to assess the effects of those human activities that may have a small radius of influence, such as shallow-hazard surveys.

For these reasons, in future studies it is recommended that spatial correlation should be investigated further and the Mantel test approach should only be considered for use when spatial correlation is demonstrated to be an important problem.

If a regression type approach is used with site-specific types of study then logistic regression may or may not be the best statistical method for use. It is very suitable with the COPAC data because whales were not present in most of the sample units, and the detections were almost always of only one whale or group of whales. Thus the data are essentially of detections and non-detections, which is what logistic regression is designed for (Manly, 1992, Section 8.8).

If there were a higher proportion of sample units with whale detections and it often occurred that a sample unit contained several apparently independent groups of whales then a log-linear modeling approach (which is also sometimes called Poisson regression) would be more suitable, with the dependent variable being the number of whale groups in a sample unit. This would then lead to an analysis that is rather similar to logistic regression, at least in terms of how data are modeled (Manly, 1992, Section 8.5). An example of this type of approach is Moulton *et al.*'s (2001) analysis of ringed seal distribution in the Prudhoe Bay area in 1997-2000.

One advantage of the logistic regression or log-linear modeling approach to data analysis is that, in principle, data from different activities of the same type can be analyzed together. For example, the effects of drillships can be assessed by combining the data from all site-specific studies of drillships in different years. Also, the data from any MMS aerial surveys in the area of a site-specific study can be used to increase the aerial survey coverage in time and space.

Area-Wide Studies

There seems to be no reason why a logistic regression analysis cannot be applied with whale sightings from the MMS surveys over the whole of the Alaskan Beaufort Sea to assess the effects of environmental variables and human activities. During each survey day, a certain survey area is sampled by transects that extend laterally out to some distance on each side of the survey line. This surveyed area can be divided up into sample units of an appropriate size. Each sample unit then either does or does not contain a whale observation, and the probability of a whale observation can be related to the water depth, the distance from the shore, and any environmental variables such as ice cover or visibility that are known either from the survey records or another source. In addition, distances from human activities of different types (seismic surveys, drilling, etc.) may also be included in the model, with one variable for each type of activity, possibly only for those activities that are closer than 100 km (say). This would then make it possible to assess whether a particular type of activity significantly reduces the probability of a detection.

Each survey day in one area could potentially provide a fitted logistic regression relationship, and it would be possible to combine these into a global model for each year, and possibly for multiple years. This model could allow for time trends within and between years if necessary, but with the effects of some variables (e.g., distance to a drilling rig) being assumed to be constant if the data support this assumption. An advantage of this approach of treating each day of surveying in a given part of the overall study area as a separate sample is that the analysis is conditional on the actual sampling design used and no complications are introduced by a highly irregular coverage of the full study area. It does require that at least some of the estimated parameters are constant across time and/or space because of the sparseness of the sightings on many survey days.

There are many issues that would need serious consideration in a study like this, including the appropriate size for the sample unit, the possibility of temporal and spatial correlation in sightings, what transformations (if any) should be made in the explanatory variables entered into the logistic regression equation, and the effect of the distance from the flight line on sighting probabilities. However, at present it seems that logistic regression is the approach that is most likely to give informative results.

One alternative approach is the selection ratio method used by Moore *et al.* (2000) and Moore (2000). However, this is far less flexible than logistic regression. As applied by Moore, it uses MMS data only, and also only addresses the effects of the natural factors of ice, distance from shore and season on whale sightings. Similarly, the method of Miller *et al.* (1999), involving a log-linear model applied to sighting rates, does not generalize in a straightforward way to multiple activities over time and space.

Feasibility of the Planned Study *Analysis of Covariance of Human Activities and Sea Ice in Relation to Fall Migrations of the Bowhead Whale*

The feasibility study is intended to determine the usefulness of the HAD database and other available data for addressing the objectives of the planned study entitled "Analysis of Covariance of Human Activities and Sea Ice in Relation to Fall Migrations of the Bowhead Whale". There are various specific tasks involved, and comments follow on some of these.

(3) Evaluate the feasibility of using the HAD to detect multiple, combined and/or cumulative effects of industrial activity on the movement and behavior of the bowhead whale ...

The area-wide analyses proposed earlier would be designed to detect multiple, combined and/or cumulative effects of human activities. In principle, models may easily allow different types of activity to have different effects depending on their distance, and can incorporate an allowance for the presence of acoustic barriers (e.g., barrier islands, sand bars) and other such complications.

(4) Describe the recommended statistical procedure and illustrate the type of product such analyses would produce

Analyses of whale distribution around a particular type of industrial activity can be conducted using all the available site-specific data, along with subsets of the broad-scale MMS data collected in the relevant areas. The most appropriate approach to adopt would probably be logistic regression to estimate the probability of a whale detection at a particular location, although this should not rule out the consideration of other approaches. In fact, logistic regression may not always be appropriate, although this will depend on the nature of the available data in each case. Also, even when logistic regression is used, this should be supplemented by other analyses such as simple comparisons of mean values for sample units with and without whale observations. It is anticipated that the analysis of site-specific data would allow the assessment of whether the particular human activity involved affected the movement of whales in the vicinity, and whether the locations of whales depended on any environmental variables that were recorded. It may also be possible to test whether similar human activities in different times and places had a similar impact or lack of impact on whale movements.

Logistic regression can also be used on an area-wide basis using data from the MMS aerial surveys and any site-specific surveys also carried out. This would potentially allow the assessment of the effects of human activities on a larger scale than the site-specific surveys, and also the combined effects of several activities if these occur at the same time. Again it is important to note that although logistic regression appears to be the analysis of choice this should not rule out the consideration of alternative approaches. The first step in any area-wide analyses should therefore be a detailed review of possible alternatives. Supplementary analyses such as simple comparisons of mean values of variables for sample units with and without whale observations would also be needed.

Both site-specific and area-wide analyses can make use of observations from all aerial surveys conducted at the appropriate time in the appropriate area. Issues of temporal and spatial correlation would have to be addressed, and also the size of the sample unit to be used. Explanatory variables could include the distance from shore, the water depth, the ice cover, the slope of the ocean floor, measures of visibility, the distances from sound sources of different types, and whether or not acoustic barriers are present for these sources. Some or all of these variables might need to be entered after a suitable non-linear transformation. Also, consideration would have to be given to the question of what effects can be assumed to be constant over time and/or space in order to estimate a logistic regression function from data that are very unevenly distributed in these dimensions.

As noted above, logistic regression appears to be the main analysis of choice for both site-specific and area-wide analyses. The product of such analyses is an equation that gives the estimated probability that an aerial survey would detect a whale in a sample unit. This probability can be used to produce a map showing the relative preference of whales for different types of unit (as defined by environmental and human activity variables) and to provide objective measures of the "take" of bowhead whales resulting from different human activities. The logistic regression equation is in fact a resource selection probability function as discussed by Manly *et al.* (1993).

In addition to logistic regression, other alternative analysis procedures such as log-linear modeling could be investigated for use with specific data sets, and supplementary analyses could be carried out to investigate general aspects of any differences between sites with and without whale observations (e.g., tests for whether the mean values differ significantly for particular variables).

In terms of a strategy for analyzing all possible data, it is recommended that the site-specific data sets be considered first, including MMS data collected near the activities in question. This will provide understanding of the nature of the effects of particular types of human activity in the local area where they occur. Gaining this understanding will be a valuable first step towards modeling the effects of several activities on an area-wide basis.

(8) Evaluate the possibility of using all data including those data sets prior to 1990

Logistic regression using several years of data is possible, but does require that the variables considered for use in the equation have been measured in all years. It appears at the moment that this will rule out any area-wide multi-year analyses including years prior to 1990.

(9) Recommend whether adequate information is available to proceed with the goals and objectives of the proposed new study

There is enough data to make at least some site-specific analyses possible and worthwhile. These analyses would go far beyond any that have been carried out before because they would include MMS survey results when assessing the site-specific effects, and the estimation of effects would be improved by combining results from studies at different times (including different years) and in different places.

Area-wide analyses for individual years are also possible back to 1990, and for earlier years or parts of years in some cases. Multi-year area-wide analyses also seem feasible including years back to 1990, possibly separated into those with light, medium and heavy ice conditions using the classification devised by MMS and applied recently in the analysis of Moore (2000).

References

Davies, J.R. (1997). *The Impact of an Offshore Drilling Platform on the Fall Migration Path of Bowhead Whales: a GIS-Based Assessment.* M.S. Thesis, Western Washington University.

Manly, B.F.J. (1992). *The Design and Analysis of Research Studies.* Cambridge University Press, Cambridge.

Manly, B.F.J. (1997). *Randomization, Bootstrap and Monte Carlo Methods in Biology*, 2nd Edit. Chapman and Hall, London.

Manly, B.F.J., McDonald, L.L. and Thomas, D.L. (1993). *Resource Selection by Animals: Statistical Design and Analysis for Field Studies.* Chapman and Hall, London.

Miller, G.W., Elliott, R.E., Koski, W.R., Moulton, V.D. and Richardson, W.J. (1999). Whales. In *Marine Mammal and Acoustical Monitoring of Western Geophysical's Open-Water Seismic Program in the Alaskan Beaufort Sea, 1998* (Ed. W.J. Richardson), pp. 5-1 to 5-109. Report TA2230-3, LGL Ltd., King City, Ontario, and Greeneridge Sciences Inc., Santa Barbara, California, produced for Western Geophysical, Houston, Texas, and the U.S. National Marine Fisheries Service, Anchorage, Alaska, and Silver Spring, Maryland.

Moore, S.E. (2000). Variability of cetacean distribution and habitat selection in the Alaskan Arctic, autumn 1982-91. *Arctic* 53: 448-60.

Moore, S.E., DeMaster, D.P. and Dayton, P.K. (2000). Cetacean habitat selection in the Alaskan Arctic during summer and autumn. *Arctic* 53: 432-47.

Moulton, V.D., Elliott, R.E., McDonald, T.L. and Richardson, W.J. (2001). Fixed-wing aerial surveys of seals near BP's Northstar and Liberty sites in 2000 (and in 1997-2000 combined). In *Monitoring of Industrial Sounds, Seals, and Whale Calls During Construction of BP's Northstar Oil Development, Alaskan Beaufort Sea, 2000* (Eds. W.J. Richardson and M.T. Williams), pp. 5-1 to 5-66. Report TA2428-3, LGL Ltd., King City, Ontario, and Greeneridge Sciences Inc., Santa Barbara, California, for BP Exploration (Alaska) Inc., Anchorage, Alaska, and the National Marine Fisheries Service, Anchorage, Alaska, and Silver Spring, Maryland.

APPENDIX B: OBJECTIVES/HYPOTHESES NOT CONSIDERED IN PHASE I

Objective 4

H_a: Shallow-hazards and similar surveys employing single-airgun and/or mid-frequency pulsed sources (e.g., sparkers, boomers, sub-bottom profilers) result in reduced probability of observing bowheads near the survey vessel at times when one or more of these sources are operating.

H_o: Shallow-hazards and similar surveys employing single-airgun and/or mid-frequency pulsed sources (e.g., sparkers, boomers, sub-bottom profilers) *do not* reduce the probability of observing bowheads in the region near the survey vessel at times when one or more of these sources are operating.

Objective 5

Quantify the probability of observing bowheads relative to distance and direction (E, W, N, S) from an active drillship, amount of exposure, and time since exposure. Addressing this objective will allow us to assess the reduction in probability of observing bowheads in the various regions and time periods discussed in Objective 1.

Objective 6

H_a: The distribution of headings for "traveling" bowheads is deflected from the typical WNW migratory direction at distances up to w km east of the drillship. [Bowheads recorded as being engaged in activities other than "traveling" should not be considered.]

H_o: The distribution of headings for "traveling" bowheads is not deflected from the typical W/NW migratory direction east of the drillship.

Objective 7

H_a: The distances within which the probabilities of observing bowheads are reduced are larger when icebreaking is underway in conjunction with drillship activities than at times without icebreaking.

H_o: The distances within which the probability of observing bowheads is reduced are *not* larger when icebreaking is underway in conjunction with drillship activities than at times without icebreaking.

Objective 8

H_a: The duration of exposure necessary to decrease the probability of observing bowheads is smaller when icebreaking is underway in conjunction with drillship activities than at times without icebreaking.

H_o: The duration of exposure necessary to decrease the probability of observing bowheads is the same when icebreaking is underway in conjunction with drillship activities as at times without icebreaking.

Objective 9

H_a: The distance within which headings of "traveling" bowheads are deflected from the typical WNW migratory direction is larger when icebreaking is underway in conjunction with drillship activities than at times without icebreaking.

H_o: The distance within which headings of "traveling" bowheads are deflected from the typical WNW migratory direction is the same when icebreaking is underway in conjunction with drillship activities than at times without icebreaking.

Given the circular (degrees) nature of the dependent variable, this hypothesis cannot be tested with the logistical regression approach discussed earlier. A separate test appropriate to directional data will be performed.

Objective 10

H_a: Caisson-based drilling operations result in reduced probability of observing bowheads within v km of the caisson.

H_o: Caisson-based drilling operations do not result in reduced probability of observing bowheads.

Objective 11

H_a: Drilling operations on gravel islands (artificial or natural), aside from those in lagoons, result in reduced probability of observing bowheads within u km of the island.

H_o: Drilling operations on gravel islands (artificial or natural), aside from those in lagoons, do not result in reduced probability of observing bowheads.

Objective 12

H_a: Proximity to two (or more) active seismic vessels and/or drillships results in a greater reduction in the probability of observing a bowhead sighting than expected based on simple addition of the effects of the individual activities; this reduction in sighting probability is greatest in the area between the two (or more) vessels.

H_o: Proximity to two (or more) active seismic vessels and/or drillships *does not* result in a greater reduction in the probability of observing a bowhead sighting than expected based on simple addition of the effects of the individual activities.

Objective 14

To quantify the relationship between the preferred distance from shore (or preferred water depth) and percent ice cover, and the effect of this interaction on the probability of observing bowheads.

APPENDIX C: DATA VALIDATION AND BACK-UP

Original Dataset Checks

MMS Dataset

An "event sequence check" was performed on the entire MMS dataset (1979-2000) acquired from MMS via the National Oceanographic Data Center. This check involved comparing sequential records (the dataset was ordered based on time) to ensure that events (i.e., transect start times, records for environmental conditions, transect end times, etc.) were ordered properly. This check found some inconsistencies in early years of the dataset. However, no errors were detected in the 1996-1998 portion of that dataset. After this event sequence check, the 1996-1998 portion of the dataset was extracted to an Excel file from a master Access database containing all MMS data from 1979-2000. All MMS transects were plotted and compared to the location of these transects produced in a GIS program (MapInfo) as part of other LGL projects that had used the MMS data from 1996-98 (Miller et al. 1999, 2002). No inconsistencies in the location of transects were found. The codes and values in each of the MMS records were checked for spelling errors and out of range values. The only errors found were some minor spelling errors in the visibility and sea state variables; these errors were corrected.

LGL Datasets

The most recent versions of the four LGL aerial survey datasets were extracted from the 1996-98 industry-funded project folders and the 1998-2000 MMS funded bowhead feeding study folders stored on a computer at LGL Ltd. These data had been validated, including checking transect locations, for previous reports. Nonetheless, we checked each variable that would be used in producing the final regression analysis database for appropriate value ranges and data coding schemes. No corrections were necessary.

Regression Analysis Dataset

As described earlier, the "regression analysis database" containing bowhead sighting and covariate data organized by 5-km transect segments, is the final database and contains the data the Poisson regression models were based upon.

A comprehensive validation was performed on this final database. The validation involved the following:

- range checks of all variables by two of the authors

- checking that all codes in each covariate were valid

- maps of transects and sightings from the 5-km sample units in the regression analysis dataset were compared with previously mapped transects and sightings for the LGL and MMS datasets relative to the seismic source location during the 0-1 hour and 12-24 h seismic periods

- checking the recoding of seastate, visibility, ice percent and distance from shore from values in the original MMS and LGL datasets to the standardized scheme used in regression analysis dataset

- systematically checking sightings in the MMS and LGL data files against sightings that are included in the final regression analysis dataset

- systematically checking the assigned seismic activity levels to each record based on previously completed summaries of seismic activity in reports completed by LGL on behalf of BP and Western Geophysical (e.g., Miller et al. 1999)

As a final check, the regression analysis results (i.e., maps) were consistent with known patterns of bowhead whale distribution in the Beaufort Sea during the fall migration.

Data Back-up

A backup of each database version was maintained locally and in an archive stored securely in an off-site location. Backups were performed as required, sometimes as frequently as 1-2 times per day during active database creation and editing. Copies of the database were shared between project staff providing off-site and multi-copy backups.

APPENDIX D: THE EFFECTS OF SERIAL CORRELATION

IN POISSON REGRESSION MODELS

Chris Nations and Bryan Manly
Western EcoSystems Technology Inc.

Introduction

Here we consider how modest levels of serial correlation affect the standard errors of coefficients in a Poisson regression model that is fitted without accounting for this correlation. To address this question, we simulated data from a relatively simple Poisson model and introduced correlated errors. We then fitted a standard Poisson regression model to these data to assess the potential effects of correlation on the estimated coefficients and their standard errors.

Cameron and Trivedi (1998, pp. 240-242) discuss so-called *serially correlated error models* that introduce autocorrelation via a multiplicative latent variable. Their treatment is oriented towards estimation that explicitly accounts for the dependencies. We used their models for simulation rather than estimation.

Consider the Poisson regression model

$$E(y_t) = \exp\{\beta_0 + \beta_1 x_{1t} + \beta_2 x_{2t} + \ldots + \beta_p x_{pt}),$$

where the *t* subscript represents time. Note that the structure of the model does not reflect any dependencies in the data. Rather, dependency is introduced via a latent variable constructed by first generating a first order autoregressive process

$$\varepsilon_t = \rho_\varepsilon \, \varepsilon_{t-1} + \delta_t,$$

where δ_t is normally distributed with a mean of zero and a variance of σ^2, and $0 < \rho_\varepsilon < 1$. The latter condition assumes that only positive autocorrelation is of interest, though this assumption could be relaxed if necessary. Taking the exponential of ε_t and dividing by the mean gives

$$v'_t = \exp(\varepsilon_t),$$

and

$$v_t = v'_t / \{ \textstyle\sum v'_t / T \},$$

where the summation is over the T data values available. The new variable v_t is then always positive, with a mean of one.

Both v'_t and v_t are lognormally distributed, though for small σ and small ρ_ε , both are approximately normal with a mean of one and a variance of σ^2. In general,

$$E\left(v'_t\right) = \exp\left[\frac{1}{2}\left(\frac{\sigma^2}{1-\rho_\varepsilon^2}\right)\right],$$

$$\mathrm{Var}\left(v'_t\right) = \exp\left(2\frac{\sigma^2}{1-\rho_\varepsilon^2}\right) - \exp\left(\frac{\sigma^2}{1-\rho_\varepsilon^2}\right),$$

and

$$\mathrm{Var}\left(v_t\right) = \sigma_v^2 = \exp\left(\frac{\sigma^2}{1-\rho_\varepsilon^2}\right) - 1 ,$$

which follow from properties of the autoregressive process, the lognormal distribution, and division by the mean.

Given v_t, the expected value of y_t is calculated using

$$E(y_t) = \exp\{\beta_0 + \beta_1 x_{1t} + \beta_2 x_{2t} + \ldots + \beta_p x_{pt}) \, v_t .$$

Finally, Poisson random variates are generated using these expected values. This process introduces both over-dispersion and serial correlation. Because v_t has a mean of one, the expected value of y_t is unchanged by inclusion of the latent variable, but if

$$E\left(y_t\right) = \lambda_t ,$$

then

$$\mathrm{Var}\left(y_t\right) = \lambda_t + \sigma_v^2 \lambda_t^2 .$$

To informally assess the effects of autocorrelation on regression estimates, data were generated from the following model

$$E\left(y_t\right) = (-2.5 + 0.25 x_t - 0.001 x_t^2) \, v_t ,$$

where $28 \leq x \leq 52$ and $t = 1,\ldots,1000$. Under each of the conditions described below, 5000 datasets were simulated. Each condition involved a unique combination of σ^2 and ρ_ε (from the equation above): $\sigma = 0.00075$, 0.0015, or 0.01 and $\rho_\varepsilon = 0$, 0.08, 0.15, 0.3, 0.5, or 0.8. The effects of σ^2 and ρ_ε tend to interact, but broadly speaking σ^2 controls the degree of over-dispersion and ρ_ε controls the level of autocorrelation. In addition to these combinations, 5000 datasets were generated for $v_t = 1$ for all t, i.e., neither over-dispersion nor serial correlation. For each simulated dataset, a Poisson regression was fitted using the model

$$y_t = b_0 + b_1 x_t + b_2 x_t^2.$$

With each regression, the dispersion parameter, lag one correlation in residuals, and slope coefficients and their standard errors were estimated. Means and standard deviations of these estimates were calculated from the 5000 datasets and results were plotted.

Results

The results are shown in Figures D-1 to D-4 below. Figure D-1 demonstrates that the estimated lag one correlation of the residuals increases with ρ_ε, as expected. However, it appears that the relationship is progressively *less* linear with smaller values of σ. At the 2 smaller values of σ (0.00075 and 0.0015), the estimated dispersion parameter was relatively insensitive to the level of autocorrelation, though very high correlation ($\rho_\varepsilon = 0.8$) produced small increases in the estimates (Figure D-2). On the other hand, at $\sigma = 0.01$, the estimated dispersion parameter increases roughly 60% as ρ_ε increases from 0 to 0.8. Standard errors of the slope coefficients (Figures D-3 and D-4) roughly parallel the patterns seen in the dispersion parameter. That is, at the two smaller values of σ, estimated standard errors were generally unaffected by serial correlation except at higher values ($\rho_\varepsilon \geq 0.5$). However, at $\sigma = 0.01$, standard errors were more sensitive to changes in ρ_ε. Results for estimated slope coefficients are not shown, but these were extremely stable, i.e., unaffected by changes in either σ or ρ_ε.

Discussion

Assuming over-dispersion is not a severe problem, we would expect the results obtained here to hold for more complex Poisson regression models (those with more covariates and larger datasets). That is, serially correlated errors should have minimal effect on estimated standard errors except when correlations are very strong. However, if autocorrelation is severe, or if both over-dispersion and autocorrelation are moderately strong, then standard errors could be inflated. In that case, one solution might be to fit the serially correlated error model (rather than the standard regression model) and then adjust standard errors appropriately. This approach is discussed briefly by Cameron and Trivedi (1998).

Other time series models for Poisson counts are also discussed by Cameron and Trivedi. In some cases, these may be more appropriate than the serially correlated error model. For instance, it may be appropriate to model the current count as depending explicitly on previous counts. Analogous to linear autoregressive moving average (ARMA) models such as

$$y_t = \rho y_{t-1} + \varepsilon_t,$$

there are integer-valued ARMA models. In some models, covariates may be introduced through either the error term, ε_t, or the parameter, ρ, or both.

Another class of autoregressive models specifies dependency on both the current covariate state and the previous observations, for example

$$E(y_t) = \exp\{\beta_0 + \beta_1 x_{1t} + \beta_2 x_{2t} + \ldots + \beta_p x_{pt} + \rho \log_e(y^*_{t-1})\}$$

Where y^*_{t-1} denotes a transformation of y_t to ensure that it is positive. Under certain constraints on this transformation, this model may be estimated using standard software for Poisson regression. However, if there are very many zero counts in the data, the performance of this model may be poor owing to the ad hoc nature of the transformation used to obtain y^*_{t-1}. And, in any case, the model's theoretical properties are not well-understood. Other approaches for time series of Poisson counts include state space models and hidden Markov models. Chapter 7 in Cameron and Trivedi includes citations for original research on these various approaches.

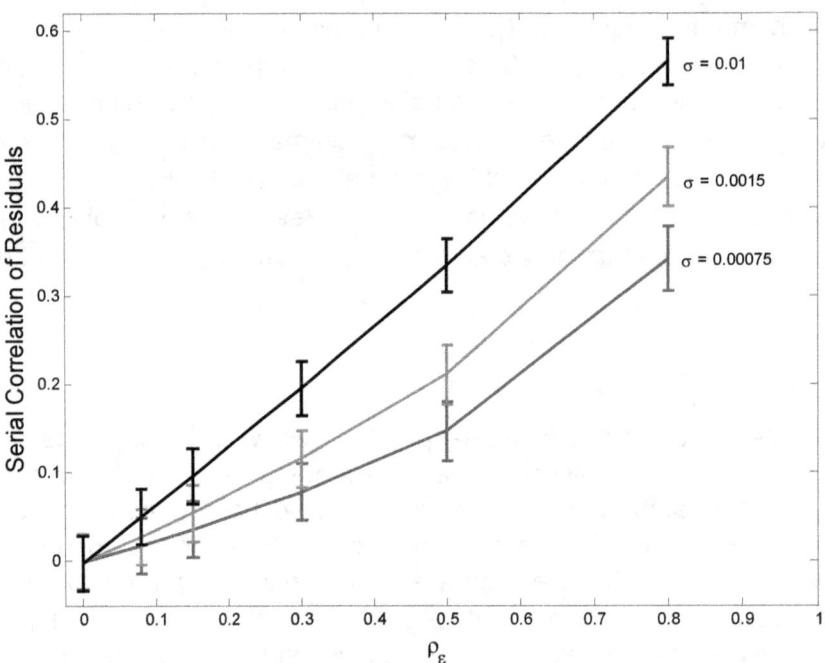

FIGURE D-1. Mean ($\pm$ se) serial correlation of residuals from 5000 simulations, as a function of σ and ρ_ε.

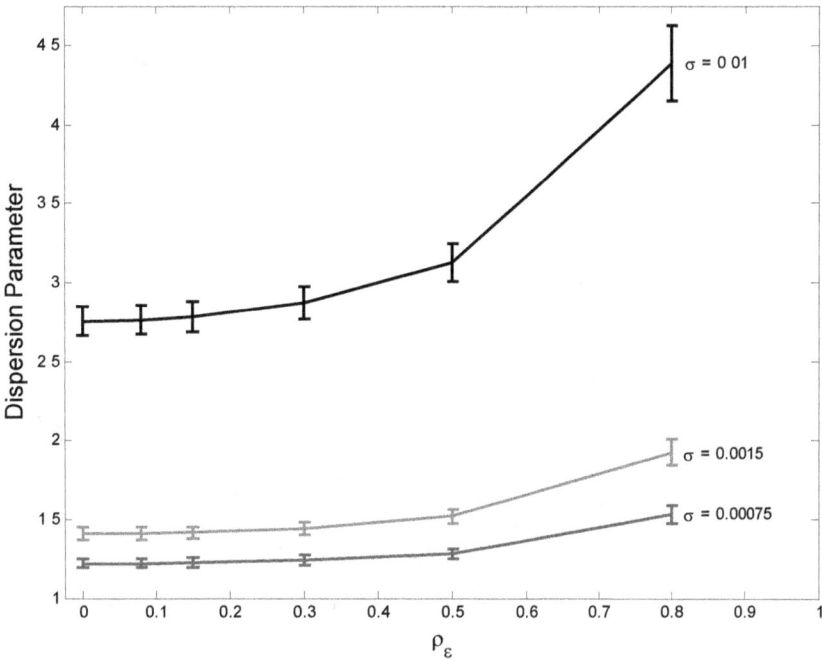

FIGURE D-2. Mean (± se) dispersion parameter from 5000 simulations, as a function of σ and ρ_ε.

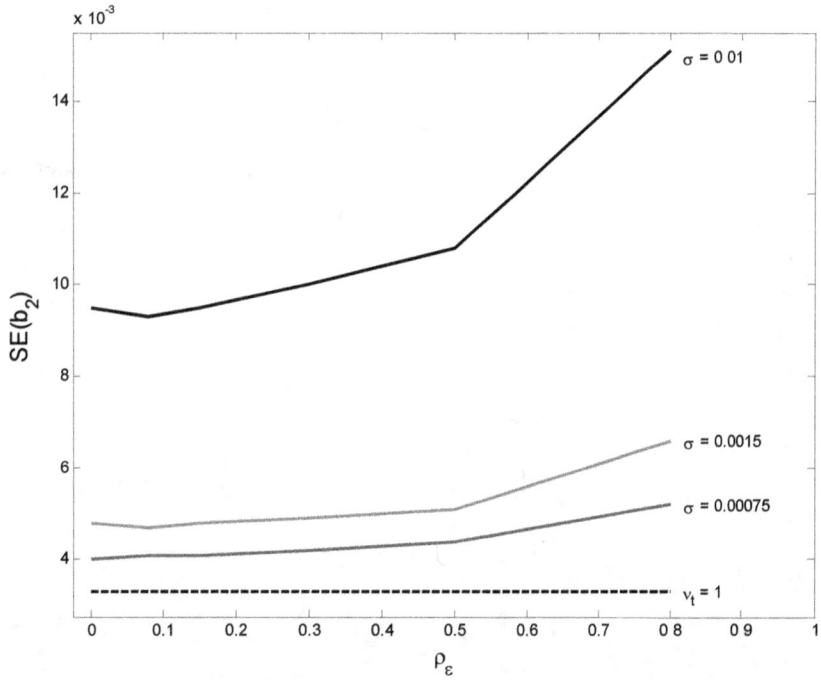

FIGURE D-3. Standard error of slope estimate (b_2) from 5000 simulations, as a function of σ and ρ_ε. The standard error without overdispersion and serial correlation ($v_t = 1$) is shown for comparison.

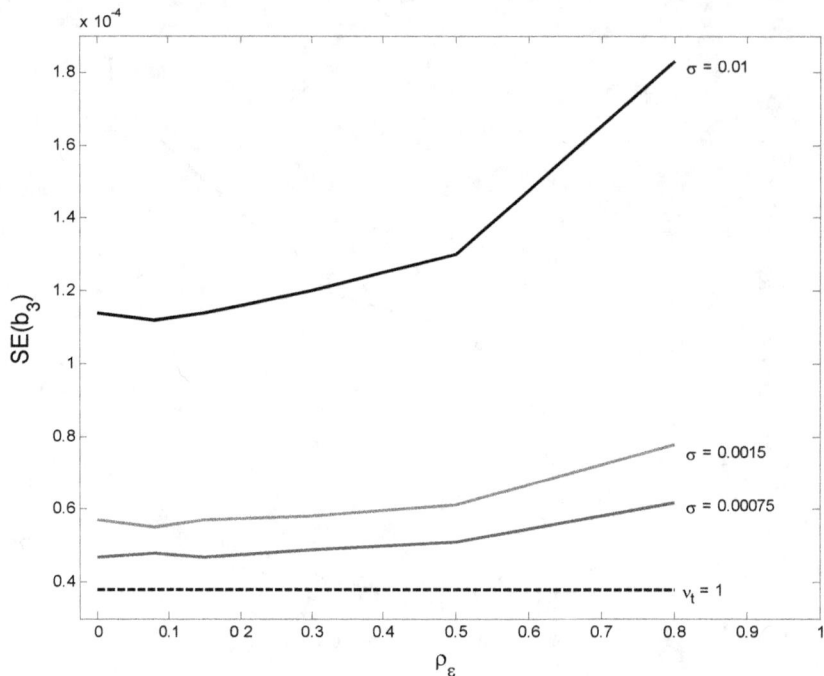

FIGURE D-4. Standard error of slope estimate (b_3) from 5000 simulations, as a function of σ and ρ_ε. The standard error without overdispersion and serial correlation ($v_t = 1$) is shown for comparison.

Reference

Cameron, A.C. and Trivedi, P.K. (1998). *Regression Analysis of Count Data*. Cambridge University Press, Cambridge.

APPENDIX E: ADDITIONAL DISTRIBUTION MAPS OF EXPECTED NUMBER OF BOWHEAD WHALE SIGHTINGS BASED ON POISSON REGRESSION MODELS

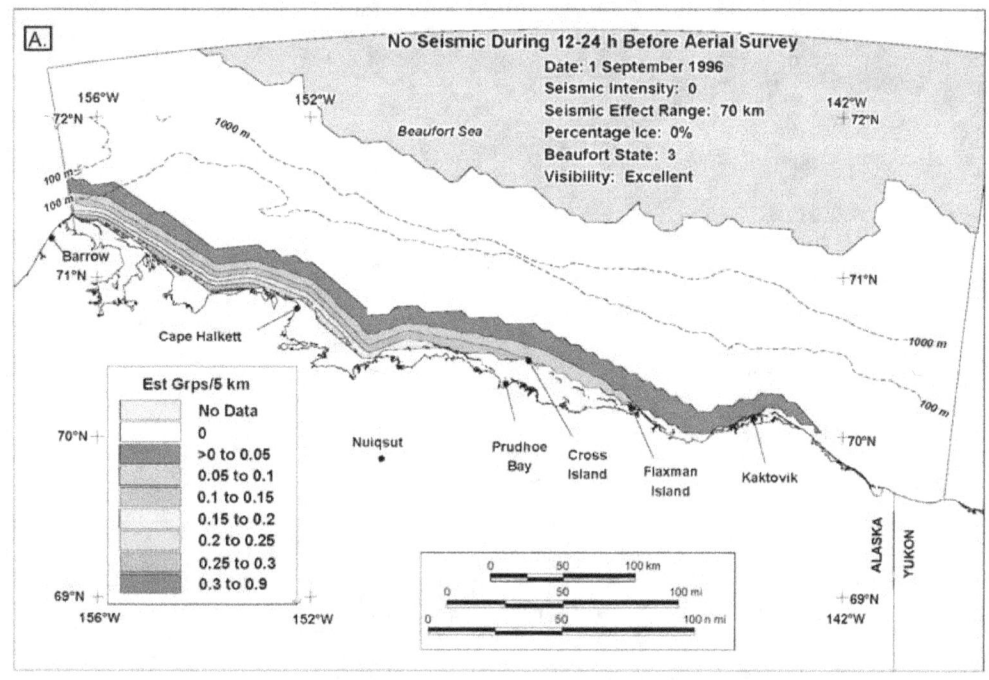

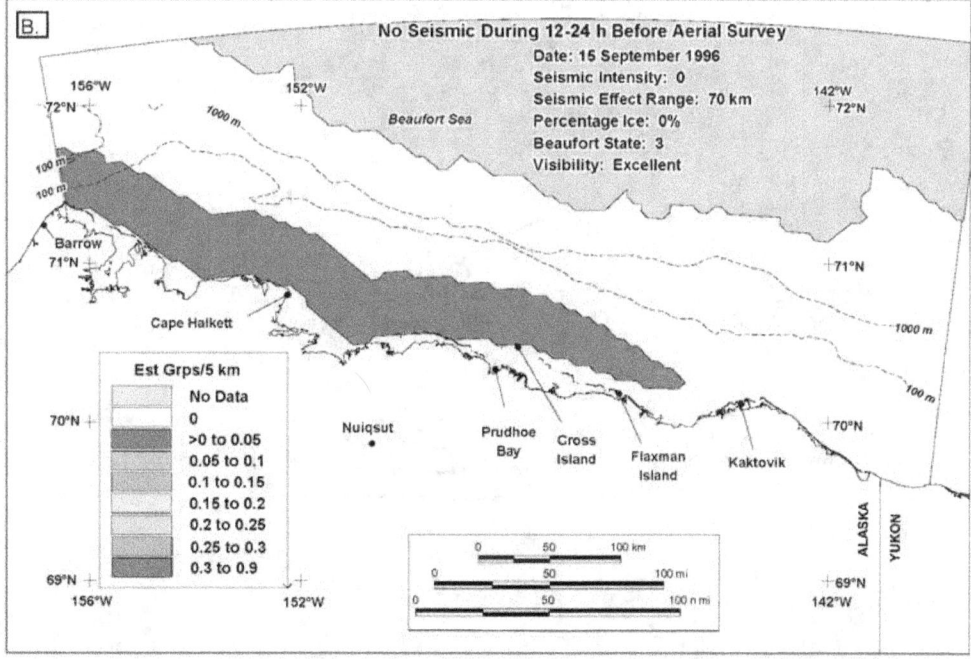

FIGURE E-1. Distribution of expected numbers of bowhead whale sightings (per 5 km transect segment) on **(A)** 1 Sep, **(B)** 15 Sep, **(C)** 1 Oct, and **(D)** 15 Oct 1996. Expected numbers of sightings are based on the estimated coefficients of the Poisson regression model (12-24 h 'version', but assuming no seismic activity), and the additional assumptions that there was no ice, Beaufort state was 3, and visibility conditions were excellent.

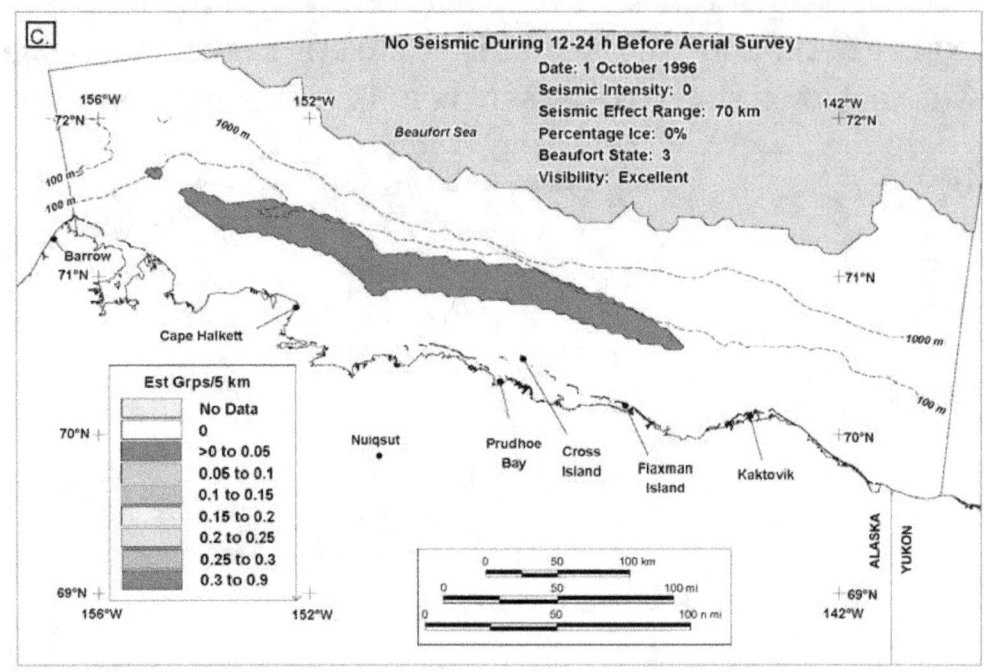

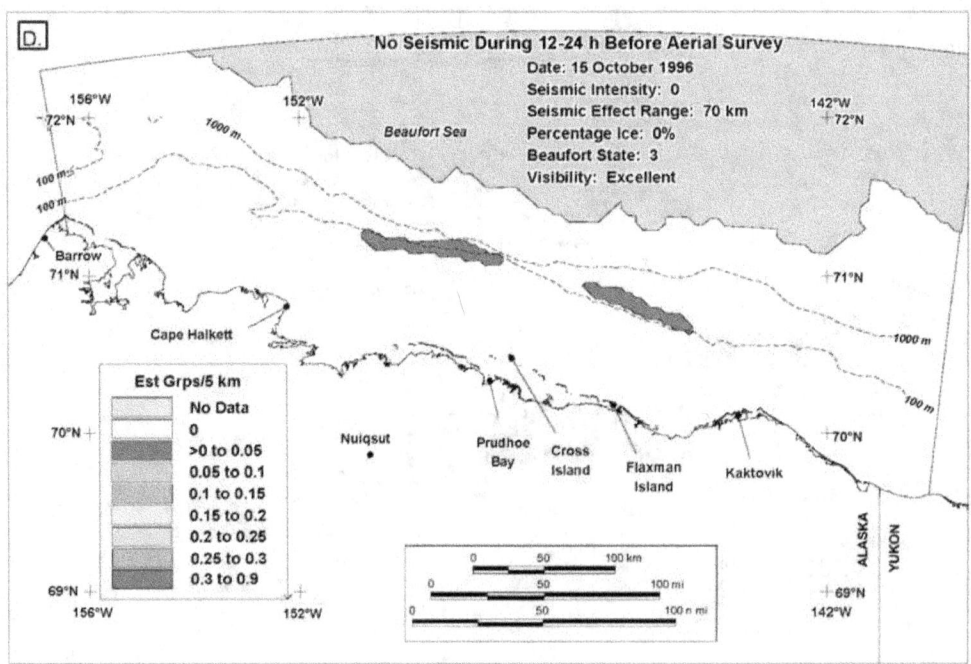

FIGURE E-1. Concluded.

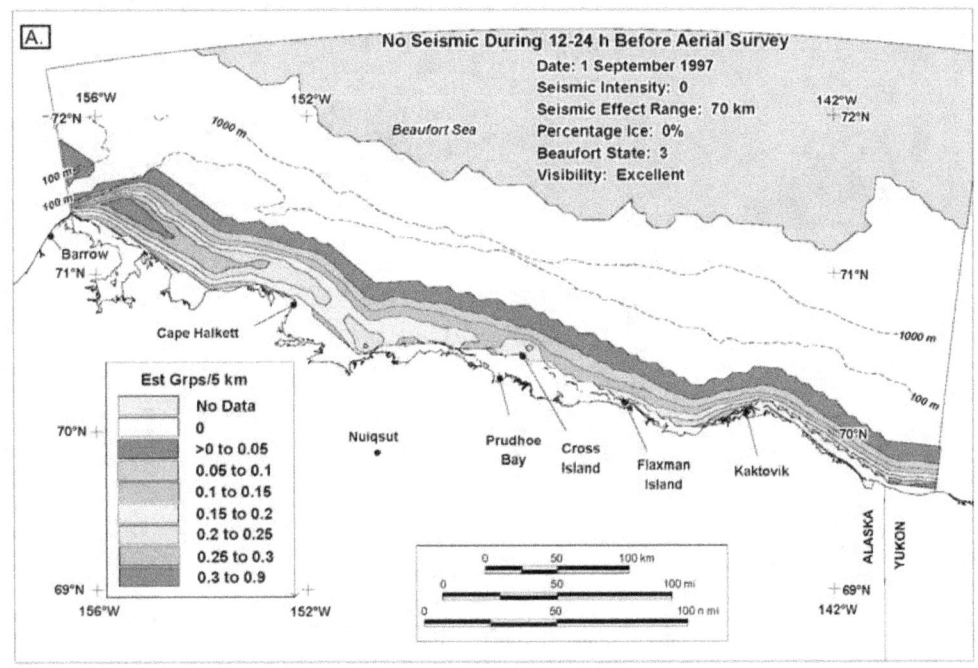

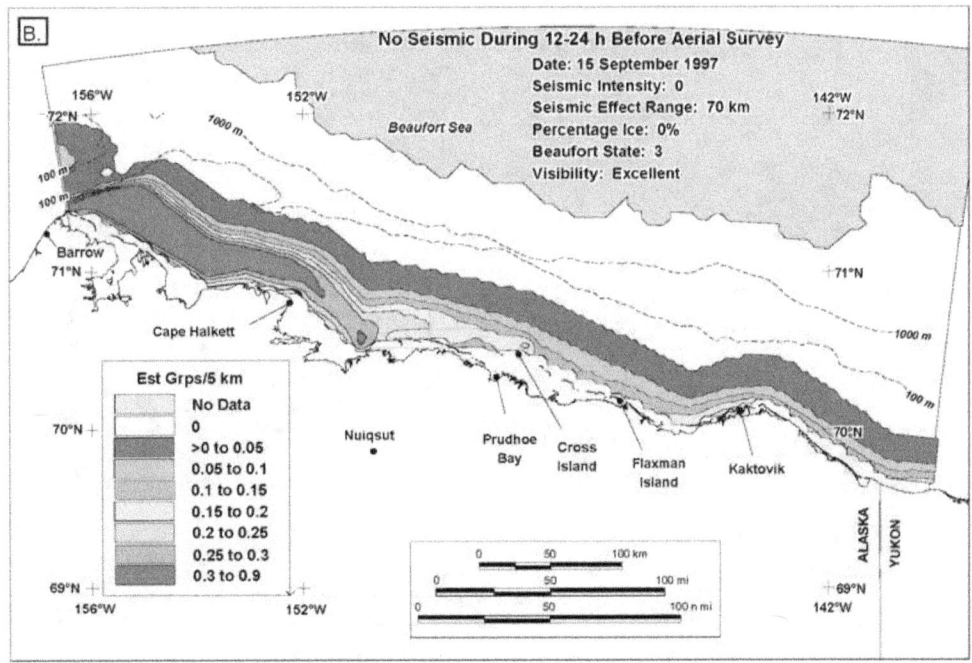

FIGURE E-2. Distribution of expected numbers of bowhead whale sightings (per 5 km transect segment) on **(A)** 1 Sep, **(B)** 15 Sep, **(C)** 1 Oct, and **(D)** 15 Oct 1997. Expected numbers of sightings are based on the estimated coefficients of the Poisson regression model (12-24 h 'version', but assuming no seismic activity), and the additional assumptions that there was no ice, Beaufort state was 3, and visibility conditions were excellent.

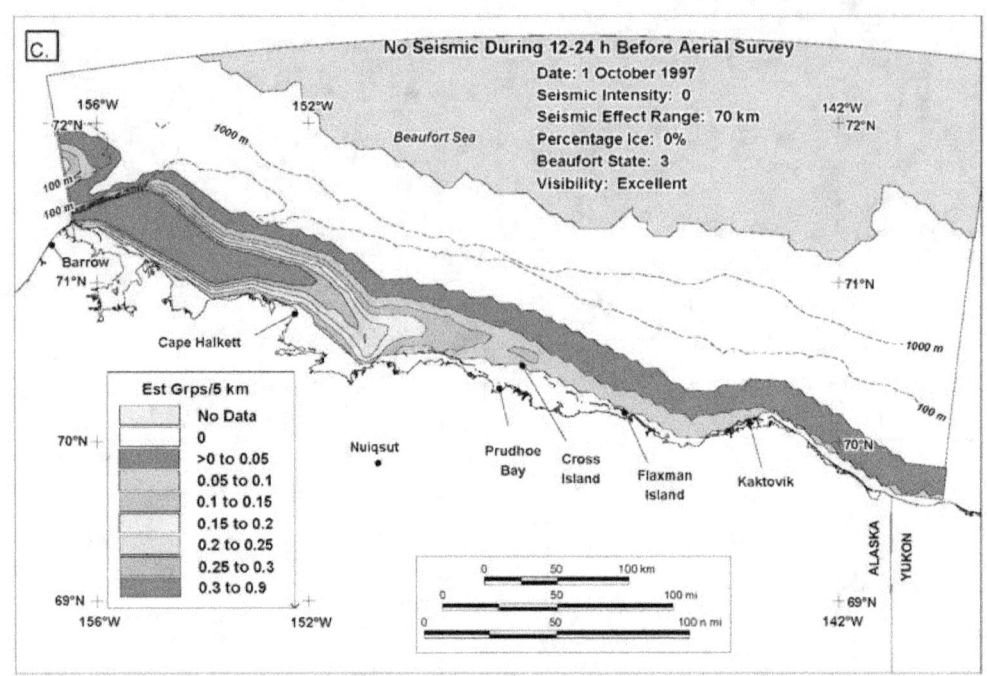

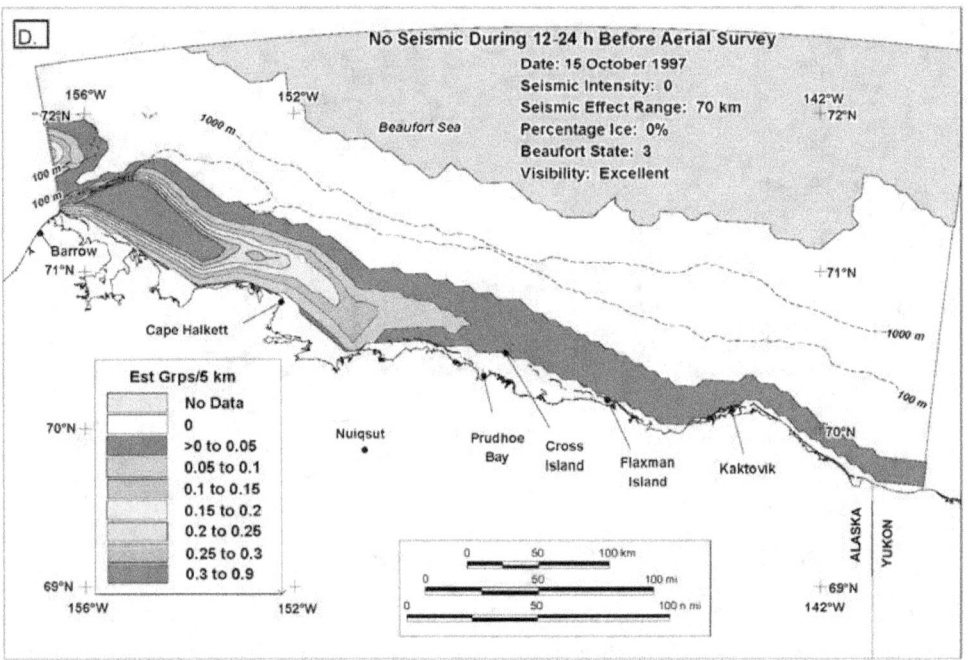

FIGURE E-2. Concluded.

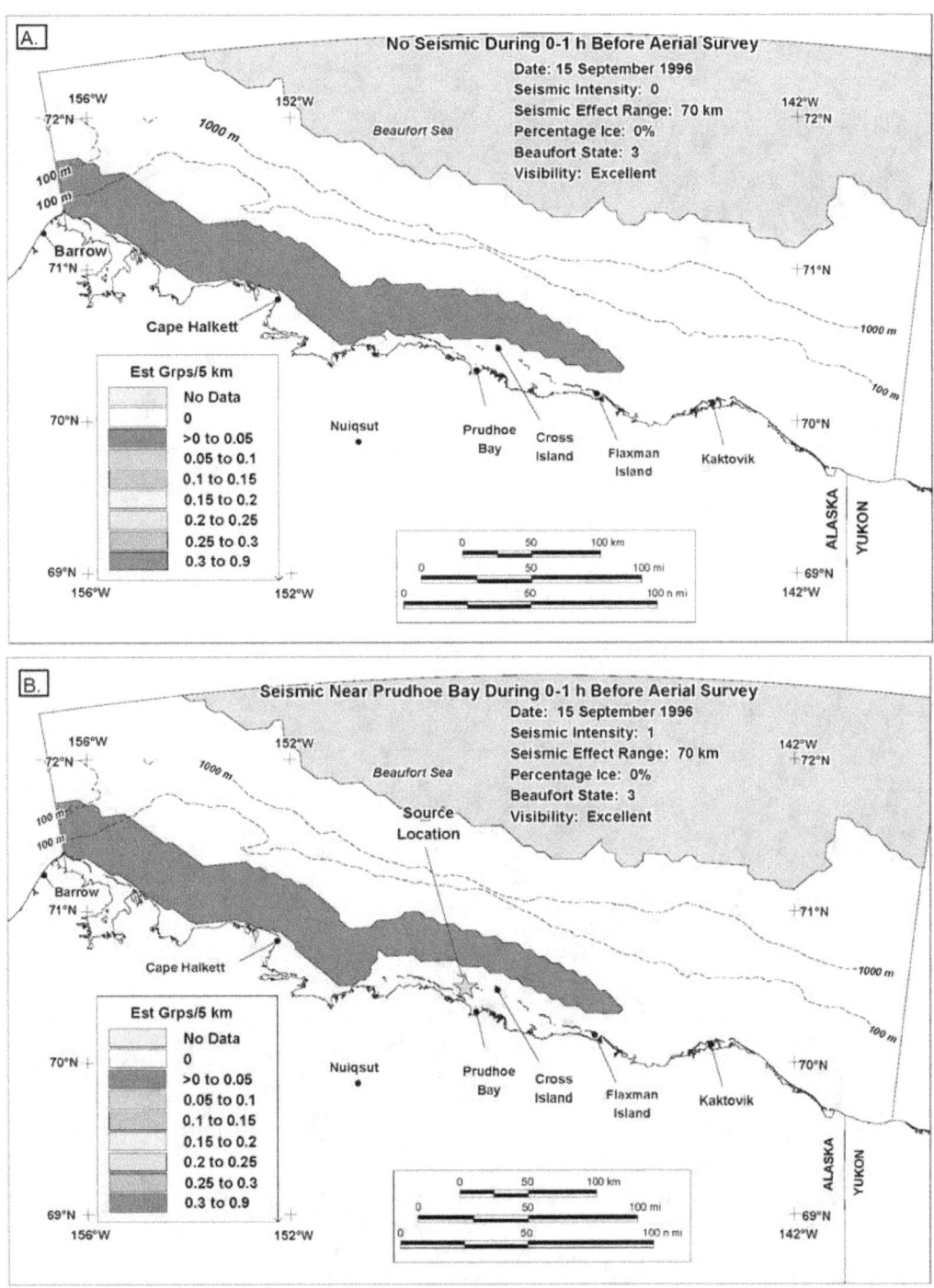

FIGURE E-3. Distribution of expected numbers of bowhead whale sightings (per 5 km transect segment) in 1996 when **(A)** no seismic activity occurred during the hour before aerial surveys and when **(B)** a seismic source near Prudhoe Bay was active for the full hour before aerial surveys. Expected numbers of sightings are based on the estimated coefficients of the Poisson regression model (0-1 h 'version') and the assumptions that the date was 15 Sep 1996, there was no ice, Beaufort state was 3, and visibility was excellent.

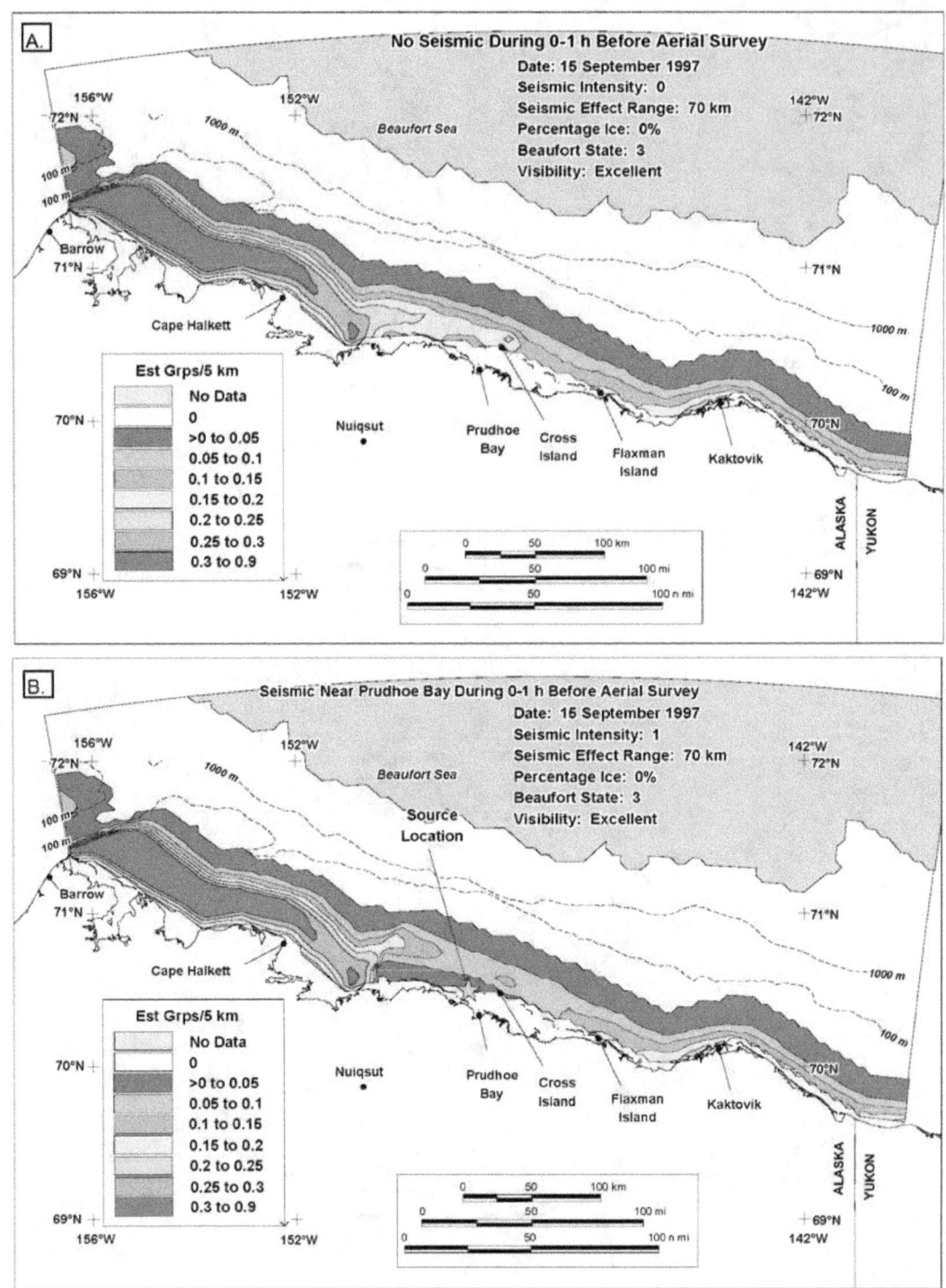

FIGURE E-4. Distribution of expected numbers of bowhead whale sightings (per 5 km transect segment) in 1997 when **(A)** no seismic activity occurred during the hour before aerial surveys and when **(B)** a seismic source near Prudhoe Bay was active for the full hour before aerial surveys. Expected numbers of sightings are based on the estimated coefficients of the Poisson regression model (0-1 h 'version') and the assumptions that the date was 15 Sep 1997, there was no ice, Beaufort state was 3, and visibility was excellent.

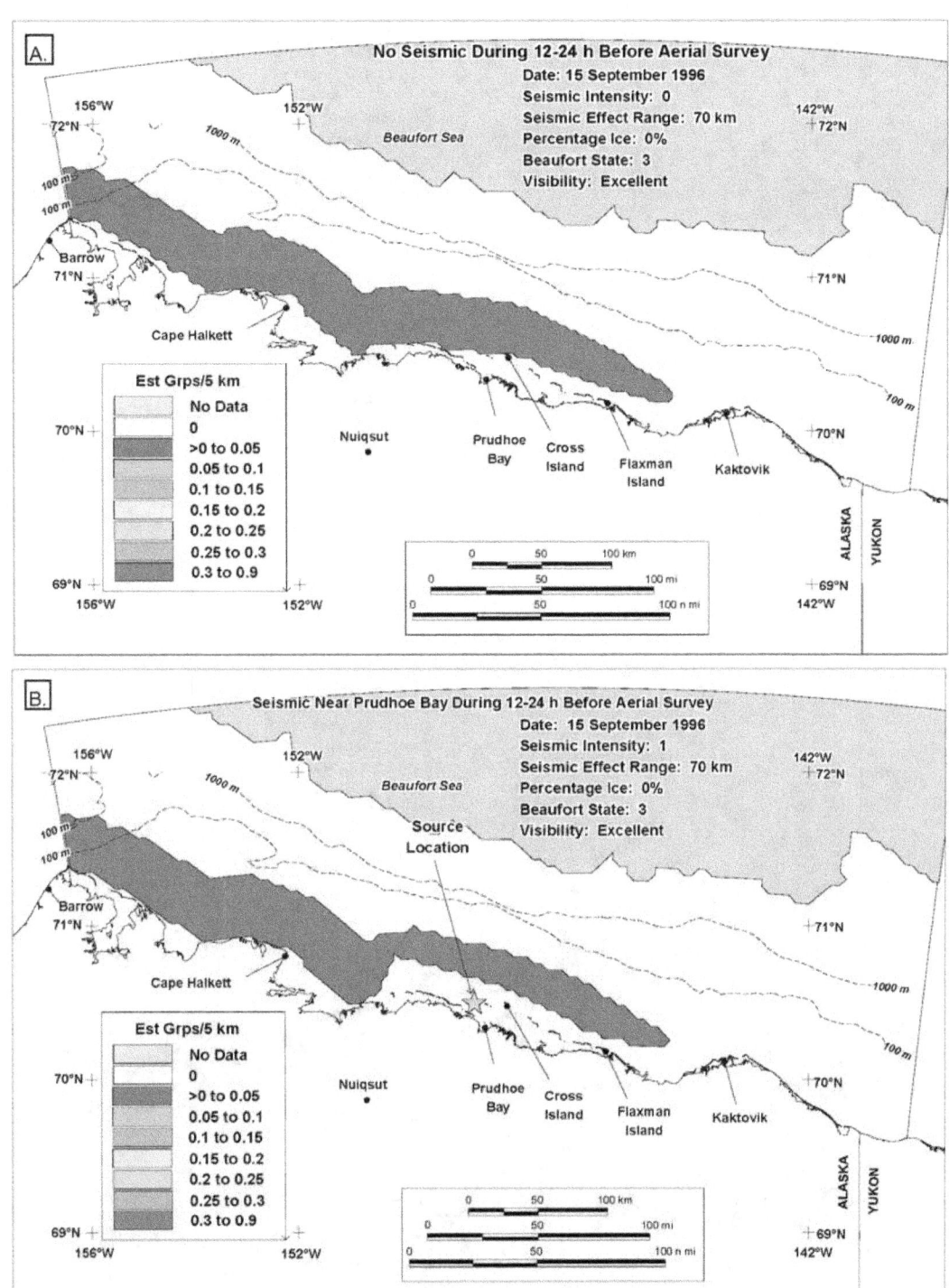

FIGURE E-5. Distribution of expected numbers of bowhead whale sightings (per 5 km transect segment) in 1996 when **(A)** no seismic activity occurred 12-24 h before aerial surveys and when **(B)** a seismic source near Prudhoe Bay was active 12-24 h before aerial surveys. Expected numbers of sightings are based on the estimated coefficients of the Poisson regression model (12-24 h 'version') and the assumptions that the date was 15 Sep 1996, there was no ice, Beaufort state was 3, and visibility was excellent.

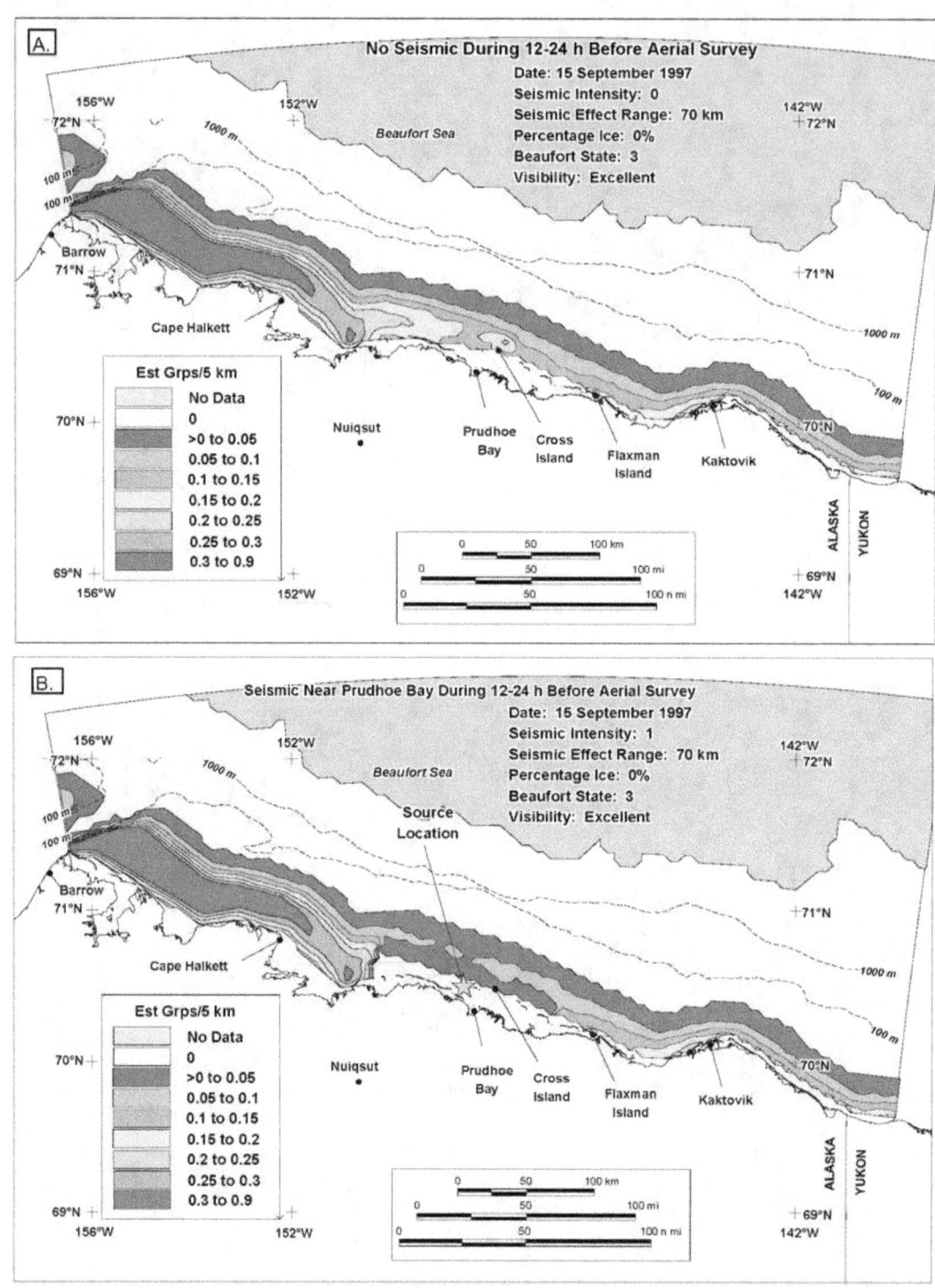

FIGURE E-6. Distribution of expected numbers of bowhead whale sightings (per 5 km transect segment) in 1997 when **(A)** no seismic activity occurred 12-24 h before aerial surveys and when **(B)** a seismic source near Prudhoe Bay was active 12-24 h before aerial surveys. Expected numbers of sightings are based on the estimated coefficients of the Poisson regression model (12-24 h 'version') and the assumptions that the date was 15 Sep 1997, there was no ice, Beaufort state was 3, and visibility was excellent.

The Department of the Interior Mission

As the Nation's principal conservation agency, the Department of the Interior has responsibility for most of our nationally owned public lands and natural resources. This includes fostering sound use of our land and water resources; protecting our fish, wildlife, and biological diversity; preserving the environmental and cultural values of our national parks and historical places; and providing for the enjoyment of life through outdoor recreation. The Department assesses our energy and mineral resources and works to ensure that their development is in the best interests of all our people by encouraging stewardship and citizen participation in their care. The Department also has a major responsibility for American Indian reservation communities and for people who live in island territories under U.S. administration.

The Minerals Management Service Mission

As a bureau of the Department of the Interior, the Minerals Management Service's (MMS) primary responsibilities are to manage the mineral resources located on the Nation's Outer Continental Shelf (OCS), collect revenue from the Federal OCS and onshore Federal and Indian lands, and distribute those revenues.

Moreover, in working to meet its responsibilities, the **Offshore Minerals Management Program** administers the OCS competitive leasing program and oversees the safe and environmentally sound exploration and production of our Nation's offshore natural gas, oil and other mineral resources. The MMS **Royalty Management Program** meets its responsibilities by ensuring the efficient, timely and accurate collection and disbursement of revenue from mineral leasing and production due to Indian tribes and allottees, States and the U.S. Treasury.

The MMS strives to fulfill its responsibilities through the general guiding principles of (1) being responsive to the public's concerns and interests by maintaining a dialogue with all potentially affected parties and (2) carrying out its programs with an emphasis on working to enhance the quality of life for all Americans by lending MMS assistance and expertise to economic development and environmental protection.

www.ingramcontent.com/pod-product-compliance
Lightning Source LLC
Chambersburg PA
CBHW081104290526

45795CB00006B/1997